To: R—

Best Wishes

Brian Magee

C000069837

Two Lives of Brian – From Policing to Politics

Two Lives of Brian –
From Policing to Politics

by

BRIAN, LORD MACKENZIE
OF FRAMWELLGATE

The Memoir Club

First published in 2004 by
The Memoir Club
Whitworth Hall
Spennymoor
County Durham

All rights reserved.
Unauthorised duplication
contravenes existing laws.

British Library Cataloguing in
Publication Data.
A catalogue record for this book
is available from the
British Library.

ISBN: 1 84104 084 3

Typeset by George Wishart & Associates, Whitley Bay.
Printed by CPI Bath.

To my wife Jean and our two sons Brian and Andrew. The former I chose, the latter I was blessed with – for their forbearance.

Contents

Illustrations

Foreword

I AM DELIGHTED to have the opportunity to write the foreword to this excellent book by The Lord Mackenzie of Framwellgate. Brian Mackenzie enjoyed a distinguished career within the police service, rising to the national position of President of the Superintendents' Association. He subsequently joined an elite group of former police officers that are elevated to the House of Lords, where he continues to contribute thoughtfully and constructively to debates about the police service, which he is obviously still so passionate about.

This is more than a book that just charts Brian's progress from Dodmire infants school, Darlington to Peer of the Realm, although that in itself is an interesting enough story. It is full of thoughtful and insightful commentary on the development of the police service at a critical point in its history. Brian's career takes place against the backdrop of key events such as the Edmund Davis and Sheehy reviews, the years of Margaret Thatcher's government and the Miner's strike and culminates with the installation of Tony Blair's New Labour Government. Brian's narrative provides an extremely entertaining read, both for those outside as well as inside the police service, and is an engaging personal perspective on a profession that is never far from the public consciousness.

There is of course a strong political theme running through this book. Brian's interest in politics is not motivated by any personal ambition but rather by a genuine desire to influence matters for the greater good of others. This was evident during his time as President of the Superintendents' Association where he did much to impact on the Home Affairs agenda and has continued in his capacity as a hard working member of the Upper House.

Brian Mackenzie is a colourful, larger than life character and I am very pleased to say that his book does him justice. It is a modestly written account of a man whose life has been characterised by achievement but who remains someone who understands the value of friendship, loyalty and commitment to others. I found it hugely entertaining, full of humour and a must read for anyone with even a remote interest in policing and politics.

Sir John Stevens QPM LL.B
Commissioner of the Metropolitan Police

CHAPTER 1

The Sting!

IT WAS AROUND 6 p.m. on Monday 10 March 2003 when I walked into the Sports and Social Club, which nestles behind the River Thames Terrace in the House of Lords, below the chamber. It's the nearest thing you'll get in the Palace of Westminster to compare with a good old English pub! I often use this bar, also known as the 'HOP' [Houses of Parliament] Inn, to meet colleagues and staff, all of whom I get on well with. I saw that there was a new lady working behind the bar. I was meeting my friend, Mick Skelton, who had retired the year before as the principal doorkeeper in the Lords.

Mick was having a drink with Lord Gerry Fitt, the former and well-respected leader of the Social Democratic Labour Party in Northern Ireland. I asked Mick Skelton who the new barmaid was, and was told that she had only been here a week and was French. When I ordered a drink, I spoke to another parliamentary employee with whom I had become friendly, a genial Irish chap called George Fleck, standing at the bar. He winked cheekily, and nodded towards the new girl, who was very well-dressed and attractive, and I noticed that she spoke very good English with a striking French accent. Later, on Wednesday of that week I was feeling pleased with myself as I had just asked a question in the chamber, with a view to increasing the penalties for causing death by dangerous driving, and had received a very positive reply from Charlie Falconer, the Home Office minister in the Lords. I was in a celebratory mood that day and being naturally gregarious, I went to the HOP Inn, where I saw that the same French lady, who was in her mid thirties, was sitting by herself at one of the tables. People tell me that my police background leads me to continually ask questions when meeting people, and I soon established that she was an interpreter, spoke five languages and that her name was Salima Kabache.

She told me she was a temporary barmaid and was very interested in politics and the workings of parliament. It did not in the least occur to me that she would have any reason to tell me other than the truth, bearing in mind that I had seen her employed behind the bar. I asked her if she had been into the chamber of the Lords before, or had had a look round the magnificent building. She said she had not. I have to say that I have taken a great interest in the history, architecture, procedures and traditions of the Palace of Westminster since being appointed to the Lords in 1998, and have shown a great many people round since then.

1

The Palace of Westminster.

In the early days I used to attach myself to official tours, listening to the expert historians describing the Palace's history, which spans almost one thousand years. I remember one doorkeeper giving a tour whilst off duty, describing to his group the Gold Tour, the Silver Tour and the Jeffrey Archer Tour. Asked what the difference was he said, 'Well the Gold Tour takes you along the complete line of route, including the Lords and the Commons, with a description of the history, architecture, paintings and procedures. The Silver Tour is identical, but is confined to the House of Lords.' Pressed about the Jeffrey Archer Tour he said, 'Well it's like the Gold Tour, but I just make it up as I go along!'

Talking of Jeffrey, Mick Skelton, the former principal doorkeeper, told me that at one State Opening of Parliament, Lord Archer turned up fully robed but late, and there were no seats. 'Mr Skelton', he cried indignantly, 'there's nowhere to sit!' Jokingly, Mick Skelton indicated the empty throne and said, 'There's a seat there, my Lord', whereupon Jeffrey Archer, typically, said in a flash. 'No, No, Mayor of London first, King later!'

But I digress, back to Salima. Because I was pressed for time and had a meeting to attend, I told her that if she came to the Peers' Entrance the following afternoon, she could see the Lord Chancellor's procession, which is a daily occurrence, I would give her a conducted tour of the Palace, and she would have an opportunity to sit in the chamber and watch the proceedings. She seemed very keen and the date was set.

The next day, Thursday 13 March, went according to plan. I went to my office at Millbank, just opposite the Lords, in the morning. Jean, my wife, rang to tell me that the Royal Mail had been trying to get the address of my London flat. When she had given them the address of the House of Lords they told her that this was unsuitable as it was 'a business address'. I became slightly concerned when she rang me later and told me that they had also contacted my son Brian, in Manchester, with the same request. Sensibly, he had not disclosed it.

I had just been to Belfast the week before on police business with 'Safecall', a company of which I am a director. Alan Long, a former detective who is the managing director, rang me also that day, to say that he had had a similar call from the 'Royal Mail'. A return telephone number, which the man had given him, was unobtainable! I was now more concerned, given the Ulster visit, so I contacted the anti-terrorist branch at police headquarters in Durham, asking them to check it out. The detective inspector was very helpful and agreed to trace the call, which had been logged by 'Safecall'.

I started the tour with Salima around two o'clock at the Peers' Entrance to the Lords, taking her along the line of the tour route. She was again very well dressed, with tight, black leather, expensive looking trousers, and she turned a few heads as we commenced the tour. We visited the Prince's Chamber, the Royal Gallery, and the Sovereign's Robing Room. I explained how the voting system worked, taking her through the 'content' voting lobby and into the Peer's Lobby where I introduced her to Mr Kirtley, the geordie Principal Door-keeper, who is also a very good friend of mine.

Throughout the tour, Salima was very talkative and showed great interest in everything. I even think she understood some of the jokes. The House sat at 3:00 p.m. that Thursday and I sat Salima in the chamber to watch proceedings for a while. The tour continued into the Central Lobby, through St Stephen's Hall and into the ancient Westminster Hall, which was constructed in 1099 by William the Conqueror's son, William Rufus. This ancient hall was saved from the fire in 1834, which destroyed the rest of the Palace of Westminster.

The tour normally takes about one hour and at the end I told her that I had time to buy her a drink in the HOP Inn, before departing to write a speech and prepare for dinner that evening with Sir Fergus Montgomery, an ex geordie schoolteacher and former Tory MP, and one-time confidant of the now Baroness Thatcher.

Having had a very pleasant afternoon I saw Salima off the premises at the Peers' Entrance around four o'clock, without the slightest suspicion that there was anything amiss. Why should I? It is something I have done over my five years in parliament with hundreds of people of all nationalities. Here was a favour being done for one of the employees of the House, all of whom I hold in the highest regard.

Dinner with Sir Fergus

I have known Fergus Montgomery since I was a police superintendent seconded to the Home Office in the early eighties, having met him at a police function in London. He was then a Tory MP and my natural interest in politics, and his northeast roots, cemented our friendship. That evening around 6:30 p.m., I walked to his flat just off Victoria Street, wearing my light mackintosh and carrying my black briefcase. I had a gin and tonic while he got ready and then we set off to walk to Grumbles Restaurant in Pimlico, no more than ten minutes away.

Little did I know at that time, the momentous events that were to unfold later in the evening!

It was a pleasant evening and as we approached a road junction I saw a dog ahead, running about in the road, in great danger of being run down by traffic. I was indifferent, but Fergus shouted, 'It has a name tag', and went to grab hold of the dog. I went to help him, put my bag down in the shop doorway and tried to read the tag around its neck, in the fading light.

I saw that there was a telephone number on the tag, which I rang on my mobile. The grateful dog owner duly arrived, thanking us profusely. I remember saying to Fergus, 'That's your good deed for the day!'

We then went to the restaurant and had a very agreeable dinner, discussing old times and joking with Issy, the very affable manager of Grumbles, whom we both knew well.

It was only when I rose to leave, put on my coat and looked for my bag that I realized that it was not there. I had last had it at the scene of the dog-catching incident earlier. Fergus was more concerned than me. I went through the contents of the bag in my mind, 'keys, spare organizer, reports, *Hansard*; nothing too critical, apart from the keys to my flat in Pimlico, where I had lived for about three years.

We re-traced our steps and my instincts told me that the bag would not be there. I was right! I calmed Fergus down and he asked if I wished to report the loss from his flat. I told him that the key-office at my apartment block would get me into the flat and I would ring the police from there. So we parted company on a rather downbeat note after such a pleasant meal. It would now be around 10:30 p.m.

I got into the apartment with the spare keys around 11:00 p.m. and watched the remainder of *Newsnight*, after reporting the loss of my bag and belongings to the police by phone. I poured myself a nightcap gin and tonic.

It was about 11:30 p.m., when I received a call on my mobile phone. It was Salima. She had the number from my business card, which I usually hand out to all visitors. She was distressed and sounded in tears. 'Brian, I need someone to talk to', she cried. I was catching an early train the following day, so I hesitated and should have said no. I didn't, I asked, 'Well where are you?'

'I can be there in a taxi in five minutes', she responded. The alarm bells should have been ringing. It was late, I'd had a drink and they didn't!

I met her from the taxi and we went to my flat. It's a nice, one bedroom apartment, and facing south with a balcony, from which you can see the River Thames. I have a few limited edition plates on the wall and a number of paintings and prints of Durham City where my home is. There is also a framed letter from the Prime Minister Tony Blair, and a photograph of my wife and family stands on a corner shelf near the window.

I offered her a drink and saw that she was dressed exactly the same as earlier during the tour of the Lords. 'Have you any orange?' she said. I called to her from the kitchen that I only had Coca Cola and she said, 'That's fine, Brian'.

I had the same; she took off her coat and started looking at the paintings. She seemed to be fascinated by politics and said that she was going to Monte Carlo at the weekend. That comment again should have sparked more interest from me, I was slipping. She did not appear to be as distressed as she had indicated on the phone, and she seemed to be a very decent, intelligent young woman. We talked and talked and talked, covering the Iraqi invasion, which was looming, Tony Blair, (she had seen his letter), and many other matters besides, including my former career as a senior police officer. At one point she called her flat mate on her mobile phone and I said 'Hi' to her, over the phone, just to be friendly.

Salima's depression seemed to have gone and after about an hour I suggested that she should get a taxi from outside a nearby hotel where there was a constant stream of black cabs. She insisted that she liked to call a particular taxi firm, as it was safer, late at night. This appeared to make sense, although it should have been another pointer, however I thought no more of it. Having booked the taxi, we waited and waited and waited! She rang the cab driver three times asking how close he was. I was starting to get annoyed, as I knew she could have jumped in a black cab outside the hotel below. It appeared that she was delaying her departure for as long as possible and now of course I know why!

I took her down to ground level and saw her into her 'cab', and snatched some sleep before catching my train to Durham next morning, thinking no more of it. Even then it still did not occur to me that there was anything untoward happening, although if I had used commonsense, there were a few things, when looked at together, which should have rung those bells. The attempts to trace my London address, the distressed phone call late at night, the delayed attempt to get a specific taxi and, the calls to her flatmate. But it is easy to be wise after the event, she was an employee from the Lords, gave a cry for help and I was taken in completely. My antennae must be starting to fail! Afterthought is a wonderful thing!

On the Friday evening, Jean and I had arranged to dine in Newcastle with a couple of friends, Anita and Peter, who live in the same village as us, Shincliffe, on the southern outskirts of the picturesque City of Durham. We had a splendid evening and returned by taxi to their house, where we had a nightcap, before walking home.

The next morning, Saturday, Jean received a concerning telephone call from another friend in the village, Debbie, who lives in a cottage about 200 yards away. Debbie described how earlier that morning she had seen a van parked near her house containing a man taking pictures of our cottage, with what appeared to be a telephoto lens. She was obviously alarmed, not least because she knows that Jean lives alone through the week. Intelligently, Debbie had taken the registration number of the van, so I intended to pass this on to my contact in the anti-terrorist branch, thinking there might be a connection with the previous telephone calls regarding my London address. There was, but not in the way I suspected!

The Confrontation

I answered the door at the cottage at 5:00 p.m. that night and was confronted by a *News of the World* reporter. She asked if she could come in, so I invited her into the study on the ground floor.

You can imagine my shock when she informed me that the friendly barmaid, Salima, was in fact a French Algerian, who was allegedly a drug-dealing prostitute. She had no official authority to be in the Palace of Westminster and had not been vetted. The reporter told me they intended to run the story of her visiting my flat the following day in the paper.

My principle concern initially was that she could have been a terrorist, so I contacted Black Rod's office regarding the breach of security. I also rang members of my family to forewarn them of what they might read the next morning, and went down to Debbie's house and explained the full story, thanking her for her vigilance.

Lt General Sir Michael Wilcocks (Black Rod) is in charge of security in the Lords, but he was away for the weekend, so I warned his deputy about what was about to break in the press.

The article was duly printed. It was an interview with her flatmate with 'admissions' to her from Salima that she had wanted to target 'powerful' men like Lords or MPs, and that she had not been vetted for her job as a barmaid, which she had got through 'a friend of a friend'. She went on to state that I did not know her background and because she 'fancied me', she had not charged at all for her 'services', which she went on to describe in great detail.

This was pure invention and I could not believe what I was reading. The paper legitimately added criticism of security in parliament together with photographs of me with Salima Kabache in the 'HOP' Inn, taken presumably, with a secret camera. I was described variously as a crime advisor to Tony Blair and the Home Office, and as a former 'Top Cop'. The tabloid Sunday paper had embellished the whole episode, 'sexed it up', I think is the current language, and it illustrated graphically to me the dangers and risks of being in public life.

The experience brought to mind a phrase used by Rudyard Kipling that the 'press wanted power without responsibility – the prerogative of the harlot throughout the ages'. How appropriate in the circumstances I thought!

I was due to do a phone broadcast on Radio Newcastle that morning on David Blunkett's proposals for anti-social behaviour. The radio presenter, Tony Cartledge, rang me and, in fairness said that he would ask me about the tabloid disclosure. I told him that I was happy to do it, to put the truth on record and denied any sexual misbehaviour of any kind. I gave a press briefing outside my home and stated that I would consider my position if I was asked to stand down from any of the positions I held. The daily papers ran fair reports the next day, but the damage was done!

Jean had organized a big party at a local hotel for my sixtieth birthday the following Saturday, and we had to consider whether, in view of the circumstances and the embarrassment, we should call it off. I pointed out that I had been trapped as the result of a 'sting', and sensible people would realize that, so we decided to go ahead with the arrangements. Jean had invited about 140 guests, with a few surprises.

I was not due to return to the Lords until Tuesday as I was speaking at a fraud conference at St James Park on the Monday. I knew that it was going to be a difficult week but I was determined to change none of my plans. At the conference, I followed the chief constable of Northumbria Police, Crispian Strachan. He was introduced as a man who was passionate about tackling fraud.

When the chairman introduced me, I opened, by commenting on the introduction afforded to the chief constable, and said that I was pleased that I was not described as being passionate! The audience of around 500, mainly police officers, loved it, and those opening words got me a loud cheer and round of applause.

That evening I had arranged to introduce the guest speaker, at the Shincliffe Village History Society, where I am a relatively new member, which I did. I prepared to go to London the following day.

The support I had that week was uplifting! I was inundated with e-mails (even from abroad – news travels far these days). I even had a call from Sir John Stevens, the Metropolitan Police Commissioner, who is a personal friend, which I appreciated, and Mike Welply, chief executive of the Joint

Security Industry Council, of which I am president, declared their full confidence in me. Even journalists came to my aid, Mark Turnbull a local radio presenter rang, as did Stephen Wright the chief crime reporter on the *Daily Mail*. I hoped it would all blow over... some hope!

The Birthday Party

The party, the following Saturday night, was a splendid occasion. Jean did me proud. Colleagues turned up from 40 years earlier, many of whom I had not seen for decades. My sons, Brian and Andrew and their girlfriends and families were there, together with other colleagues and relations. It was magnificent.

Ray Mallon, the elected mayor of Middlesbrough, the former police officer, dubbed 'Robo Cop', came to the function and made a magnificent speech of support. It was much appreciated and in a sense a form of reciprocation, as I had stood four square with him during his period of suspension and investigation on corruption allegations for many years by Cleveland Police in 'Operation Lancet'.

My old buddy, Eddie Marchant, the former deputy chief constable of Durham, was the master of ceremonies for the night and did a brilliant job. He read letters of congratulation from Tony Blair, Jack Straw and David Blunkett. There was even a letter from my favourite local TV interviewer, the legendary Mike Neville, with whom I have become friendly over the years, but the highlight of the evening was a video of about 30 minutes, which Jean had organized, helped by Eddie. It showed highlights of my career, with clips of television broadcasts, my OBE investiture, my introduction into the House of Lords, together with my maiden speech. The video was crowned by personal messages to camera from Sir John Stevens, the Commissioner of the Metropolitan Police and the Rt Hon Michael Howard QC, the then Shadow Chancellor of the Exchequer.

We sang and danced until 3 a.m. on the Sunday and then the bombshell fell again. The *News of the World* ran the same story again, this time in the words of Salima Kabache herself.

I could not believe it! It was pure fantasy island! She described me squeezing her leg in the 'HOP' Inn, which was totally false, fictitiously going to my office at Millbank (they even got the address wrong!) where I allegedly kissed her. She never went near my office, as I never left the Lords with her!

She described me wearing a police cap (and little else!) and holding a truncheon. Total rubbish! I do not have a police cap or truncheon in London. Then the penny dropped – in my study in Durham where the reporter from the paper had been invited to speak to me, was a superintendent's cap on a shelf and a truncheon hanging on the wall! The pieces fell into place.

They had transferred the 'uniform' to London to feed the fantasy!

The whole thing was so bizarre, it was pure invention and all sensible people understood that. I took legal advice from no less a figure than the present Lord Chancellor, Charlie (Lord) Falconer QC, then Home Office spokesman in the Lords, who cautioned me against taking legal action because it would give the story 'legs'. As well as the publicity, the costs would be high and, at the end of the day it would be my word against hers. He did suggest, and I considered it, writing an article setting out the facts in a 'quality' paper. However, having discussed it with Jean, I decided against it, as it would simply cause another media feeding frenzy.

My good friend Nazir (Lord) Ahmed of Rotherham, has told me since that on the Thursday I was 'stung', he had seen the investigative reporter, whom he knows, from the *News of the World*, outside parliament with a photographer, presumably hoping I would come out with Salima. He was the same reporter, by all accounts, who posed as an Arab Sheik and duped Sophie Wessex into making indiscreet comments. I suspect also that the reason they wanted my London address was to send Salima round to my apartment. The wonderful world of the tabloid press! Still, I have done extremely well out of raising the profile of the Superintendents' Association over the years through the media, and have therefore had the fruits of publicity. I can have no complaint therefore, about the press taking an interest in me. I repeat the story of Salima, not in bitterness or angst – more in amazement that such trivial invention, sells mass copy!

The local Constituency Labour Party was magnificent. I received an email from Mathew Teale, the constituency secretary, informing me that at the AGM on 29 March the following resolution was passed unanimously:

> This Labour Party values the contribution made by Lord Mackenzie of Framwellgate, a member of this Labour Party, to public debate in recent years, especially in matters relating to public order and the need for a safe and just society, and urges him not to deprive this community and this party of his experience, knowledge and expertise because of matters which are essentially domestic, private and not relevant to his work for this community and party.

I even had a note from the chairman of Sunderland Football Club, Bob Murray, exhorting me to 'Keep your chin up!' It was wonderful support like that which kept me going during this difficult period!

Some other good news! On the Tuesday after the 'sting', when travelling by train, back from Durham to London, I received a message from the House of Lords to ring a Mary Hughes in London. Her husband had found my briefcase in the shop doorway. I called and collected it personally; we had a glass of wine, a good chat and a laugh about the 'sting'. Mary and her husband restored my faith in human beings! I later sent them a nice bottle of House of Lords whisky as a 'Thank you'.

It is said that the press like to build celebrities up – before knocking them down again; that there is no such thing as bad publicity. Tell that to my family! I apologized to them then, for the embarrassment caused, and willingly do so again. I had been well and truly conned, completely set up. Still I had no one to blame but myself for letting Salima within 100 miles of my apartment. As many people have told me since, 'You are too friendly with people!' You certainly live and learn!

I had arrived at the age of sixty with a bang! What timing! One thing is certain – you soon find who your friends are… The letters of support and solidarity I have had from friends and colleagues have been absolutely amazing. It is what keeps you going at times of adversity.

But how did I find myself being 'set up' in the Palace of Westminster, 40 years almost to the day, since joining the police in Durham. It was a long road from policing to politics. So I will start at the beginning of an intriguing lifelong journey from the terraced back streets of the north east of England, to the House of Lords, the mother of all parliaments…

CHAPTER 2

The Early Years

DARLINGTON WAS A railway town on the River Tees, which flows from picturesque Teesdale in the west of the County of Durham, down to the sea through industrial Middlesbrough. I was born at 51, Brighton Road in Darlington, on 21 March 1943, where I was brought up. Situated in the Eastbourne area of the town, it was pleasant enough, with two-up, two-down, terraced houses, with a toilet in the yard and a cobbled back lane where the washing hung from wall to wall. This made it difficult for vehicles to pass down on washing day, not that many people had vehicles in those days.

The jewel in the crown of the area was Eastbourne Park, which nestled at the bottom of the parallel streets which ran down from Neasham Road. The kids would play on the swings and roundabouts, or kick a ball about from dawn till dusk. It also had a bowling green and pleasant well-tended gardens. My soul mates at that time were Derek Hawdon, 6 months older than me, who lived a few doors down the street. A little younger, was Ronnie Knight who lived a couple of streets away. A few streets the other way, was Lawrence (Tom) Sawyer, who was to play an interesting part in my life. Another pal who I have since lost touch with was Robert Liddle. I remember I saw television for the first time at the house of a younger boy by the name of Geoffrey Wilson who lived with his mother, Marjorie and his father who I believe was in the Territorial Army. I used to go along and watch the 'Grove Family' on TV in black and white in the 1950s. I recall that Geoff's dad left a live bullet lying around the house and Geoffrey started to play with it and blew the tip of his finger off!

We did all the things that raggy-trousered kids did! We played football, went cycling, and built 'runaways' (pram wheels, with wooden boards to sit on). I remember when, on one occasion, whilst I was pulling Derek on a home-made 'runaway', he fell off and broke his arm! His mother was not best pleased!

I would go exploring with Tom Sawyer, to waste land where we would swing on ropes hung on trees. 'Jelly Island' was a favourite place on the Firth Moor (now a housing estate), which was a swamp-like piece of land just like jelly, as its name implied.

School
We all went to Dodmire School, which was nearby the park, the infants

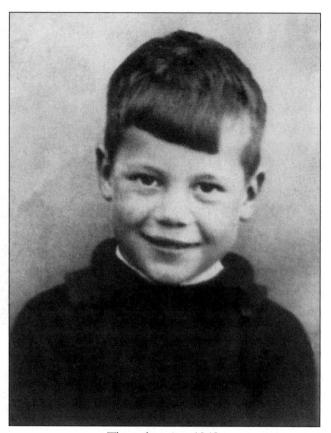

The author, circa 1948.

being housed in a large tin hut, which had been built 'temporarily' in 1920. It has only recently been demolished – but more of that later!

My mother, Lucy Ward, was a large, pleasant lady, who at that time did not work outside the home. She had married Frederick George Mackenzie on 9 November 1929 and moved to Darlington from Catterick, in North Yorkshire, where he had worked on a farm. Dad was a slim, dark wavy-haired man, who worked hard as a farm labourer. An ex-RAF man he looked very handsome in his younger days, in uniform. I never knew my grandparents, although I am told that the Mackenzie's forebears came down from Scotland as stonemasons and worked on Richmond Castle in North Yorkshire, which would account for my father's family settling at Catterick.

My earliest recollection is being wheeled in a pram in the South Park, where I recall there was an aviary, and I remember my mother going into the greenhouse to buy lettuce! Isn't the memory amazing?

Mum and Dad, circa 1943.

I was the third child of four, the eldest being Raymond followed by Margaret (a stunning, dark-haired, award winning beauty when she was in her teens), myself, born in 1943, followed by my younger sister Sylvia, born 4 years later.

Dad worked for the local council as the driver of a refuse wagon. He and his team would go up and down the back lanes and empty the pivoting bins, which were purpose-built into the wall of each house. The job had its perks. He would get overtime for 'washing off' the lorry at the end of a week.

I recall that he would collect parts of discarded bicycles on his round, slowly and painstakingly building them up in our back yard, buying the odd part here and there. He would then paint the finished bike and put it up for sale at an auction house called 'Fred Robinson's'. I can recall the household jubilation if the bike brought six or seven pounds.

I did not take a great deal of interest in education at that time and like most of my contemporaries, failed the 11 plus examination, which was the key to grammar school. My sister, Sylvia, on the other hand, 'shone' and passed with flying colours to the Darlington Girl's High School.

We rarely took holidays, apart from a day trip with the East End Working Men's Club to Redcar on the east coast, where we kids got half a crown each – twelve and a half pence today – as pocket money. My mother later took a

Dad (Frederick George Mackenzie), 1940s.

job at Hundens Lane Nursing Home as a housemaid, and having saved a little, our parents took Sylvia and me to a country cottage for a week in West Burton, Wensleydale. It was a hot summer and I recall that dad burnt his feet!

So I went to the Eastbourne Boys' Secondary School, the headmaster of which, George Welford, was to have a great influence on my life. I was no academic, but the headmaster was a strict man with good values, who talked straight. I respected him. He was a magistrate and dispensed justice in the school, as well as in the community.

Many years later when I was designing my family coat of arms on becoming a Peer, I recalled the values of George Welford and chose as my motto what I thought were the values he had instilled in me – *strength*; *humour*; and *determination*. These words in Latin are the motto on my Coat of Arms. But more of that later…

Wildlife, Music and Work

My passion as a teenager growing up in Darlington was wildlife generally, birdwatching in particular and hiking around High Force in Teesdale, with my school pal Alex Walker, who still lives in Darlington.

I always kept sticklebacks (minnows), newts or frogs, which I delighted in breeding in a glass tank in the back yard. I used to be amazed, watching the female Great Crested Newt laying her eggs between the leaves of water plants and folding the leaves over with her back legs. I would take zoology magazines, and still have the binoculars I bought for £12. I remember saving up for them and the excitement of their arrival by post from Denmark Hill, London.

Much to the despair of my mother, I moved on from fish and amphibians to reptiles. I became an amateur herpetologist (the study of reptiles). Grass Snakes and Green Lizards were kept in a vivarium in the back yard. On one occasion I vividly remember hearing my mother scream. She had seen a lizard escaping from the tank, tried to catch it and it had shed its tail. To her horror, the tail continued to wriggle frantically, jumping about the yard (a defence mechanism to distract a potential predator). We caught the lizard and it lived on, with a stump for a tail!

I also discovered my gift for music as a child. We had a piano in the front room and I discovered that I could play any tune I knew, with one finger. If I could whistle it – I could play it – starting with 'God Save the Queen!'

As the years wore on, I used to amaze my pals by playing the piano by ear in pubs where live music was allowed. I also started to sing in public and mimicked the Jewish singer Al Jolson, whom I loved to hear. I saw the film *The Jolson Story* many times. I still sing to this day, and for a few years sang in the Durham Constabulary Choir. I often play my Hammond electric organ,

Catterick Band, circa 1915.

which stands proudly in our cottage where we now live in Shincliffe Village. I use both hands, playing the tune with the right and the chords with the left. I can even simultaneously use the foot-pedals and it seems to sound all right, yet I still cannot read a note of music!

Years later I once mentioned my gift of music to my ageing aunt Edith Robinson. She was my dad's sister and one of the few relatives who kept in touch with us, as we were not a close, extended family. She was living in retirement at Darlington and I used to call and see her when I was in town. I told her that I could not understand where my musical ability came from. She smiled, walked across the room and took out an old book. Inside was a picture of Catterick Brass Band (circa 1915). Pictured in the band were two of my dad's uncles and my grandfather. All had been fine musicians!

I left school in 1959 with no qualifications to speak of, and did what most young lads did at that time, applied for an apprenticeship at the local factory. I mentioned earlier that Darlington was a railway town, and it seemed perfectly natural to apply to British Railways' North Road Workshops, to become an apprentice fitter.

My family were delighted when I was accepted and went to the training school in Whessoe Road, beside the workshops at the opposite end of the town. I still remember the instructor George Pickering, who was disabled and walked with a limp. Mr Barnes was the other instructor. In my class were people I have rarely seen since, such as Terry Johnson, Joe Smith, Jeff Gibbon, Walter Metcalfe, John Bates and Kenny Kilcran.

North Road Railways Training School, 1959. (The author is standing 5th from right.)

Holidaying in Great Yarmouth. (The author, Derek Hawdon, Ronnie Knight and David Robinson.)

Derek Hawdon and Alex Walker also accepted apprenticeships, and we made many new friends during that time of our lives. These included Malcolm Sturdy whom I had lost touch with and was delighted to see again at my sixtieth birthday party!

Derek and I used to cycle across the town to work and the apprenticeship involved work-experience in different departments; fitting shop, turning metal on lathes, boiler work, the diesel shop and the drawing office. There was also an academic side to it. I was attending the local technical college studying mechanical engineering (City & Guilds), and for the first time in my life I started to blossom!

I recall winning the Group Class Prize for engineering and was asked to stay on longer in the drawing office, which I was delighted to do, because it was clean and 'white collar' employment.

In 1959 at the age of sixteen, our attention was turning to other things – girls, sport and alcohol. We started going on 'lads' holidays to Butlins, at Great Yarmouth and Skegness. These were drunken, fumbling affairs and all part of growing up. We listened with wide eyes to the exploits of the older men in the factory. We started playing Sunday league football. 'Eastbourne Rovers' was our team with Derek, Ronnie Knight, David Robinson, who now lives in Coventry, and Ian Oliver. Ian married Brenda Peaks and they built their own bungalow in Shildon, where she was born. They have lived there ever since. Ian and David, along with their wives, also came to the sixtieth birthday party.

Together with Derek, Robbo, Ronnie and others, we would catch the train at weekends from Darlington to Stockton to go drinking in the many lively bars. Why Stockton, I don't know, it must have been because we were spreading our wings! There was a particular bar just off the High Street called the Brunswick Arms, which had live music, a pianist and a drummer, whom we dubbed the 'drug addict' because of his unkempt appearance. The early 'entertainer' in me must have surfaced then, because during the interval I would sit at the piano and play sing-along tunes. If the weather was inclement I would borrow my dad's mackintosh, which was far too large, and Derek would always pull my leg about it.

Romance

We used to practise football in Eastbourne Park and it was there that I met the love of my life, Jean. She told me afterwards that she liked my legs. (We used to practise in shorts.) I certainly liked the look of her! She was only fourteen, with three years between us, and she was a very pretty blonde, with a curvaceous figure. She had come to Eastbourne Park with her friend Linda Walker, who subsequently married Ronnie Knight and lived in the Eastbourne area of the town. They were both pupils at the Technical School where they were taking a secretarial course.

We started courting in the conventional way. I would take her to the pictures, go to her house in the north of the town and she would visit me. I remember that Jim, her father, was unhappy at first when this big lad started seeing his daughter. Eventually however, he came to accept me and later we used to go out for a pint on a Sunday and put the world right. Jim and I became great chums.

Attending night school with me at this time was Lawrence 'Tom' Sawyer, whom I had grown up with. He was serving an apprenticeship at Stephenson's, a local factory servicing the railway industry. We would call at the Red Lion public house in the centre of town on the way home from evening classes, have a couple of pints and plan the rest of our lives.

I particularly used to hate having to crawl inside dark, damp, engine tenders to push bolts through for the fitter to secure. Neither of us was happy with our lot, and we considered a range of options, the strongest of which was joining the navy. Tom was courting a friend of Jean's, called Sylvia Parks, a tall, pleasant, attractive girl who Tom eventually married. I recall that Jean was working in the same offices as Sylvia at Paton & Baldwins, a woollen manufacturer, so we would often go out in foursomes.

I was still wrestling with the question of what to do with the rest of my life, when Jean changed her job and started work in the British Railway offices, at Bank Top Station. I recall being extremely jealous during those teenage years and I would interrogate Jean about whom she had spoken to and where she had been.

The bicycle was my main mode of transport and I had a couple of bikes stolen from outside Jean's house in Katherine Street. This brought me into contact with the police, when I called to report the thefts, and I remember a sergeant at Darlington police station commenting that I was a big fine lad and that I would make a good 'bobby'. It was then that I started to ponder the possibility. I was still doing well as an apprentice at North Road Workshop and at night school, but I became more and more attracted to the police service and sent away for further information. Tom Sawyer could not believe it when I told him, because although we talked a lot about changing careers, he was witness to my academic successes at night school, and thought it was a retrograde step. But my mind was made up!

I recall another lad at North Road called Mike Hoy, also joining the police and moving down to West Yorkshire as they were advertising for recruits, so I decided to do the same. My parents were not happy when I told them that I was giving up the much-coveted apprenticeship at North Road, but I could not be budged. I was now excited at the prospect and was determined to see it through. It was when I went to get measured (there was a height limit in those non politically correct days), and I remember the sergeant asking me why I was leaving Durham. I told him that I believed there was more chance of getting appointed in Yorkshire. 'Don't be daft lad, try Durham first, then you can go down there if you don't make it here!'

The Police

It was good advice and altered the course of my life. I applied to Durham County Constabulary in the autumn of 1962. Following simple spelling and maths tests at Darlington police station, I was called for interview to the police headquarters at Newton Aycliffe, just north of Darlington.

The chief constable AA (Alex) Muir was in the chair, with his deputy William Hogg and one other, as I recall. It was a very easy-going interview and I was there with one or two contemporaries. I remember Keith Readman and Barry Simpson were ex RAF, the remainder were civilians from a broad range of jobs. Ken Morrison, Billy Laws, Ron Parks (who was to later hang himself), Harry Dawson (who was to be a groomsman at my wedding), Bob Hall (who retired from Durham as a detective super-intendent) Harry Morton, and Trevor Brown. I could go on – it was a large intake.

We were all working class lads and I don't recall any women joining

Tom Sawyer's bachelor party, 1962. The author is 3rd left, front row; Tom Sawyer is 3rd from right.

Durham County Police in that intake. I was absolutely delighted when I discovered that I had been successful in my application. I was told however that there was a long waiting list and it would be some time before I could be appointed.

Shortly after my acceptance, I was invited to the bachelor night of 'Tom' Sawyer, who was marrying his girlfriend Sylvia. We all went out on the town, round the pubs in the centre of Darlington. I knew most of the lads, but they were mainly Tom's pals, not really mine. We finished up I recall, at a Chinese Restaurant on the corner of Crown Street in the town centre. There is little doubt that our group were noisy and caused the trouble. In any event I remember all hell breaking loose with tables being overturned and Chinese waiters coming out of the kitchens with the most horrendous weapons, knives and clubs with nails in the end. My only thoughts were for my future as a police officer and I 'legged it' down the stairs and out of the restaurant as quickly as I could. I saw the police cars going to the premises as I ran away. My career had nearly ended before it had begun!

1963 was a terrible winter. It was a long one too, as I waited for details of my appointment to come through. I waited right through the Christmas period and in February I got word that my appointment date was 1 April 1963, which of course was April Fools' Day! Before that I had to go to Aycliffe to get measured and kitted out with new uniform. Durham was, and still is, an excellent force. Not all were so lucky. Some of the smaller forces,

Sunderland Borough being one, kitted out their new recruits in second hand uniforms and I recollect one recruit, who was a former surveyor, resigning out of sheer embarrassment because of his shoddy kit.

In Durham we were given the very best. A winter and a summer uniform, a mackintosh, a great warm overcoat, two helmets, one with a dark badge for nights and the other with a silver badge for days. New cord gloves and a couple of pairs of new shoes. I was as proud as punch when I took them home to show my parents and Jean.

I was slim, 6 feet 3 inches and looked quite a commanding figure with the helmet on. As I mentioned earlier, there was a height restriction in those days and we were all young men with a certain presence. Without being disrespectful, I still feel embarrassed, usually in London, when I see an extremely short police officer, of either sex, not because they are less competent, but because they simply lack that certain 'presence', which I think the public expects of a police officer.

CHAPTER 3

A First Taste of Discipline

M Y POLICING CAREER started with a week at Harperley Hall, near Crook in County Durham on 1 April 1963 on a wage of £11.75 a week (or 11 pounds, fifteen shillings as it was then). Harperley Hall was a former mansion house, which had been acquired by the police many years before. It was the force training school and also housed the mounted section, with the stables at the back, and the dog section. I recall that the first week was spent gardening and generally improving the grounds, before we went to Newby Wiske Hall, the Home Office training school, near Northallerton in North Yorkshire, for initial police training with officers from surrounding forces.

This was the year of the great train robbery and the moors murders. The Beatles were still holding centre stage on the music front and Harold Macmillan was handing over the Conservative premiership to Sir Alec Douglas-Home. It was to be two years before the death penalty was abolished!

The significant thing about policing in England and Wales is the uniqueness of the (now) 43 individual forces. Forces were reduced to 43, by compulsory amalgamation, in 1968 and 1974. It follows that although recruit training was national in content, and delivered regionally, forces had differing forms and procedures, which could only be taught locally. This local training would take place at Harperley Hall, after the initial 13-week course at Newby Wiske Hall.

I still make the humorous point that when I joined the job – there was a police force and a postal service. Now we have a police service and a parcel force!

Life was fairly easy at Harperley Hall. I was bonding with my colleagues on what was, in effect, the first lengthy spell away from home. The pleasantries were to change, because the following week we were going to Newby Wiske and I would have to get used to it with many more officers from surrounding areas.

Newby Wiske was another imposing former country mansion with a parade ground at the front, classrooms, dining facilities and dormitory style bedrooms in the main building. The first thing that struck me was the discipline of the regime. It was a military style of training in which you did not question orders, boots had to be bulled, there were inspections of bed-packs, which had to be prepared in a certain way, and woe betide you if you got it wrong!

Newby Wiske initial course, April 1963. The author is 2nd from left, middle row.

Our intake was so large that the group was split into two syndicates, a] and b]. Understandably, the two syndicates became rivals and I believe that this drove up performance, both academically and on the sports field and drill square.

I have to say that at first I didn't like the regime and felt a little nervous. Our class sergeant was an imposing figure with a balding head, from Hull City, a chap called Harry Poller. I grew to like him. But all the recruits were apprehensive and some didn't last a week. The ex-military recruits were totally at home and I have to say, the disciplined life started to grow on me. I started to take a pride in my 'turn out'. I used enjoy drill on the square and marching to our syndicate marching tune 'Sussex by the Sea'.

Part of the training involved us doing a night patrol of the old building, in full uniform, and at various fire points throughout the old mansion, recording the time and signing the record. I suppose looking back it was also designed to get you used to patrolling in the dark alone. One of my fellow recruits was a northeast lad called Billy Laws, with a broad local accent (what we used to call 'pitmatic'). He was a loveable character who felt he might have difficulty on the academic side of the course. He made the mistake of telling people that he was nervous about patrolling alone in the dark, as he had heard strange noises. There was a strong rumour about the hall being haunted.

We hatched a wicked plot to give Bill the fright of his life! Because we did the night patrol by rote, we knew when PC Laws' turn to do a night shift was due. One of the fire points requiring a signature was down a long dark corridor with a shower at the end nearest the door. The fire point was at the bottom of the other end of the corridor, which was a cul-de-sac.

On the night in question, we got the tallest constable to stand in the shower behind the curtain, wearing his helmet and covered by a sheet. A frightening apparition on a dark night! He had a green torch and a red torch for eyes through the sheet. We all pretended to be asleep as we heard Billy Laws getting ready to do his fire check. He went out into the dark night to perform his duty, during which incidentally, you were not allowed to put the lights on, as it would disturb other residents.

He went on his rounds flashing his torch nervously and we all listened in anticipation. As PC Laws got to the bottom of the corridor with the shower curtain, our ghostly colleague switched on his green and red 'eyes' and let out a low groan. You can imagine the response. Billy Laws had to run towards the 'spirit' to get to the door out of the corridor. Word has it that he bounced off the wall until he came to the opening. When he ran back to join us in the dormitory, we all pretended to be asleep and I swear that he had turned as white as a ghost himself!

It was not until we were due to pass-out from the college 13 weeks later that we admitted what we had done. When I think about it now it was a silly prank, because he could have had a weak heart and there could have been disastrous consequences.

I travelled back and forth between Darlington and Newby Wiske by car, sharing with one or other of the few who had their own transport. As I recall it Ron Parkes, who later tragically committed suicide whilst a serving constable at Darlington, and Ken Lavery, the son of a middle class business man from Stockton, who later became a superintendent, gave me a lift. Colleagues were very generous in this regard.

I did well on the course and found criminal law a fascinating subject. We used to learn 'definitions' by rote and I found it extremely useful to be able to recall matters quickly. For example to prove an offence you were required to know what the definition was without having access to a textbook. If you ran through the definition of larceny, now theft, it became apparent that you had to 'take and carry away property, belonging to another, with the intention of permanently depriving the other of it'. These were the points to prove when you put the file together. Similarly with powers of arrest, it was essential that you knew in your head the fact that, to arrest someone for what was then a felony, you needed, not evidence at this stage, but 'reasonable grounds to suspect him of committing the offence.'

I was very fortunate that in my newly discovered determination to do well, I used to write definitions, the Judges' Rules, powers of arrest and the like on small cards and commit them to memory whilst travelling on buses or any other 'dead' time.

I seem to have the same ability now with jokes, being able to pull them down off the shelf to fit the conversation. They are often triggered by a comment someone has made. I suppose I have become a bit of a raconteur in that respect.

But back to initial training. I passed out with flying colours, with above average results. Jean attended the pass-out ceremony with Harry Dawson's girlfriend, also called Jean, on a hot July day. One recruit, a tall solid lad, Arthur Charlton, collapsed with the heat and burst his lip. We gave displays of point duty, marching to 'Sussex by the Sea' and generally we were proud to be fully-fledged constables. We were then scattered to the winds, some of course, were never to be seen again. It rather saddens me as I write this, that military style pass-out parades are being abolished. I think there is a lot to be said for discipline, marching to drill and the team spirit engendered by being part of a proud group of uniformed officers. It was always a very proud occasion for parents and loved ones.

The modern day recruit still undergoes a two-year probationary period, consisting of a two-week induction and familiarization course, followed by a 15-week residential course delivered by Centrex, the newly branded central training body. Then there is the two-week local procedure course; followed by ten weeks patrolling with an experienced tutor constable. There follows a two-week review of additional needs, with the remainder of the two years consisting of further development work. Although it sounds similar 40 years later, the content has changed dramatically with less emphasis on learning by rote and more on evidence gathering, intelligence, race and diversity issues, as well as understanding the society we live in. No doubt there will be a move to embrace electronic learning and the increasing use of technology in due course.

Tyneside

My first posting was to Jarrow-on-Tyne on 7 July 1963, together with Harry Dawson, also a Darlington lad, who had been in my syndicate at Newby Wiske. The policy seemed to be to post recruits to the farthest point of the county from their homes. Harry and I decided to travel together on the train from Darlington with our kit in suitcases, as neither of us had a car. I was quite excited, said goodbye to Jean and the family and headed north to Tyneside.

Harry had been allocated a room at a police hostel; I think it was Henry Study House in Bedeburn Road. I was placed in 'digs' in Hebburn with a lady whose memory I treasure. Susie Forster and her husband Jess lived in Victoria Road East, near Reyrolles' factory, where Jess worked. They were a lovely couple and Susie became my surrogate mother. In the digs with me was one of the most unusual characters I have ever come across in the police, Michael Coverdale. He has since retired on Tyneside as a constable. I suppose you would describe him as eccentric. He was extremely bright but I discovered that he got very excited during crises. Not the most useful qualities in a police officer.

Professional wrestling, which is more about showmanship than sport, was very popular on television at that time and, would really excite Mick. He would contort his face and vigorously rub his hands together. It got to the point where Susie, Jess and I would enjoy watching the antics of Mick rather than watch the telly!

Even worse than that was the occasion when I was patrolling the Viking Shopping Precinct in the centre of Jarrow and, came across PC Coverdale watching the wrestling from the pavement, on a television in a shop window. He was reacting in exactly the same way in full uniform! I could not believe it and I cannot imagine what the shoppers thought on that Saturday afternoon.

On another occasion, a barking dog, again in the shopping centre, was annoying him so he did no more than take out his truncheon and proceeded to attack the dog with his 'stick'. I think his sergeant gave him advice!

After a week we returned to Harperley Hall for the local procedure course for two weeks, which was quite relaxing after the pressures of Newby Wiske. Then back to Jarrow.

I took to foot patrol in uniform like a fish to water. The superintendent was a quiet, wiry officer called Chris Wills who talked with a slight lisp. The chief inspector, his second in command, was Norman Bell, a pleasant avuncular, fair-haired man, who was the main prosecutor in the magistrates' court. There was no Crown Prosecution Service in those days. I was fortunate in that superintendent Wills took a shine to me and became my mentor, but more of that later. The inspector who welcomed us to Jarrow was a real eccentric called Derek Amos. He was a pleasant, rotund man who reminded me of Benny Hill. He had worn 'spats' on his shoes when he had been in the CID a few years earlier. Inspector Amos was a well-read man who made us feel welcome.

Policing in those days consisted of leaving the police station on foot with a whistle, truncheon and note book, after being briefed by the shift sergeant as to which 'beats' you were to patrol. You did not return to the station until your meal break, some 4 hours later, unless you made an arrest, keeping in touch with the office by 'making a point' at a particular public telephone kiosk. If the office needed to contact you, they would ring you there.

You were also subject to surprise visits by the sergeant, or less likely, by the inspector, when he would usually sign your notebook, known as 'giving you a chalk'.

For the first two years of service a police officer served a probationary period, during which time duties were varied to provide a variety of experience. Initially a more experienced officer, often a fellow probationer, accompanied you. He is now called a tutor constable. In my case the guide was PC Roger Reed, an extremely bright, well-read officer whom I became extremely friendly with. Roger introduced me to 'The World at One' on Radio 4, and I have been a devotee ever since! Little did I know that I would broadcast regularly on the programme many years later as president of the Superintendents' Association and also as a member of the House of Lords. Roger retired from Northumbria Police as a superintendent and has toured the Lords with his family and kindly turned up at my sixtieth birthday party.

As I got to know the area, I became acquainted with shopkeepers, licensees, and elderly people on the beat, as well as criminals. But it was the young who provided the bread and butter work. Kids causing a nuisance, drunkenness, urinating in doorways, breaches of the peace, and of course the poor old motorist – always a fertile source of law breaking. In my view however, that was not real police work, necessary though it was to gain experience. The real job was crime!

I hit the jackpot one night when, with only six months service, I was patrolling the back of the shops in the Viking Centre in Jarrow around

02:00 a.m. A brick wall surrounded the shops with a gap to allow delivery trucks to get in. I saw a movement and a chink of light and it was then that I saw two men coming from the back of one of the shops, carrying something. I later discovered it was the cash box. I went towards the entrance to the walled area to investigate and realized that they had broken into the wine shop. I knew that I could only arrest one of them as they rushed towards me. As I grabbed one of the burglars, a 22-year-old called Vincent Ronald MacDonald, he pushed past me and I fell to the ground losing my helmet and torch. When I gave chase, I saw that he was running towards a builder's compound, which was a cul-de-sac. A fence surrounded it with barbed wire on the top.

I called on him to stop, he looked around and picked up a large piece of cast iron guttering and threatened me with it. I took out my truncheon and told him not to be silly, whereupon he threw the guttering directly at me. I remember thinking 'They didn't tell me about this at the training school!'

I ducked and the guttering smashed onto the floor behind me. It then dawned on me that this was a serious matter. If the guttering had hit me it would have taken my head off! MacDonald attempted to get over the fence and I closed with him. I struck a couple of blows on the back of his head with my truncheon and tried to pull him down, but he just became more violent. It wasn't like the movies, where when someone is hit they get knocked out!

We both fell to the ground and started rolling about the builder's compound. I was determined that he was not going anywhere without me. It was then that I became aware of the blood. My truncheon blows had split his head, he subsequently required nine stitches and, we were both covered in his blood. I remember shouting to people outside the compound to call the police. Then the cavalry arrived!

It was the divisional car on routine patrol. In those days one car patrolled the whole division – there were no panda vehicles. Ken Kerr, an inveterate, experienced thief taker, was driving it. He told me later that he thought it was two drunks rolling around in the compound. He then realized that I was wearing uniform and came to my aid. MacDonald was arrested. My prisoner was taken in custody to hospital and I got cleaned up.

I spent some time with Ron Bradley the detective constable assisting with the preparation of the case. Although we knew who MacDonald's accomplice was, I could not identify him and he would not admit it, so Vince carried the can alone. He received six months imprisonment, the magistrates' court maximum. The court commended me for the arrest, as did the chief constable subsequently. The headline in the local paper read 'Young Jarrow PC is praised!' The commendation was published in force general orders. I had made my mark as a thief taker!

I was still courting Jean and going home to Darlington on the No 46 bus on my rest days. I used to enjoy calling in the local pub where dad would be drinking and I could see the pride on his face when he introduced me to his pals. 'This is Brian, he's a policeman' he would beam.

Everything was too good to last however. My father was a smoker and suffered badly with his chest. He had been off sick for some time and had to occasionally sit in the back yard at home to get his breath. I recall a lot of people like that in those days and I just cannot understand people who still insist on destroying their lungs by smoking. I have ardently campaigned against it all my life.

Christmas of 1963 was a disaster. I was on leave fortunately, and on the morning of Boxing Day I heard a scream from my mum and dad's bedroom. I went in and saw that my father had stopped breathing. I couldn't believe it. Mum was distraught, so I took his false teeth out and tried to revive him, but could feel that he was cold. His heart had given up at the age of 56!

Jean came round to our house that Boxing Day and we walked round Eastbourne Park and I unashamedly cried my eyes out. My great regret is that dad did not witness my ultimate destiny – or even a hint of it! At least I have the satisfaction of knowing that he was proud of me being a police constable.

I was quite frugal with money as a youngster, and it was about this time that I read an article about the value of regularly investing in unit trusts. I therefore set up a direct debit of £1 per month from my salary to the Barclay Unicorn Unit Trust. As time went on I increased the amount to £5 and then to £20 a month. The investment was never touched and increased over the years to quite a sizeable sum.

Susie was looking after me at Hebburn and my widowed mother spoiled me at home. I enjoyed the job and did my probationer studying with relish, both law and education subjects. There was a general education promotion exam in those days. I attended a civil defence course at Sedgefield, worked in the divisional administrative office for a week and constantly attended the weekly probation classes. We had homework to do and were set exams from time to time, which, much to my surprise, I started to excel at.

It was just before I went on my refresher probationary training course that I went home to Susie with a burst lip and a black eye. There had been a disturbance at the Jarrow bus station around 11:00 p.m. I told the instigator, a youth called James Wynne, that he would be arrested if he did not desist. He continued to cause trouble so I put a hand on his shoulder and he said, 'You touch me again and I'll stick one on you'.

There is a golden rule of policing that you never bark unless you are prepared to bite, so I went to arrest him and he punched me in the face. I fell to the ground and another man came to my rescue. He got punched as well for his bother. Four youths were eventually arrested and Wynne got borstal training. Incidentally, the man who came to assist me was a special constable, a bus driver, and I have valued the work that these brave volunteers do ever since.

We spent our off duty time playing sport and socializing with the locals. I got to know Peter Hepburn very well and his friend, Derek Armstrong, a local businessman. Peter was a local character who eventually rose in the council to become Mayor. Coincidentally I still have a drink with his son, Steve, in the Palace of Westminster. Stephen Hepburn is the current Labour Member of Parliament for Jarrow. It's a small world!

Did joining the police change my personality? People had told me that it had made me a harder person. I am not so sure. What you do is adapt to the circumstances. The police culture is very macho, and you are conscious of being in the public eye, particularly when patrolling in uniform. When dealing with incidents, from road accidents to lost children, you are conscious of being watched and not being expected to show emotion. I think therefore that what happens, is that when dealing with such matters, you disguise your true feelings and become a bit of an actor. It may well be of course that you take the emotional stress home with you and let off steam there. It is for that reason that there seems to be an affinity between individuals in the emergency services, which occasionally results in a culture of alcohol abuse when off duty.

In February 1964 I returned to Newby Wiske for the two-week refresher course. This was where officers could re-live interesting occurrences experienced in the first 12 months of their service. I recall that I did well in the examination at the end of the course.

The highlight of 1964 was my six week CID training. I used to work long hours, quite often from 09:00 a.m. until 02:00 a.m. if it was busy. Experienced detectives under the command of detective chief inspector 'Matty' Pallister, showed me the ropes: Ron Bradley, Fred Dixon, who tended to specialize in juvenile offending, Keith Tweddle, a young, good looking, well turned out detective, Jack Marriott, who was just the opposite, but a very effective fraud investigator, whose appearance let him down. He reminds me of detective Columbo in retrospect.

I loved CID work and learned as much as I could in the short time available. I was of course still attending probation classes and fitting in studies and homework.

Wedding Bells

Meanwhile, on the domestic front, Jean and I were an item, so we decided to get married. Even though we had very few means, other than our respective jobs, I knew we would be allocated a police house.

In December of 1964 I was posted to administration duties at divisional headquarters, Clervaux Terrace, for two months. Police Constable Billy Weddle worked in the office with an admin clerk called Hilda. I quickly learned how to deal with correspondence, accident forms, petty cash and the like. What I did not know was that my mentor, Superintendent Wills, was grooming me.

I had applied for permission to get married. Headquarters had to approve your choice of partner – strange as that might sound these days. Jean obviously got the seal of approval so we started making plans for the wedding at Darlington on 6 March 1965.

I had by now moved into a new hostel near the police station and Susie, my ex landlady, had secured a job there as a housemaid – so I did not lose touch with her. In January I went on my final refresher course, this time to an overspill training school at RAF Leeming in North Yorkshire. Again I was excelling in the examinations – I must have been a late developer!

When I returned to my admin duties, you can imagine my surprise when Superintendent Wills walked into the office at Jarrow, stood beside my desk and said, 'There's a wedding present for you son', dropping a set of house keys onto the desk. It was a brand new police house at Whitburn, near Sunderland, with a sea view. Jean and I were to be the first occupants after our wedding. Superintendent Wills then said, 'You'd better get the divisional car and go and have a look at it then.' PC Billy Weddle took me to see the marital home and it was a dream house, with gardens, front and back, but completely unfurnished. I had a couple of months to get it habitable as I was told I was transferring to Whitburn as a detached beat officer from 6 March, our wedding day.

A detached beat was a coveted posting, normally reserved for officers with lots of experience and many years service. You worked 'discretional' hours, which amounted to being available round the clock. I could not believe that I had secured such a posting whilst still a probationary constable – the stars were shining favourably on me!

We were duly married in Darlington at St Paul's Church, which was later burnt down, and held the reception at the plush Imperial Hotel in Darlington. It was a great day, with many from Jarrow attending. Susie and some of the ladies from the hostel came down. Harry Dawson was a groomsman and my brother in law, Margaret's late husband Martin Deacy, was best man.

After the reception Jean and I caught the train to London and spent a thoroughly miserable week in a hotel near Kings Cross. It was cold and we got tired of walking round and came home early to our new home.

A Country Bobby

Life at Whitburn was magical. Jean was now working at a local solicitors'
firm in Sunderland and I was one of a team of police officers at Whitburn
Section in the Boldon sub-division. It was just like *Heartbeat* on the
television. The sergeant was a big, jovial man called Jim Anderson. The other
constables were Eric Smith, a sarcastic, bitter man, who lived in the police
house next door to me. Bill Burt, a powerful man, who always had an eye for
the ladies, and they for him. The other officer was Jimmy Thompson who
reminded me of a ferret. He had a wrinkled face and, unusually for someone
of his age in those days, a crew cut.

We would all assemble at 9 a.m. in the office; the sergeant would go
through the complaints book and allocate tasks. We were allowed one evening
off, in addition to our rest days. This meant that even in a small village like
Whitburn, there were always three officers plus, except for his rest days and
leave, the sergeant. A luxury indeed by today's policing standards!

It is not often realized that with the advent of the 8-hour continuous tour
of duty introduced in 1968, police coverage was reduced five fold at a stroke
in rural areas. To provide the same round-the-clock cover in Whitburn, for
example, remember we were on call during the night, it would have required
20 constables. Now you can see where all the police officers have gone.

Having said that, the days of officers being exploited round the clock had
to change. Another factor of course was the increase in squads as the service
became more specialist in nature. But much more of these matters later.

The job also had the services of the police wife of course. With Jean and
me living in an identifiable police house with an office attached, members of
the public would call to report incidents. If I was not at home, Jean would
have to deal with it. I recall one day she rang me asking me to come home as
a car had collided with a horse just outside the house!

I used to travel to Jarrow for swimming practice and of course the
probationary classes, but mostly, I was learning the trade of the omnipotent
country bobby. The end of my probationary period was over at the end of
March 1965 so I was now a fully-fledged police constable. I kept on studying
law however as I had my eye on the promotion examinations. There was no
stopping me now!

It was the evening of 10 September 1965 that I was called to the youth
club at Marsden, just north of Whitburn Colliery on the Coast Road. There
was a massing gang of youths from South Shields, who were taking on the
local Whitburn youths by the youth club. Richard Reed, a brilliant advocate
who was confined to a wheelchair, rather like Ironside the American attorney
on television, described it later in court as follows. 'Two armies of young
thugs had formed up and were using the road as a battlefield. They were
armed with all sorts of weapons. PC Mackenzie who had told them to go

Jarrow Lifesaving Team, 1965. The author is 2nd left, front row. Inspector Derek Amos is in the centre.

away realized that the hysterical and stupid young men were starting something of a magnitude seldom seen', said Mr Reed. 'The officer was surrounded after arresting two of them. They closed in on the officer, who drew his truncheon and backed against a wall.'

I recall that the experience was a very hairy moment, as the warring groups united against me. Fortunately the youth leaders had dialled 999 and I remember my relief when I saw PC Bill Burt cycling towards us from Whitburn. It is surreal when I think about it now. Bill was a big man in every sense and was a judo expert so the two of us grabbed a prisoner each and held the fort until reinforcements, in the form of traffic patrols, arrived on the scene. One of the traffic officers was PC Rod Mackay, who was married to the policewoman sergeant at Jarrow, Nora Mackay, whom I still see from time to time at pensioners' functions. Their son became a police officer in Durham.

The youths scattered in all directions and we managed to arrest four or five of them, one in the yard of the Souter Point Lighthouse. Again the newspaper headlines were graphic '100 "frenzied" youths mob two policemen' [*Northern Echo*] 'Police take on 100 in gang war' [*Shields Gazette*]. This incident resulted in my second commendation for good police work.

My swimming, particularly lifesaving, was coming on a treat. Jarrow Division of the force had been fortunate in having a very keen young training sergeant called Ray Thompson who had been an instructor at Newby Wiske. Also, working in special branch at Jarrow, was another keen swimmer called Stan Hall.

We had entered a team in the force lifesaving competition and won. We also won the Northumberland and Durham competition and the No 2 regional finals, which consisted of all the forces in the north. As a result we were entered to represent the region in the 'Silver Baton' competition nationally.

All the team were Jarrow officers and we trained at South Shields Derby Street baths. Other members of the team were PCs Harry Dawson, Stan Hall, Eddie Simpson, Arthur Pringle, Dave Robson, Stuart Hamilton and Sergeant Ray Thompson. It was a great time to be young, fit and enthusiastic and I loved it.

In the national finals held in London we came sixth out of twelve and everyone was very proud of our achievements.

In December 1965 I was one of several members of the team to be awarded the Diploma of the Royal Lifesaving Society. I still have it framed to this day in my study, signed by Lord Mountbatten of Burma, the Grand President of the Society. Incidentally, the award of the Diploma earned me my third commendation from the chief constable for achievement.

CHAPTER 4

The CID
(Criminal Investigation Department)

I WAS STILL beavering away at Whitburn, and studying for my sergeant's examination, which I was not qualified to sit until 1966. It was a pleasant surprise therefore, when I received notification that I had been selected to attend a two week 'Potential CID Officers' Course' at Harperley Hall.

Durham was a very innovative force at this time and the head of training was a chief superintendent called George Fenn, who was a tall commanding figure with black hair, a man bubbling with enthusiasm for police work and an inspirational leader, who later became chief constable of Cheshire. I did well on the course and was delighted when I was appointed to the CID at Jarrow on 5 July 1966. I had become a detective in just over three years. It was a remarkably early appointment in those days and, I felt I was unstoppable. My career change had been a masterstroke!

I took to the CID like a duck to water, working all the hours I could. In retrospect it must have been a lonely life for Jean, but she supported me wholeheartedly. We were a busy team in the CID, with plenty of crime to deal with, but I also had my studies as well. I studied methodically, going through each subject and memorizing those important facts that I thought were relevant. I would go into the empty magistrates' court, which was adjacent to the police station in Jarrow, and study during the lunch hour. The chief constable commended me for the fourth time in 1966 when I detected a difficult case of shop breaking and receiving. I was now really getting into my stride.

On the domestic front, we had moved back to Jarrow when I was posted to the CID, to a semi detached police house in Stirling Avenue on the 'Scotch' estate, near to the John Reid Road. Our neighbours were Harry and Ruth Turnbull. Harry was a quiet, nice natured detective, who worked in the scientific aids department. This job consisted of, in the main, examining scenes of crime for forensic evidence, fingerprints and the like. Harry and Ruth moved on, eventually to work in special branch, and tragically he died shortly after he retired, but I was delighted that Ruth came to my sixtieth birthday party.

A young PC, Tom Marjoram and his wife, became our new neighbours in Stirling Avenue. Also in the scientific aids department at that time was a fascinating, swashbuckling character, called Derek Wright. He was always suntanned, was a brilliant gardener and fisherman, and could drink any of us under the table. We became firm friends.

The culture of the CID at that time was to work hard and play hard. If there was not a great deal happening late at night, we would go to Franchi's Nightclub at Jarrow, or to the Beach Club at South Shields, to see the cabaret. In those days, before gambling was controlled by the Gaming Act of 1968, the profits from the gaming side of the club would support excellent shows with top stars. Tom Jones, Dusty Springfield, Shirley Bassey, and Bob Monkhouse, were just some of the performers on the circuit at that time. Drinking and driving was not so frowned upon then and I suppose we reflected the attitude of most people at that time.

The money in clubs and gambling also attracted criminals however and the northeast had visits from the Kray twins and others, to try and muscle in on the rich pickings. But the local hoodlums sent them packing and, the new legislation to control gaming came in before they managed to get a foothold.

The Special Course

Whilst all this was going on, I was still studying hard for my sergeants' examination. For someone who had not been ambitious at school, I now had the bit between my teeth and realized that I could compete up there with the best of them. About this time a new accelerated promotion scheme was being introduced nationally. Pioneered by a man called Johnson it became known as the 'Johnson Scheme', although its proper title was the 'Special Course'. Initially, officers were selected for interview on the basis of the highest marks in the national promotion examination.

Successful selection meant attendance at the Police Staff College, Bramshill, in Hampshire for twelve months with the rank of sergeant, and then rapid promotion to inspector.

I was well prepared for the examination in November of 1966 and was delighted when the results came out. I was top in the county with 78% in every subject! Superintendent Chris Wills, needless to say, was delighted. His investment in me was justified. Forces were competing for successful places on the course, and I attended a Special Course Candidates' Course at Harperley Hall for three weeks in February 1967 for coaching preparation for the interviews in London in April.

I attended the interview at the Royal Scottish Corporation Hall in Fetter Lane, London on the 17 April 1967 but was unsuccessful.

At that time an officer could not sit his inspector's promotion examination until after he was promoted sergeant. It follows that in a sense I was at a roadblock until I was promoted, but I had only been in the job 4 years! So undaunted, I got my head down again and decided to sit the sergeants' examination for a second time, with the sole intention of qualifying again for the 'Special Course'.

In the meantime of course I was a working detective and attended a junior CID course at 'Tally Ho' Training School, in Birmingham in the summer of 1967. This again was right up my street, as I was fresh from studying for the exam. What a summer that was. Birmingham was a long way in those days and I could not afford to come home every week. The vivid memory I have is of the 'flower power' music of the time, particularly a song called 'San Francisco' sung by a guy called Scott Mackenzie. Another song which still haunts me from that time is 'A Whiter Shade of Pale'.

I thoroughly enjoyed the course and met a fair-haired Scotsman called Jim Kelly, who was in the Hampshire Constabulary. Jim and I became buddies and he stayed at 'Tally Ho' the same weekends that I did.

I recall on one occasion going with Jim to a club called the 'Dolls Club', a striptease club with an entrance like a football turnstile. We showed our warrant cards to gain admittance and were watching the 'entertainment' when a big rough guy came over and said, 'Are you the guy from Durham?' They must have seen it on my warrant card. I nodded and he said, 'The boss want to see you upstairs'. I followed the gorilla upstairs where I was introduced to the owner of the club, coincidentally a middle-aged man called Jimmy Mackenzie.

He told me he came from Darlington and had moved to Birmingham a couple of years earlier. We established that we were not related and he was an extremely good host, buying us dinner before we left. I never went back to the 'Dolls Club' and it was some time later that I discovered that a few years earlier, Jimmy Mackenzie had been involved in a road accident, I think in Neasham Road in Darlington, when a police officer had been knocked from his pedal cycle and killed.

Mackenzie denied driving the vehicle, but was strongly suspected. The detective inspector in charge at Darlington at that time was a tough character called Les Newton, who retired as a chief superintendent and now lives in Spain. Jimmy Mackenzie's life was made so uncomfortable that he moved to the Midlands. He was virtually run out of town. I felt sick at having accepted his hospitality.

I worked hard on the course, using the same cramming technique as for the promotion examination. It worked and I came top of the class of 34 in the final exam with 84%, the class average being 68%.

Once back to Jarrow in the CID, it soon got round to the sergeants' promotion exam again in November of 1967. The CID course clearly helped, because I came top of the county again, with high enough marks to qualify for the Special Course interviews once more. Off I went to London, but again failed to make any headway and came away disappointed.

I remember about this time that I lost my voice and had to go for treatment to the South Shields General Hospital. One of my vocal chords was paralysed and it made talking above any noise impossible. Eventually it came back, but the problem was to recur later in life.

I got involved with DC Jack Marriott in a complicated fraud case. Jack was a master at file preparation and presentation. A car salesman had been bouncing cheques and systematically defrauding his employer, by false pretenses, fraudulent conversion and theft of cars. It amounted to thousands of pounds, with over 19 charges. We gave evidence for over three hours at the Newcastle Assizes and Jack had prepared meticulous schedules for the court showing how the fraud had been perpetrated. At the committal hearing, the chairman of the bench said, 'Particular praise for Detective Constable Marriott for the excellent and fair way in which he gave his evidence, and also to Detective Constable Mackenzie for the hours of long work he must have spent preparing this complicated case'. He expressly asked for his remarks to be passed on to the chief constable. I had secured my fourth commendation for good police work and it was Jack Marriott who had done all the work!

The 'Special Course' rules changed shortly after that, allowing officers to apply for interview through their own force, which I did and I was selected again. I did go to London for a third and final attempt but failed once again to be selected for the course.

I was even called in for a one-off interview before the last attempt, with the chief constable, Alec Muir, himself a Hendon trained graduate, who took a special interest in me, but to no avail.

On the domestic front, in the middle of 1967 Jean announced that she was pregnant, which caused a flurry of excitement. She would of course have to give up work at Lennig's Chemicals and we prepared ourselves for the happy event.

Brian James Mackenzie was born at Darlington's Greenbank Maternity Hospital on 21 March 1968, exactly 25 years to the day after my birth. How's that for timing! He was a big healthy baby and I recall wetting the baby's head a few days later, with colleagues in the CID, at a special party night in a pub called the Queen's in Jarrow. The detective sergeants at that time were complete opposites; Ted Woodhall was a determined, eccentric single purpose police officer, whereas Jim Selkirk, a former British Transport officer, was a fat, jovial officer who did not drink a great deal and was a prize-winning gardener.

I recall one unusual case at Jarrow involving a young lad on a bike. He would ride past a woman on a lonely track and squeeze her breast. He had committed a few cases on different women, but the youthful description was always the same. Keith Tweddle was dealing with the case, with me in support. Keith was a methodical, dedicated detective who did not miss much, Tall, slim and good looking, he later became a statement reader on murder enquiries because of his attention to detail.

In Jarrow at the time there was a local man called Mallon who had a riding school. People could ride the horses, either with a saddle or with a cart. He would also lead hay and his horse and cart was often seen passing the police station at Clervaux Terrace. Keith and I were leaving the back entrance to the police station, still pondering the identity of our youthful 'titty squeezer'. Descriptions had been circulated, informants alerted, enquiries exhausted, when Mallon's horse and cart went past. Sitting on top of a bail of hay was a young man. Keith suddenly exclaimed, 'Brian, there he is. That's our man!' I glanced across and sure enough, the youth answered the description of the assailant. We stopped the horse and cart, interviewed the youth and he admitted the offences. The value of astute observation was proven.

Life went on pretty much the same, staff came and went and I recall a new aid to CID was appointed. He was a Ferryhill lad called Alan Edgar. A big, jovial fellow, Alan was an excellent cricketer, but above all a comedian. He was always laughing and telling stories.

In October, before Alan was aiding in the CID, I had been to a large burglary at Centenary House, the Cooperative department store in the centre of Jarrow's new Viking Shopping Centre. Thieves had entered through the roof and stolen thousands of pounds worth of clothing and electrical goods.

I did the routine detective work, but it was clear that it had been well planned and executed and we did not get very far. We drew up a list of the stolen goods for the crime report and for circulation to other police forces. The secret of good detective work is to have a good source of intelligence and at that time I was running a very useful informant, who I shall call X. I was in the office one evening in December, when I received a telephone call from X. He told me of a house in Hebburn, where the stolen goods from the Co-op burglary would be found.

I alerted detective sergeant Ted Woodhall of our intentions and then Alan Edgar and myself immediately went to the house in question in Hebburn. It was the home of a burglar well known to the police. We knocked on the door and at first the occupant refused entry. I told him that we could obtain a warrant and he allowed us inside. It was obvious that there had been strenuous efforts to hide property but a quick search revealed goods from the Centenary House burglary. Indeed guilty knowledge was proved by a ham-fisted attempt to conceal property by hanging it outside from a bedroom window. A good catch indeed, leading to my fifth commendation from the court and from the chief constable.

Boards and Interviews

I was still enjoying crime fighting but wanted to use my legal knowledge so I applied for a position as an instructor at a CID training school, without success. My detective inspector at that time was a round, former newsagent with a sarcastic manner called Tommy Garside. He was not very well liked in the department and considered a bit of a bully. When I got the result back he sarcastically told me that he knew I was wasting my time, as I did not have the qualities to be an instructor. I was determined to prove him wrong!

I had seen an advertisement for a student instructors' course at Dishforth Police Training College, another RAF base 'borrowed' by the Home Office. I duly applied and was successful in being selected for the course.

I did not wish to leave my beloved CID, but felt this was a tremendous challenge and could add another dimension to my qualifications. It was a 6-week course and I have to say, probably the hardest course in the police service. Talk about burning the midnight oil. Again, I threw myself into it and discovered the 'entertainer' in me was given an opportunity to blossom further. I had always enjoyed the 'theatre' of giving evidence in the Crown Court and I also warmed to standing before a captive audience and teaching law.

I did extremely well on the course and was told by the course director, Chief Inspector Dennis 'Chalky' White, that I would be selected as an instructor when I got back to my force. I was excited with the prospect, because instructors always held the rank of sergeant.

Jean and I had a good social life when we could get a baby sitter, going to local clubs to watch entertainment, singers or comedians, or going to social events at the police club in Jarrow police station. Superintendent Wills had retired by now, a short retirement – he sadly died soon after, nearly blind. The new boss was Superintendent John Punshon, a tall, lean pleasant natured man, with a forceful, attractive wife called Betty. John unfortunately is now dead, but I still keep in touch with his brother Jim, who lives in the village of Sacriston, near Chester-le-Street. Jim, a keen historian, kindly researched the origin of my title 'Framwellgate', and in consequence I discovered that there was once a 'Fram Well', which supplied water to the ancient city of Durham. One of the gates of the city was near the well; hence it was the 'Fram Well Gate'. Other gates in the city were 'Walkergate', 'Gilesgate', 'Owengate' and 'Milburngate', which are still areas of the city. I am indebted to Jim for his interest and advice.

The CID at Jarrow had now changed and I was working with John Wile, an amiable Geordie of the old school; Owen Rogers, a well educated, Darlington grammar school lad, who loved a pint of beer; Alan Paley, an ex butcher, and Brian Clark, the scientific aids fingerprint officer. I thought I worked long hours in those days, but Brian Clark and his colleagues, Harry

Jarrow CID, 1970s. (The author is centre back.)

Turnbull and Derek Wright, were constantly called out at night, sometime two and three times, to visit scenes of crime. Eight hour continuous tours of duty were a blessing to officers such as these! I remember distinctly, in July 1969, sitting in the Conservative Club in Jarrow, with Owen Rogers, watching the Apollo astronauts, Neil Armstrong and Edwin 'Buzz' Aldrin, land on the moon!

It was about this time that Durham Constabulary was amalgamating with the smaller borough forces of South Shields and Sunderland, who as I recall it, were not that enthusiastic about the idea. The promotion examination rules were changing also and officers at constable rank were allowed for the first time to sit the inspectors' examination. So in January 1969 I sat the promotion exam to the rank of inspector and passed with flying colours, coming fifth in the county.

I had applied for a promotion board, which is a selection interview of qualified officers in order to create a list of officers to be considered for promotion to sergeant. I appeared before the board at South Shields, where the new divisional headquarters was situated. It consisted of Assistant Chief Constable Dobson, Chief Superintendent Young, ex South Shields, and Superintendent John Punshon from Jarrow. I had a successful interview and qualified for a central selection board at the new force headquarters at Aykley Heads in Durham.

The summer of 1969 was taken up with interviews. In April I had attended a force selection board in yet another attempt to qualify for the accelerated promotion scheme. I was successful and was put forward for interview in London. On 30 April I attended a central promotion board at police headquarters with the chief Constable, Alec Muir, the new ACC, Jack Hallett, former chief constable of Gateshead, and the deputy chief constable, Bill Hogg. On 4 July I once more trooped down to London to be rebuffed yet again in my application for the Special Course. It was as though I could not put a foot wrong in the north, but in the south, disaster. I still wonder whether or not my northern accent was a factor?

In any event, I was pretty demoralized by now. I had heard nothing since I had qualified as a law instructor, so I rang Chief Inspector White at Dishforth who had told me I was about to be selected as an instructor the previous year. He seemed a little embarrassed and told me to keep my head down. What really brought it to a head was when a sergeant at Jarrow, Harry Rogers, since then a lifelong friend, came to me and asked if I could help him with an instructors' course he was attending at Dishforth. Harry was a smiling, avuncular figure and I had no hesitation in lending him the course notes that I had brought back from my course.

You can understand my surprise when following his successful completion of the course, Harry Rogers was posted to Harperley Hall. I was understandably aggrieved. I then took a course of action which I have only taken twice in my police service – I applied for an interview with the chief constable. Chief Superintendent Young came through to Jarrow to see me first. I explained my sense of frustration, because the skills I had acquired on the instructors' course were withering on the vine, through lack of teaching practice. He was a fair and a just man, said he agreed with me and arranged for me to go to police headquarters at Aykley Heads in Durham.

I did not see the chief constable, but Bill Hogg, the deputy, who had a formidable reputation as a hatchet man. I put my case to him as best I could and he listened intensely. He went to a filing cabinet and took some papers out. 'You're right', he said, 'You've been overlooked'. He then went on to tell me that he would arrange for me to be transferred to the training school at Harperley Hall as soon as there was a vacancy. But he added, 'there have been too many officers jumping the promotion ladder by getting into training, and it has to stop. You realize that I am not offering you promotion. You will go as an acting sergeant.' I was happy with that, knowing that I would get a sergeant's pay and unless I fouled up, I would surely leave as a sergeant!

CHAPTER 5

Teaching Law

HARPERLEY HALL was a wonderful posting and I went there as an acting sergeant on 18 March 1970, seven years after joining the police. I was with some interesting people. Harry Rogers was still there of course, living in the nearby village of Fir Tree with his wife Jean. A chap called Ramsey Hall, a straight, genuine man who did not appear to relax a great deal, but was a dedicated instructor nonetheless. The Commandant of the training school was Ted Pointon, an ex South Shields officer, with his wife Vera. He was a quiet, helpful superintendent, who could be forceful when necessary.

We lived in the police houses about 200 yards from the hall and were surrounded by other residents, including Matt Hedley, the sergeant on the mounted branch and his wife, Anne. Another was the RAF man I had joined with, mounted officer Barry Simpson and his wife Marion. PC Eddie and Dorothy Simpson from the dog section were also part of the police community, as were mounted PC Jeff Ridley and his wife Christine. All had children and it was a happy, self-contained community. Another mounted officer Bill Maltman and his wife, Edith also lived at Fir Tree. Then there were the cooks, cleaners, drivers, some of whom were characters, such as 'Old Walter' who fetched and carried and won more premium bond prizes than anyone I knew. 'Jack' the Kennel man, who lived in a caravan in the grounds and could drink more Guinness than Brendan Behan the Irish writer; more than anyone I have ever come across before or since!

This was a happy community, the social life was good and we had a full quota of students of all ages through our hands. It helped me to get to know the 'new' officers from Sunderland, South Shields and Gateshead. We had farmers' 'socials' from time to time in the hall, to show our appreciation of the local community whose lives the police community touched. Local people would come to the hall for bingo, food and drink. The instructors' responsibilities extended to running the bar and the shop.

Jean and I still kept in touch with our old pals from Darlington, with nights out at weekends with the Olivers, who were still at Shildon. Derek Hawdon had joined the fire brigade in Darlington and married June, a Liverpool born journalist with the now defunct *Evening Despatch* in Darlington. David Robinson was to move to Coventry in search of work and is still there, working for Rolls Royce. 'Tom' Sawyer had married Sylvia and they had a son. He had left Stephenson's factory and joined Cummins'

Engines in the 'work study' department. He was moving to the left politically however, and became a regional representative of the National Union of Public Employees (NUPE). I followed his career with interest and he eventually became the deputy general secretary of NUPE at national level and to some extent, a disciple of Anthony Wedgewood Benn, well to the left of mainstream Labour politics. We had drifted apart and did not keep in touch. But more of Tom, later.

I specialized in teaching the Theft Act (theft, robbery, burglary, deception etc) and I recall the Commandant coming into my office one day and saying, 'You'd better start learning about that – you're teaching it next week'. He then dropped on my desk a copy of the new Gaming Act, 1968 which regulated the gaming industry and set up the Gaming Board for Great Britain. I studied the new Act and read everything I could about gaming law and started to teach it. The thing about teaching is that the questions you get help to hone up your knowledge even more, and you continue to research.

I wrote articles on the new law and became somewhat of an 'expert', receiving queries from senior officers from other forces. I was in my element, studying law and getting paid to teach it. I had found my vocation.

A visiting lecturer was an inspector called Tommy Cundall, a lovely man who I got to know very well later on in my service. He was married to Vera, a quiet lady who always had a smile. He was later to influence my decision to seek further academic qualifications.

Humour
I had learned very early on that as an instructor, I could get a message across far more effectively with a little humour. I would prepare my lectures therefore with a humorous anecdote at the beginning, somewhere in the middle and if possible insert a rib-tickling ending. I would build stories into the lecture such as when teaching cruelty to animals: This man got onto a bus with a baby crocodile under his arm. It started to bite the bum of the bloke in front. He looked round in horror. 'You shouldn't be allowed on a bus with a thing like that! In fact you should take it to the zoo.' 'I took it to the zoo yesterday, I'm taking it to the pictures today', he replied. It seemed to go down well, and even to this day ex PC Alan Lunn, a round jovial man with an infectious sense of humour, is one of many to remind me of a lesson I gave on sexual offences, when I asked the class, 'What is the definition of 'gross indecency'?' PC Lunn said, 'Is it 144 men in a room playing with themselves?' Peter Johnson, my fellow instructor and I looked at each other and I said, 'So endeth the first lesson!'

I then usually followed on with a quick one-liner, 'I can remember my first sexual experience, I only wish there had been someone else there to share it with me!' The power of humour to sell a message cannot be overestimated.

Speaking on theft and deception, I would interject, 'My wife had her credit card stolen last week. I didn't report it to the police however, as the thief is spending less than she was!'

Talking of Jean, she was now working part-time as a waitress at the Duke of York, a village pub at Fir Tree on the A68 road. She enjoyed the break from the routine of the house and looking after Brian junior. I was baby-sitting on the nights that she worked as I lived on the job and could work at home. In late summer of 1970 Jean announced that she was pregnant again and we prepared for our second child.

We eventually acquired a new member of staff, Ivan Cliff and his wife Sylvia. Ivan was a thin, short cropped, sergeant with a dry sense of humour. He was very visual in his presentations and we developed a bit of a double act, of which I am still reminded by people from time to time. We used to love end of course parties, when Ivan and I would make speeches and run the bar. Bliss indeed! To add icing to the cake – I was promoted to substantive sergeant on 12 May 1971. I was beginning to think that they had forgotten about me again.

Our second son Andrew Craig, was born at Bishop Auckland Hospital on 18 May 1971. There was a minor problem when he turned blue whilst being bathed one day. Jean was magnificent and he was quickly taken to Bishop Auckland Hospital for checks. He has grown into a fine, healthy sport-loving young man.

Whilst at Harperley I was encouraged by Tom Cundall to study for a GCE in law. Tom and I started to go to classes together at New College Durham studying law at A level. This was different. I had mastered criminal law, but this whetted my appetite for constitutional law, tort, land law, trusts and many other aspects of civil law. It was an extremely successful venture, with Tom and me passing the exam, in my case with a grade A.

Having acquired a taste for it, I now embarked on a real challenge. I applied for permission to take an LL.B course in Law at Teesside Polytechnic, leading to an external degree from London University. I was granted permission on 18 September 1971, commenced my studies, and every Friday travelled to Middlesbrough for classes. We had a great instructor, an Asian academic called Andy Khan, with whom the students became very friendly. I recall that DC Derek Lindsay and Terry O'Connor, who was a former successful Special Course applicant, also enrolled on the course, which in the main, was made up of police officers.

The work was long and hard, with me still teaching at Harperley and studying at every opportunity on the degree course. During the weekends I would take my books down to the Hall and go into the lounge to read. It was quite spooky on the winter nights, as there were strange noises in the old hall and there had always been rumours of a ghost! One evening I was sitting reading law when I heard a noise. I looked towards the large panelled door in the corner and swear I saw the handle turn. Being a police officer I controlled my reaction but felt the hairs on the back of my neck bristle. I went across to the door and pulled it open. The hall outside was dark, but in the half-light I could see what appeared to be a figure standing at the top of the staircase, wearing a hat. My heart missed a beat and I quickly switched the light on to see that what I had seen was the post attached to the banister. Tricks of the mind! But after that I always took my truncheon down to the Hall with me!

Being Orphaned

The downside of my time at Harperley Hall was that my mother's health was failing fast. She had a dread of doctors. My eldest brother Raymond was still living at home in Darlington in Brighton Road, and I would get back whenever I could. Jean and I would take the children to see their 'Nana', and we would go down to Eastbourne Park when the weather was nice enough.

The LL.B studies were going well and I passed the intermediate examinations in September 1972 and my Part 1 finals in September 1973. It was becoming a hard slog and I realized that when I left Harperley Hall it would be more difficult to study whilst performing operational duties on shifts round the clock. I therefore took the risky decision to reduce the final two years work into one. This required intensive study so I stepped up the visits to the Hall in the evenings that winter.

Meanwhile, Jarrow, South Shields, Gateshead and Sunderland were swallowed up by Northumbria Police, which was created to serve the new metropolitan county of Tyne and Wear and the county of Northumberland, and Durham contracted in size.

There had been some political fall-out following the corruption enquiry into the architect, John Poulson and 'Mr Newcastle' T Dan Smith in the north east, which resulted in Poulson, Smith and the former chairman of the Durham Police Authority, Alderman Andrew Cunningham, going to prison. It was a massive police enquiry and showed an unhealthy relationship between the architect and elected officials, particularly in respect of planning matters. It was often stated that the map of Durham County was redrawn to reduce the power of the mighty Durham County Council.

My mother's health was becoming critical and she became housebound. She had a fear of going into hospital and was in some considerable pain, and the doctor referred her to a specialist. It got to the point where I felt the delay was such, that I wrote to the Darlington Memorial Hospital stating in terms that if action was not taken quickly 'I would be relating this sad story to HM coroner!'

I sent a memo to police headquarters, dated 8 June 1973, applying for a posting to Darlington when my term as an instructor came to an end, as surely it must after over three years at Harperley. I gave two reasons for the request. The first was that travelling for my continued studies at Middlesbrough for my finals would be made easier. Secondly, I pointed out that there was a domestic factor. My widowed mother, living at Darlington, was shortly due to undergo a serious operation and I felt that my presence would be a great help.

I was not aware of it then, but my mother, who was now bedridden, was dying of cancer of the bowel. In August of 1973 I received an urgent call from my sister notifying me that my mother had fallen out of bed. I raced through to Brighton Road, found that the doctor had been out to the house, simply put her back into bed and left a prescription.

I was incandescent with rage. I immediately rang the doctor and demanded that an ambulance be sent to take mother to hospital. It arrived within five minutes and she was at last admitted. Alas, it was too late. The family constantly visited her and I was at her bedside when she passed away about three weeks later, on 16 September 1973.

I was devastated, believing that I should have done more to expedite her admission for treatment. I wrote a powerful letter of complaint about the general practitioner concerned and the hospital, particularly after a nurse told me that my mother had been neglected by being left on a trolley in a corridor all night. There was an official tribunal hearing before a committee of doctors chaired by a solicitor, at which I gave evidence. The hospital refused permission for the nurse to give evidence. I called members of my family in support, but my allegations were dismissed.

This incident illustrated to me the difficulty of the individual taking on large organizations, and I include in this the police. It probably shaped my decision later on in my career to become involved in police politics as an elected representative, and ignited a passion in me for justice, that would endure. Little did I know then how that decision would affect my future destiny!

I now saw little reason to confine myself to Darlington when I left the Training Department, so I sent another memo to the chief constable on 7 October 1973 requesting consideration for a re-appointment to the CID. I had a simple rule in the police service, and it has in the main, served me well. If you don't ask – you will rarely get, and trying loses nothing!

I heard nothing more from headquarters regarding my request for a posting, until I received a transfer notice posting me to Bishop Auckland Town with effect from 21 January 1974.

Back to the Streets
I was a disappointed officer in the New Year of 1974. My mother had died, I

felt guilty about not have kicked up enough fuss with the medical services soon enough, and my requests to be transferred first to Darlington, and then to the CID, had, it seemed to me, been ignored at headquarters. Still I had to go somewhere to start operational duties as a sergeant, so after the New Year I went to Bishop Auckland.

I met the Chief Superintendent, Bob Hill, to whom I took an instant dislike. He was a thin, tall figure coming to the end of his service, and was quite unwelcoming. I was offered a police house, which had been a senior officer's house, at Shildon. I took Jean to see it and it seemed nice enough and of course it was near our friends, Ian and Brenda Oliver, so we decided to accept it and I sent a memo to that effect.

It was not until the chief inspector at Bishop Auckland, a gruff, sarcastic Scotsman, called Archie Campbell, popped into the sergeants' office that I had second thoughts. He said mockingly, 'I see you've accepted that house in Midridge Lane, I knew you would!' 'Well why shouldn't I?' I said. 'You'll find out in the winter, it's impossible to keep warm!' Well that was the last straw! I had not been made at all welcome and now it appeared that I was being offered poor housing. I rang Jean and told her that I had decided not to accept the police house at Shildon and submitted a memo to that effect.

Within an hour I was wheeled in by Archie Campbell to see Chief Superintendent Hill. He was not happy! After explaining why I had changed my mind, in front of an embarrassed Chief Inspector Campbell, Bob Hill said, 'Look, I didn't ask for you to be posted here, in fact I don't want you here!' I barked back, 'Mr Hill, I didn't ask to come here, and if that is your attitude I do not want to stay!'

I went back to my office and for the second and last time in my service, I requested an interview with the chief constable.

Within seven days I was summoned to headquarters. As is normal in such requests, I saw the deputy chief constable. Bill Hogg had now retired and the new deputy was the former chief constable of Gateshead Borough, a quiet, unassuming, white haired, pleasant man, with whom I became quite friendly in later years, called Jack Hallett. He heard me out as I went through the saga of my mother's illness and death, my previous request for a posting to Darlington and subsequent application for CID. He said, 'What I am prepared to do is offer you a detective sergeant's job at Peterlee, but you will have to prove yourself as a sergeant in uniform first.'

I was happy with that. Like Harperley Hall, I was being sent on approval, but that was no problem. If I set my mind to something, my strength, humour and determination would see me through.

On 22 February 1974 I was transferred to Peterlee on the east coast of Durham, just one month after going to Bishop Auckland.

I later discovered that Jack Hallett, who did not really know me, had consulted the respected rising star Ray Basham about my qualities. Ray, a career detective, was working as the chief constable's personal assistant. Ray told me many years later that he had told the deputy chief constable he didn't know me, but that I had a good reputation as a detective at Jarrow. He advised the deputy chief that he should send me to Peterlee under the wing of Detective Inspector Bill Grundy, who would soon assess my qualities.

CHAPTER 6

Peterlee

PETERLEE WAS A NEW TOWN, developed in the 1960s to mop up residents from various mining villages in Durham which had now become unviable to sustain with decent housing and services. It was named after a nineteenth century miner, Peter Lee, who in 1919 when Durham County Council became the first Labour county council in the country, was elected its leader. It was a young town and had peculiar, modernistic housing, many with flat roofs. We were allocated such a house. It was modern, warm with plenty of green spaces – a typical new town in fact.

We settled in and got Brian junior fixed up at the local school and got to know one or two neighbours. Peterlee had a thriving police club where we would socialize when the shifts fell right. I was a uniform sergeant, which was a relatively new job to me, as my last operational work, apart from the short unhappy spell at Bishop Auckland, was as a detective constable. I had one tremendous asset now though – I knew the law! I was still studying for my finals on the degree course, trying to cram two years study into one. It had not been helped by the trauma of my mother's death and the transfers. On Fridays I was still travelling to Middlesbrough, work permitting. Some of my contemporaries, such as DC Derek Lindsay, had dropped out of the course, but I was determined to see it through. Incidentally, Derek, my colleague on the course, later achieved academic distinction at Durham University after he retired, some years later.

Superintendent Ron Thompson, a former River Tyne officer, was my first Superintendent at Peterlee. He was a real gentleman and his chief inspector was a quiet officer who had been in training roles for many years, Frank Cooper. Then there was a change and the new superintendent was a 'John Cleese' look-a-like, called Hugh Blenkin. Hugh was a public school type, with a 'plummy' accent who was a good cricketer and squash player. He had transferred to Durham from the Metropolitan Police, as his father was a friend of the then chief constable, Alec Muir.

Frank Cooper as I said was a relatively shy, quiet officer, who had written a quote in wonderful handwritten script when an instructor. I copied it and it remained in a frame throughout my service on the wall behind my desk. It was by Lord Chief Justice Mansfield and read: 'True liberty can only exist when justice is equally administered to all – to the king and to the beggar.' I believe that says everything about a liberal democracy! Incidentally, it still adorns my study at our cottage.

Hugh Blenkin was full of new ideas and liked innovation. He was a man I could do business with, although his street credibility was not that high in the sub-division nor, I found, with his fellow superintendents.

My initiation at Peterlee was in a drink driving case. A man had been arrested for driving a vehicle over the limit; he failed the breath test and insisted that the blood sample be taken out of his big toe. I had never heard of this and decided that it amounted to a refusal, having taken the advice of the police surgeon that such a sample would not be large enough. The prisoner was charged with refusing to give a blood sample and I submitted a detailed report justifying my decision. I was vindicated at court and Hugh Blenkin was pleased.

The shift inspector was an ex-guardsman called Ray Brammer, a former Sunderland officer who had remained in Durham after Sunderland became part of Northumbria. He was very smart, with a slashed cap and polished shoes. He guided and helped me practically through those early months and I was very grateful. Another Inspector was Fred 'Bomber' Harris, who was also enthusiastic and helpful. The 'character' at Peterlee was an inspector called Frank Watson. He would lead from the front in every sense of the word, and had picked up numerous bravery awards. He ultimately transferred to Cleveland as a superintendent, as did Terry O'Connor.

I saw no signs of a transfer to CID, and I felt a little let down again. I had no reason to think that the promises were not going to be kept, but during my day release studies at Teesside Andy Khan and others encouraged me to consider a switch of careers. There were vacancies at the polytechnic for lecturers in law. I gave it great thought, and having discussed it with Jean, I applied for a position. I recall that I asked my old school friend 'Tom' Sawyer, who was now the Area Officer for NUPE in Middlesbrough, for a reference, and he gave an exaggerated account of my values and abilities, for which I was very grateful.

The pay at that time for a lecturer was better than a police sergeant, as police pay was again falling behind, and I had taken to 'teaching' at Harperley Hall. I was invited for interview and was successful. I was at the crossroads of life. It was of course subject to me getting my law degree in the summer.

Bearing in mind why I had gone to Peterlee, I was very interested in the staff in the CID. The detective inspector was a lovely character called Bill Grundy, whom I mentioned earlier. He was an ex-miner from Craghead, although to all intents and purposes, he looked like a farmer. He was a keen gardener and dedicated to the fight against crime. One of the detective sergeants was Ted Jackson, an old fashioned, reliable detective who got on with the job in a methodical way. It was interesting to me that there was a vacant sergeant's post and 'acting up' was DC Alan Miller, a young up and coming CID officer with a quiet disposition.

As for the detective constables, Max Currah was a chunky, no nonsense detective who told it at it was. Married to Marion, they were both from Weardale, in the rural west of the county. We became very firm friends over the years, as we still are. Indeed Max reminded me recently of a case we had at Durham Crown Court with a lady barrister called Mary MacMurray defending. The Judges' Rules, which governed police conduct when interviewing suspects, required officers to complete their pocket book notes as soon as possible and allowed officers to collaborate in this. Following me into the witness box, Max was told by Ms MacMurray, 'I don't suppose there is a lot of point in going over all this again as no doubt you will have been the parrot on Sergeant Mackenzie's shoulder!' Courtrooms could be very humorous places and this comment caused not a little mirth. Peter Taylor QC, later to become Lord Chief Justice, practised on the northeast circuit and I recall many years later attending a reception at the offices of the then Director of Public Prosecutions, Barbara Mills. Lord Justice Taylor was present and I surprised him by reminding him how he had cross-examined me as a detective in my former life.

Clive Brooker, Jimmy Briggs, Bob Walker, Les Bainbridge and Gerry Rogers were all in the CID at some stage during my spell at Peterlee and most if not all, are now retired. Again I got to know the local licensees well. In particular the 'boss' of the Hearts of Oak, in Oakerside Drive, Bob Hather and his wife Betty. Bob was a cheery, friendly man with a son and daughter, and was very pro police. I would often call in for a pint after my shift at 10:00 p.m. as it was near to my home.

On 1 August 1974 I received notification that I had been awarded a Bachelor of Laws Degree with Honours (LL.B) by London University. I was delighted and received a personal letter from the new chief constable A.G. (Peter) Puckering.

My determination had paid off and having thought long and hard about the lecturing job at Teesside Polytechnic, I made one of the most important choices in my life. I decided that it was better to be a well-qualified police officer, and that was where my future should be. It was one of the best decisions I have ever made!

Back to CID
August of 1974 was a good month. On the 5th, I was transferred back into CID as a detective sergeant. It raised a few eyebrows and Alan Miller lost his 'acting up'. He took it very well and was totally loyal thereafter.

Peterlee was a busy sub-division and one of the early cases I dealt with in September with DC Alan Miller was that of a man called John Coxon who set fire to Wingate Parish Church. He pleaded guilty to Arson and also admitted stealing a pig from an allotment in Wingate and killing it. Judge Alistair Sharpe QC gave him 3 years when he appeared before Durham Crown Court. It caused quite a few smiles when Coxon stated that he had been sleeping with the pig.

I had always taken an interest in police 'politics' and regularly attended Police Federation open meetings, where the chief constable addressed the assembled masses in the Federation. I wrote letters to papers and magazine voicing my opinion, usually on legal topics. I recall one such letter to the *Police Review* in October 1974, in response to an article, which in essence decried the need for uniformed police officers to visit licensed premises. The gist of my response was 'that anything which keeps the police in touch with the public is to be welcomed... Far from being wrong, it is essential!' It is a view that I think is even more relevant thirty years later.

Since my days as a detective at Jarrow, I valued the importance of communication, as a major ingredient of policing. This is particularly important in the CID. Thieves and burglars like to spend their ill-gotten gains. They spend them on the good life, drink (or drugs these days), women, and gambling. It follows that a good detective would have knowledge of these lifestyles, cultures and language. I certainly count as some of my best friends, even today, people in the licensing trade.

I can remember close friendships from my Peterlee days. One unforgettable character was Ronnie Hall and his vivacious schoolteacher wife, Maureen. Ron was the steward at the 'Big' Club, at Horden. It was a good match, as Ron was a large, generous man with a warm personality. His hospitality was legendary and he had a delightful daughter Caroline, and a nice natured son, Kieran, who in his late teens had ambitions to join the police. Ron later moved to the Bird in Hand at Trimdon and then to Coxhoe Club, near Durham and is now enjoying retirement at Easington Colliery. Ron has been a good friend of my wife and me throughout my police service and I am delighted to say they attended my sixtieth party, as we attended many of his parties in the past.

It was at Peterlee that I first met John Fyffe and his wife Lynn, a petite, blonde lady. They ran the village pub at Old Shotton on the A19 road near Peterlee, called the Royal George, which was named after an 18th century ship which had been lost with all hands. John was a tall, trendy, good looking young man with longish, dark hair. He was about my age and I was fascinated to find that both he and Lynn had been members of a 'pop' group called 'The Settlers'. They had decided with the onset of a family to leave showbiz and go into the licensing trade.

They later moved to the Sun Inn at Wackerfield near West Auckland and then to the Hope Inn at Sedgefield, finally settling at the Beeswing pub and restaurant at East Cowton, just south of Darlington. Jean and I called and saw them from time to time at every hostelry they had. They are now retired in East Cowton, but their daughter runs the Dunstanburgh Castle Hotel at Embleton in Northumberland and John keeps a watchful eye and helps out from time to time. I was delighted that John and Lynn came to my sixtieth birthday party, where John and I sang a duet to a Willy Nelson version of 'Always on my Mind'.

Another licensee I am proud to have called my friend, was Nicky Spooner. Nick had the Plough Inn at Shadforth Village on the outskirts of Durham, where I used to call on my way home from Peterlee. He then later took the licence at the New Inn at Church Street Head at the crossroads near the university colleges in the centre of Durham. Again we socialized with Nick and his wife, Beverley and latterly with his girlfriend Lesley, after the break up of his marriage. Nick and I became very close and it was a tragedy of momentous proportions in my life when he died a young man in his early forties. To this day we still see his mother and father, who still live in retirement at Nick's home village of Shotton Colliery, where he is buried. But, more of those sad events later.

I think of Jim Andrews and his charming wife Brenda, who has Uno's Restaurant at Newcastle Quayside. Again, lovely people whose friendship I value greatly. There are Derek and Lesley Crehan who used to have the Three Horseshoes at Running Waters near Durham. Friends of Nicky Spooner, they retired and moved to Totnes in Devon, and then to Spain, where they now reside. We still keep in touch and visit each other from time to time.

There are Ken and Pat Rowe who had a pub at Hawthorn near Easington Village. Lovely people. Ken came to my birthday celebrations.

Another birthday attendee was John Hudson, an ex-military man, who is the licensee of the Crossways Hotel at Thornley, between Durham and the coast. We met 'by accident' you might say, when John was travelling on the A167 towards Chester-le-Street with Eileen his wife. I was driving, in full superintendent's uniform, out of the back road to Newton Hall just north of Chester Moor. I was in the centre of the dual carriageway waiting to turn right when John's car 'clipped' my front bumper and took it with him. He stopped further on and got a shock when I approached the car in police uniform. John shares my tendency to 'warble' and often runs his own karaoke nights at the Crossways, where I have been known to contribute.

Jean's good friend Dorothy, with whom she worked as a receptionist at a local doctor's practice, married Steve Valenti who had the Newton Grange Hotel, near Brasside in Durham. We often socialize and enjoy meals together.

An enduring friendship was with a self-made, highly successful millionaire, Stan Henry, who with a business partner owned the nightclub chain in the north, known as the Bailey Organization. Stan is an affable, sociable man whose club I used to frequent in Stockton-on-Tees many years ago. I have kept in touch with Stan over the years and when, many years later, he moved into health clubs with his 'Springs Leisure' chain, I had the pleasure of formally opening a couple of his clubs at Hartlepool and Sunderland. Stan and I also share a love of singing and one of the features of his clubs was his karaoke nights!

I could go on, suffice it to say that my friendships were cemented by attending the local licensees' dinners and dances and, the ladies auxiliary functions, where I was often called upon to provide the after dinner speech. Keith and Pauline Draper from the Half Moon in Elvet, Durham, were main players in the LVA and very good friends with Nick Spooner. Keith and Pauline are tremendously generous characters who over the years, along with their colleagues, have raised many thousands of pounds for very worthwhile causes. Lovely people all of them and, I greatly value my friendship with each and every one.

Indeed my love of pubs and licensees is such that I used to regularly frequent the Rose Tree at Shincliffe and got to know Arthur and Jan Walsh very well. Similarly, in the same village, Nigel and Debbie Gadd, who had the Seven Stars. We would socialize together in a perfectly proper way, none of us compromising the other. Indeed, the friendships endured so well, like the man who bought the electric razor company; in 2002 we bought the cottage next to the Seven Stars in Shincliffe Village, where we live to this day. I suppose it is an illustration of the importance of networking in a modern society. No man is an island and the importance of using our collective knowledge and abilities has never been greater.

In April 1975 I attended an Advanced CID Course at West Yorkshire Police Academy, Wakefield for six weeks, which again I passed with flying colours. On the course with me was another Durham detective sergeant, Ken Fisher, with whom I became a very firm friend and in fact he later worked with me on the drug squad some years later.

On finishing the course, I returned to Peterlee to continue dealing with the routine of burglary, rape and robbery.

Moving House

It was during this time that I was conscious of the fact that we were still in 'provided' accommodation, even though the police were paying it for. I was not particularly happy living at Peterlee because, although the house was modern, the town had no character. We decided to look elsewhere and I decided that a good move would be to the centre of the county, in the cathedral city of Durham.

We did not have a great deal of money, although I have always been a saver, and Jean is sensible with the housekeeping. What I had done since I was a young constable, as I said, and I don't know why, is invest about £5 monthly in Unicorn Unit Trusts. The money went directly out of my pay and it was not missed. We scanned the adverts and saw a new development advertised by the house builder Leech, at Newton Hall, just near the police headquarters at Aykley Heads. The attractive feature was that Leech was offering a £500 interest free loan towards the deposit. We would not have been able to afford to buy the house without that lifeline.

We had full support from Jean's mother, Betty and her father, Jim. Indeed I discussed many aspects of our future with Jim over a pint on a weekend when we were at Darlington. I always recall him saying that his boss at work could not believe that I had studied for a law degree in my own time in three years, and Jim could not understand how gaining such a qualification had not been rewarded more by the police. I smiled and told him to bide his time, as we would have to see what the future held, little realizing then, the significance of that comment!

The day of moving came near. The weekend before, I was out for a pint with my old school pal Derek Hawdon, in Darlington. We always stayed at Jean's parents' house in Katherine Street. I remember about nine o'clock getting this terrible pain in my side. It was so bad that I bade farewell to Derek and trundled home. Jean complained that I had obviously drunk too much and I went to bed. I woke her up in the middle of the night in agony, and insisted that I be taken to hospital. Jim kindly obliged and I was admitted to the Memorial Hospital with acute appendicitis!

They would not give me any painkiller until they determined what the problem was and I spent a very uncomfortable night. The next day they operated and I remember the doctor telling me that my condition was so advanced that it was on the point of bursting and possibly causing peritonitis. He also said I had an unusual appendix, tucked round the back and therefore the incision had to be larger than normal. My hospitalization meant that I missed the removal date and lay in bed while Jean and her parents, helped by Max Currah and Marion, moved our furniture from Peterlee to Durham.

Newton Hall was a massive new development. It was at one time said to be the largest private housing development in Europe. We had a nice, new semi-detached house with a virgin garden. I have vowed since then never to buy a new house again, and haven't. Bricks, concrete, piping and all manner of rubbish had to be removed before the garden could be planned. However once I had recovered from my operation, I got stuck in.

Being a dedicated CID officer, I have always liked a glass of beer! We developed an extremely good social life with the people in Chillingham Road. Most of them, like us, were newcomers with young families. I started to brew my own beer in the summer, after seeing an advertisement for a special home brew kit with a 'beer sphere'. I brewed it in the garage in a large vat and then when it had fermented once, transferred it to the 'beer sphere' where gas built up under pressure. I left it for the required time and then tested it one summer evening. It was a perfect pint of 'export', clear as a bell.

Living opposite was Tony Bannister, a draughtsman, and his wife Eileen, Billy Dixon, a builder, and his wife Marjorie, Johnny Craigs, a manufacturer, and Lynne. Next door to us was Jeff Burns, an ex soldier now working as a manager and his wife Jean, and at the bottom of the street Brian Longstaff and his wife Elsie who kept a corner shop. We would all meet at weekends at the Newton Hall pub and have a laugh when duty permitted. I used to test my new jokes on the assembled throng.

Tony was a born extrovert; he loved to show off, but could also be a manic-depressive. In any event, he was coming home from work on the night I pulled the first glass of home-brew at around 5:00 p.m. I called him across. 'Try this', I said, handing him a glass of the golden nectar. I then called on Jeff next door. Tony called Eileen. Billy and Marje came over and before long we had a crowd in the front room. I can honestly say that it was one of the best nights we ever had. We drank the whole five gallons of home brew, along with anything else that people brought along. I have said ever since that the best parties are those which are not planned!

That really set the tone for our stay in Chillingham Road. Our lads went to the local Bluecoat School and then onto the successful Framwellgate Moor Comprehensive School nearby. Things were progressing well and I even picked up my sixth commendation from the court and the chief constable, for solving a case of Robbery, Theft and Burglary.

Domestic Violence

One particularly horrifying case involved a woman called Edith McGhin from Seaham. Detective Inspector Bill Grundy came into my office over the Christmas period of 1975. Edith was a woman who was about thirty, but looked much older and had made allegations about orgies that she and her three sisters had allegedly attended with local businessmen and police officers. She alleged that she had been 'tortured' by the men when she tried to quit the sex group.

When we saw her in hospital, she said she had been attacked with an axe handle. She had a broken breastbone, nose, jaw, three fingers, and leg. Her ribs were cracked and she had extensive bruising. Most horrifying of all, she had been branded with a red-hot poker between her thighs! She named a particular businessman in Seaham as being responsible for the assault, which she said, took place in the back of a van.

Bill and I started our enquiries but the evidence did not seem to stack up.

We interviewed the respectable, alleged assailant and, he had no idea what we were talking about. We went to McGhin's house where she and her husband, one Michael McGhin, lived with their numerous children. I saw that there was blood on the stair walls and splashed in the living room. It was clear to us that this was the scene of the crime.

Edith McGhin would not change her story until we arrested her husband. We went to the house and he was standing near the fireplace where there was a poker. I thought he might be violent, so with other officers, I quickly overpowered him and we took him into custody. He was clearly deranged and when we interviewed him he talked irrationally of 'naked men in cowboy outfits making love to my wife'. Again he named prominent business people in the town.

Once he was locked up and Edith his wife knew it, she started to tell the truth. Michael McGhin had stripped her naked at home, battered her with an axe handle and branded her with a poker, causing the dreadful injuries. Then in the ambulance taking her to hospital, he whispered in her ear the false story she was to give to detectives. An open and shut case you may think. Not a bit of it. McGhin was remanded to Durham prison and unbelievably, when Edith was discharged from hospital, she went to visit him and came under his spell again. Apparently this is a well-known medical condition where a person can come under the dominance of another. It is similar, I suppose, to the 'Stockholm Syndrome', where hostages grow attached to their captors.

In any event she changed her story back again and our main witness had vanished. Not to be deterred however, Bill and I pressed on with the prosecution of Michael McGhin and, unusually in a criminal trial, the victim, Edith, gave evidence for the defence. He was found guilty of causing Edith grievous bodily harm and got four years. He was later committed to Rampton Hospital for the criminally insane.

A final twist, Edith was prosecuted for perjury and was put on probation for two years in January 1976. She was lucky to be alive. It was a remarkable case, by any standard.

I was now getting itchy feet again. I was missing teaching and, although there is a rule that you cannot take other employment without the permission of the chief constable, I had an idea. I applied to the chief constable for permission to teach law at New College, Durham where the police sent cadets for training. To my pleasant surprise I got permission, provided it did not interfere with my operational duties. It was quite unique to have a detective sergeant teaching and the class, a mix of cadets and others, seemed to like it. I set them homework and marked it, kept the register and picked up a little income along the way.

I had now been a police officer for thirteen years and wanted to move on.

I had qualified to inspector some years before. I had done a little 'acting up' as a detective inspector in the absence of Bill Grundy and felt I was ready for greater responsibility. I applied for a preliminary promotion board and attended the interview at Durham divisional office on 11 October 1976. I remember it well because I had the most chronic back pain and had difficulty getting out of the chair. The interview panel consisted of Assistant Chief Constable Cook, the ex-chief constable of Sunderland, together with Chief Superintendents Hunter and Harry 'Nobby' Clarke. I was told afterwards by Detective Chief Inspector Charlie Organ that I had had 'an excellent board'. I was quite content, in spite of my aching back.

On 15 November I went to Police Headquarter at Aykley Heads where I had my central promotion board. The chief constable, Peter Puckering and his deputy Jack Hallett, interviewed me. Again, I was comfortable and believe I gave a good account of myself.

CHAPTER 7

The Drug Squad

CHRISTMAS AND NEW YEAR passed uneventfully and I was pleasantly surprised when I was transferred to take charge of the drug squad at police headquarters at Aykley Heads, as acting detective inspector. I had been recommended by a dedicated detective chief inspector called Don Moody in charge of the Crime Support Unit who lived at Darlington. I really got into the role, grew a beard and got to know the job and the staff. Stuart Robson was the detective sergeant, a bright, enthusiastic detective, married to a woman inspector, Jan, who had been on the Special Course. Hardy Jones, a detective constable, was a streetwise cop who knew his stuff. There were two women on the team, Pat Haig, who later married the detective super-intendent, Clayton Whitaker, and Helen Sutherland, a policewoman who spoke broad Geordie and was a bit of a risk taker, but with a lovely personality. She had a sister who was a professional singer so I warmed to her immediately!

Drug misuse was an emerging problem in Durham, focussing upon cannabis use, growing and dealing. The team were good and the role I had was not demanding as I could leave them to get on with it. I had a couple of chemist shop sergeants, Ken Fisher, who as I mentioned earlier attended the CID course at Wakefield, in the north, and Gary Waine in the south. Their role was to periodically check chemists' registers and prescriptions, and generally enforce the chemist shop regulations.

Being in the nature of the beast, I decided to read myself into the law on drug misuse and became a bit of an 'anorak' on the legislation. I studied the Misuse of Drugs Act and relevant case law and wrote an article at the end of December for the *Police Review*. They printed it as an eight-page pull-out supplement and I found out years afterwards that many people throughout the country had kept it for reference.

The drugs problem is often described as being as big as the squad set up to deal with it. The bigger the squad, the bigger problem they will uncover. To some extent that is true. The drug squad, being attached to the Crime Support Unit, also provided a valuable pool of trained detectives based centrally for emergencies and major incidents when drug work would just cease as a priority.

A murder at Darlington is a good example of how this worked during my time in charge of the drug squad.

Crime Support Unit presentation to DCI Don Moody by the author.

Murder Most Foul

I was still acting detective inspector when the call came through on Sunday 29 May 1977. A woman's body had been found in bushes in Haughton Road in Darlington. She had been battered to death. It was a case of all hands on deck.

Stephanie Spencer had been to the Flamingo nightclub in Victoria Road, Darlington and had last been seen when she left the club in the early hours of the morning. Detective Superintendent Clayton Whitaker was in charge of the enquiry and I was involved with teams of officers performing house-to-house enquiries in the area. The hot money was on the husband Eric, as there was a history of domestic violence, but he denied having any responsibility for his wife's death, even though he had insured his wife's life only a few weeks before.

Gary Waine and I were teamed up doing house-to-house enquiries in the Victoria Road area talking to taxi drivers and others, and the name of a Michael Hodgson kept cropping up. He allegedly lived in Dundee Street with a couple called Raper. He did not show up however in the house-to-house forms. Olive Raper, Hodgson's lover, gave unconvincing reasons for not including him in hers. This rings alarm bells with any detective.

Gary and I continued to check and double check and established that a taxi driver had taken the murdered girl home on the night of the murder with a man answering the description of Hodgson. We thought we were home and dry. When we interviewed the taxi driver however he denied any knowledge of picking them up. I could not figure out why he would tell lies.

This threw us, but because we were so certain of our information, we brought the taxi driver in and interrogated him fairly severely, pointing out the seriousness of obstructing the enquiry and perverting the course of justice. It was still difficult to see why he should not tell the truth. Eventually he admitted that he was scared of Hodgson and, admitted taking them both to near the scene of the murder.

Hodgson, when arrested by me, at first denied any knowledge of Stephanie. Eventually however, after he had been charged, he admitted that his mind had gone blank when Stephanie Spencer provoked him. 'Something snapped', he said. Stephanie had called him a 'freak', when he couldn't manage sex. It was a classic motive for murder – sexual inadequacy and taunting by the female.

Hodgson was convicted of murder and got life imprisonment, which, on appeal, because of the provocation, was reduced to manslaughter, and he received seven years.

What I found interesting about that case and have used in lectures since, is the importance of the senior investigating officer retaining an open mind. He can have a great influence on his team. Clayton Whitaker was a brilliant, professional detective who everyone greatly respected, but in this case, at the end of every briefing, I can still recall him saying, 'But I still think it was the husband.' It became a bit of a joke, but who knows how it influenced the detectives looking at other suspects. In other words it could have become an inquiry simply looking for evidence to connect Eric Spencer with the murder and, subconsciously or otherwise, we could have been encouraged to discount any other evidence.

Another important lesson is the possibility that not only the suspect might be lying, but important witnesses, for whatever reason, may be also being economical with the truth.

If I have a criticism of modern policing, it is that we have devalued the importance of detective work. Several forces in the 70s had been rocked by corruption, often in drug or pornography squads, and this led to a massive assault on the problem by a hero of mine, Sir Robert Mark, Police Commissioner in London. Then later we had the introduction of 'tenure', recommended by the Inspectorate, which limited the time specialists could remain in departments, ostensibly to combat associations leading to corruption, In my view it was a big mistake. It is now being reversed, but has damaged professionalism and lowered morale. By all means tackle corruption and move officers who are suspected of being too close to 'dirty' money, but surely you don't throw out the baby with the bathwater and apply the rule rigidly across the board, destroying careers and losing years of invaluable experience!

The Metropolitan Police even abolished its highly regarded detective training school. This policy is also being reversed by the consummate professional Commissioner, Sir John Stevens, who as a career detective himself, understands the importance of professionalism coupled with firm, but fair, management.

On 1 July 1977, I was delighted by the news that I was being confirmed as head of the drug squad in the substantive rank of detective inspector. By now I was really getting into the part, with my beard and my hair a little longer than the conventional short back and sides.

In September of 1977 I attended a five-day drugs course at Hutton Hall near Preston, run by Lancashire Constabulary, where half of the men on the course wore trendy beards.

Elected Office

As I said earlier, I was taking an interest in police politics, attending Police Federation meetings, speaking to resolutions, sometimes proposing them. Pay in the police is cyclical and was falling behind comparable professions. It was beginning to become an important issue. It was about this time that the police showed their discontent with the Labour government of the day by a silent demonstration at the Police Federation conference at Blackpool. During the speech by the then Home Secretary, Merlyn Rees, the audience of police officers simply remained silent. I have since spoken to Lord Merlyn Rees about that demonstration, and it clearly shocked him and his wife at the time. It is very difficult to give a speech with pauses built in for laughter or applause, against a backdrop of total silence.

In any event, I had previously taken over the chairmanship of the CID section of the Durham Branch of the Police Federation (the Joint Branch Board), following the death of Detective Chief Inspector Ted Gibson in a road accident.

I was now invited to stand as the chairman, not just of the CID, but also of the Durham Constabulary Joint Branch Board as a whole. I accepted the nomination and was elected unopposed. I was totally comfortable with the politics of it all and took a great interest in the political world generally, although clearly police officers cannot take an active part in party politics.

My personal political stance at that time was left of centre, although I was becoming more and more disturbed at the unions appearing to dictate to the government and the increasing number of strikes in car factories and in the public sector. We were then known as the 'sick' economy of Europe, not least because of the number of industrial disputes which seemed to be plaguing the country.

Rape

Another example of the drug squad being brought in to assist with a major enquiry was the terrible beating and rape of an 84-year-old widow in the Gilesgate area of Durham, in early May of 1978.

Because it is a rape case I will not mention the names of the victim or assailant. The old lady lived by herself in a semi-detached house but, because of her infirmity, she slept in a bed downstairs.

Early in May of 1978 she had gone to bed in her lounge when she was disturbed by a noise around midnight. It was a wet night, and from the corner of her eye she saw a dark figure enter the room. The man went up the stairs and returned to the old lady's bedside. He then attacked her, striking her in the face causing it to bleed. He climbed on the bed and committed a number of sexual assaults. He struck her again and then placed a pillow over her face and applied pressure. She later described how she thought she was about to be killed and feigned death. It worked. The man got off and left the house.

The old lady was truly remarkable. Members of the drug squad were called in to assist the divisional detectives under the command of Detective Inspector Arthur Meek of Durham City. I was assigned to running the inquiry jointly with him, with particular emphasis on the house-to-house enquiry team. I went to see the old lady in the Dryburn Hospital at Durham, where she had been admitted. She was badly bruised with black eyes and lacerations. She described the circumstances of the attack in fine detail and although she did not see the assailant in the dark, she gave a graphic description of the man she had felt, as she warded off the assault. He was in his twenties, quite broad build, with straight hair, cut short. He was wearing dry, casual clothing and significantly, wore his watch on his wrist with the face on the inside. He was not wearing a jacket.

It was a good description all considered, so we started work with house-to-house inquiries, known offenders, informants, taxi drivers, public houses; in fact a normal routine major enquiry.

The house-to-house team threw up a house where a youth was never at home when we called. He was out each time the house was visited and his father said that he often went away for days, fishing. We were interested because he answered the general description of our suspect – but so did many others. After a few days, I started taking more interest in him because he had not been in touch. We checked his background. He was an ex-soldier of 17 years and I went to see his girlfriend.

She described how on the night of the attack they had fallen out and he had stormed off in a rage. She eventually got the bus home on her own, as it was a wet night. I then asked her if her boyfriend possessed a watch. He did.

'How did he wear it?' I asked hopefully. 'On his left wrist, with the face on the inside,' she replied. We had hit the jackpot!

The suspect was circulated as being wanted for questioning about the sex attack and we continued the routine of a major enquiry, not ruling out anything and keeping our options open. It was a delightful surprise when I was told that our man had been detained in The Hague in Holland, having hitched a lift on a continental lorry.

I flew with Arthur Meek to The Hague, to interview our suspect and could not have timed it better. The Dutch police officer who was our host had just been promoted to head the homicide squad in The Hague, so we went to his party that evening, enjoying a very pleasant evening. The following morning we got down to business. Before long our man was telling us how he had fallen out with his girlfriend and gone drinking. He got the bus to near where the elderly widow lived. He was angry and knew she lived alone. He broke into the house and took off his coat, hence his dry clothing. He went upstairs to ensure that nobody else was in the house and then came downstairs and attacked the old lady. We took a voluntary statement from him and he showed little remorse. He agreed to come home voluntarily, rather than subject himself to the drawn-out extradition procedures and we arranged a flight back to England. He even allowed us to bring duty free drinks back in his name!

He was charged with Burglary and Rape and was sentenced to 7 years imprisonment. The case had an interesting sideline. The old lady was such a star, that the incident team in Durham had a collection, we called it a whip-round, and bought her a lovely bouquet of flowers, which I duly presented her with in hospital. When I explained this to our Dutch counterparts, they were amazed. 'You bought the victim flowers?' they said. 'Yes, why?' I responded. 'If that had been in Holland they would have thought we were covering up the fact that a policeman had committed the offence', was the surprising answer. I believe that says a lot about our style of policing, our culture and our values. Like our soldiering, our policing is respected throughout the world!

During this period I was working extremely hard and was keeping fit by playing squash, swimming and running each day. I would rise early and go for a run around the estate, before showering and going into the office for around 08:30 a.m.

The Police College
The British police are probably the best trained in the world and I was still being trained in a variety of topics, including war duties, (the threat of nuclear war still existed) and more significantly, attended a pre-staff college inspectors' course at Solberge Hall in North Yorkshire. On this course were

old and new colleagues; Joan Armstrong, now in North Yorkshire, Randy Walton of Cleveland, Arthur Smith now retired from Durham, are just some that I recall. This course was to prepare us for the national eleven-week inspectors' course at the Police Staff College, at Bramshill House in Hampshire.

The problem with Bramshill is its location. It is a long way from Durham and I went down in the summer of 1978 with a heavy heart, simply because of the long travel. We used to share transport and I travelled regularly with a fellow inspector from Durham called Terry Eales. He used to continually play Shirley Bassey records on the car cassette player. I used to like Shirley before those long journeys!

It was a useful course, grooming inspectors for sub-divisional command (either as chief inspector or superintendent). I did quite well and met an academic called Rod Adlam, for the first time. He was a young, eccentric, psychologist with curly, ginger hair, rather like Dr Who and, was the most unlikely member of a police-training establishment you could imagine. I liked him and he taught me a lot about writing, communicating and thinking.

One of the projects on that course was a visit to the BBC where we watched Angela Ripon read the six o'clock news. She then joined us in the bar for a convivial drink and I recall a superintendent from Humberside, John Taylor, unashamedly trying to get his daughter an introduction to television. Many years later I hosted a dinner in the Lords at which Angela Ripon was the principal guest and needless to say, she could not recall our earlier meeting!

We also had a question and answer session with the producer of the 6 o'clock News and as one of my favourite programmes on Radio 4 was, and still is, *Any Questions*, I told him that I thought that such a programme would make interesting television. I will to my dying day remember his response. He said, 'One thing I have learned over time is that talking heads do not make good television.' That had put me in my place! Within two years Robin Day was chairing the very successful *Question Time* on BBC 1, which is running to this day, with David Dimbleby, the brother of radio's *Any Questions* presenter, Jonathan Dimbleby, in the chair.

On my return to Durham in September I started teaching Banking Law at Ordinary National Certificate level in my spare time at New College in Durham. I don't know how I found the time, but I enjoyed teaching!

Gangsterism at Seaham

Perhaps one of the most interesting cases I found myself investigating was on my old patch at Peterlee sub division towards the end of 1978. The drug squad was called in to assist in an enquiry being conducted by a special team under the command of detective superintendent Ray Basham. Ray was a tough detective out of the same stable as Bill Grundy. They trained together at Hartlepool many years before. Ray was and, still is, a tall, dark good-looking man, with black, thinning hair, who had been identified as a candidate for rapid promotion. Indeed he was at one time the chief constable's staff officer at police headquarters. The CID was his love however, and he was good at it. In many respects he portrays to me the same image as the actor Jack Nicholson, in that when he is making a serious point, he talks through gritted teeth.

Ray was tasked with investigating the activities of one Benny 'the brick' Mottram, a Seaham scrap dealer and taxi owner who ruled the Seaham area by fear and intimidation for three years. In his early thirties, Mottram had formed the habit of reacting violently to people whose decisions he took exception to, whether they be councillors, planning officers or business rivals. He would direct the criminal operations, but get other people to carry out his retribution.

An example of his activities was a lady whose Robin Reliant car had been hit by one of Mottram's taxis from behind. Because she, quite rightly, intended to claim compensation for the damage, Mottram ordered his henchmen to set fire to her car, on which she totally depended. So the car was put to the torch, much to the distress of the owner.

When planning decisions went against him he would think nothing of arranging for the officials' windows to be broken at their places of residence. These activities in the dead of night can cause absolute terror and were intended to do just that. He 'arranged' arson at garage premises, when the proprietor refused to give Mottram's car priority for repairs. When some of his associates were barred from the Engineers Arms in Seaham, Mottram saw that the windows were broken. A newsagent's shop; a rival scrap dealer's car; rival councillors' homes; all were targets of what the sentencing judge described as, 'disgraceful, cowardly and despicable behaviour'.

One of the difficulties with this type of criminal behaviour is for the investigating team to break down the barrier of silence caused by fear and intimidation. Ray Basham did a brilliant job and when eventually we had gathered sufficient evidence, Mottram was arrested and charged. It was a 12 month enquiry, but well worth it when he was imprisoned for four years.

One humorous offshoot of the Benny Mottram enquiry was the arrest and charging of his solicitor, David Hammond, on suspicion of fraudulent property deals on behalf of Mottram. Bill Grundy and I were conducting this 'wing' of the enquiry and arrested the solicitor, who went to trial, but was subsequently acquitted. Mottram was in a cell in the police station at Peterlee, when we brought the solicitor in and put him in the cells. Benny spoke to me later that day and made the classic comment, 'Mr Mackenzie, I knew the game was up when I saw my solicitor carrying his mattress along the cell corridor!'

It was around this time that Jean and I started looking for a larger house. A detached house was our objective. Eventually we found what we were looking for at Etherley Close on the same estate in Durham. It had a delightful garden with mature trees, back and front, and the potential for expansion. We paid around seventeen and a half thousand pounds for it and moved at the end of 1978.

New Blood at the Top

Jack Hallett, the deputy chief constable, had now retired and we had a new deputy chief constable, a tall, dark haired, 'no nonsense' ACC from a nearby force. His name was Kenneth Henshaw and he was to have a significant effect on my life.

It is normal, when an officer has been to Bramshill, not least because of the cost, to have an interview with the chief constable or his deputy on return to force. In this case it was the new deputy who I saw on 19 January 1979. I liked his style and I believed he liked mine. What he saw was what he got; I was still quite forthright, in the northern style. I still think this might have been my downfall in the Special Course interviews many years earlier in London. We chatted about the course and, naturally, about the branch board of which I was still the branch chairman. It was, I thought, an instructive first meeting with the new deputy chief constable.

The detective inspector's office in the drug squad was on the first floor of police headquarters at Aykley Heads, with a wonderful view from the building of the cathedral and ancient castle, pivoted as they are on the high ground encircled, moat like, by the River Wear. There is a fine sports complex at Aykley Heads and I was a regular swimmer and squash player at the facility. I was also jogging regularly around this time. I would run a few miles round the Newton Hall Estate where I lived. I recall that it really took a hold of me and I became obsessive, feeling guilty if for some reason or other I did not get to run. It got to the ridiculous state that when I was working extremely long hours on a major inquiry, such as a murder, I would rise at around 5 a.m. to do my run before I went to work. Eventually I packed it in as it was taking over my life and I stuck to swimming and squash, although I did start running again when I started training with the FBI (more of which later).

On the same corridor as me in the headquarters building was the research and planning department headed up by a mature superintendent, who unfortunately has since died. His name was Bill Pratt and he had been in the communications and then the research and planning departments for many years. He was a specialist in communications and had made a career out of it.

Bill was what some would call 'an old woman', in that he liked to gossip and was very set in his ways.

Mistaken Identity

As we were in the same building, I would see him from time to time and pass the time of day. Also working at headquarters was a detective constable called John Reay. He was in the scientific aids department, and was a tall, thin officer with longish dark hair and a large, droopy, Mexican style, moustache. I was in my office one day, when John came in. 'Can I have a word with you boss', he said. 'Come in, John, sit down. What can I do for you?' I responded. 'Well I'm a bit embarrassed', he said, 'but I think I should tell you'. He then went on to tell me a remarkable story.

He described how Superintendent Bill Pratt had taken him to one side and asked him how he was getting on. The superintendent then told him that he had been identified by the new deputy chief constable, Mr Henshaw, as a candidate for the new computer project team which was about to be set up. John had protested that he knew nothing about computers, but Bill Pratt insisted that he would soon pick it up. Then the give-away; after describing what the new project would be involve, Superintendent Pratt said, 'I have been asked to sound you out, it could improve your career prospects. There could be promotion in the long term.'

Whatever else John Reay was, he was not ambitious. Indeed he was not qualified in the promotion examinations, so such a comment was a mystery to him. 'But boss, I haven't passed the promotion examinations!' he exclaimed. Bill Pratt looked shocked. 'What! You are Brian Mackenzie, aren't you?' John explained the mis-identification and no doubt smiled inwardly. Bill Pratt was terribly embarrassed and worried. 'I'm sorry', he said, 'not a word of this to anyone.'

I laughed out loud when DC Reay told me the story; after all, I had worn a full beard for about twelve months, although to be fair, I had a dark, droopy moustache before that. I was fascinated by the story and waited for Bill Pratt to approach the right Brian Mackenzie. Sure enough, a day or so later, in walked Superintendent Pratt. He sat down and told me that the new deputy chief constable was setting up a computer project team and that having met me, he thought I might be the right man to join. He was looking for four inspectors with different backgrounds. I was doubtful, as I liked what I was doing in the drug squad, and, was still settling in.

Although computers were used for the payroll and the like, operational data was still kept on card indexes, but there was no doubt that information technology was the up and coming thing. It was an ideal opportunity to be at the centre of things at police headquarters and, as it was not in my nature to shirk a challenge, I told him I was interested.

I saw Mr Henshaw shortly after that and he said he was still identifying other members of the team. He told me that in the meantime he would like me to transfer to the research and planning department on a temporary basis to 'read' myself into the new job. This I did and was transferred back into uniform, although wearing it was optional, with effect from 5 February 1979. Whilst working at headquarters I had got into the habit, at lunchtime, of swimming for thirty minutes in the excellent pool at Aykley Heads. Quite a few retired officers did the same. Alf Charlton and Frank Pickering were regulars, as were serving officers, Tony Robinson and Alan Miller.

Edmund-Davies
This was also a fascinating time politically. Following disagreement in the Police Council, the statutory police pay negotiating body, on whether to make a joint approach for exemption from the second round of the government's incomes policy, the Police Federation of England and Wales, together with Northern Ireland, but not Scotland or the Superintendents' Association, had withdrawn from the Council in 1976.

The Labour government was hanging on by a thread. Merlyn Rees, the home secretary, had been forced to set up an independent inquiry under the chairmanship of Lord Justice Edmund-Davies, to review the police negotiating machinery, and later, police pay. The result of that inquiry endeared Edmund-Davies to a generation of police officers. Reporting in 1978, his committee reaffirmed the unique position of the police in the country's unwritten constitution, particularly in view of the restrictions and limitations to which they are subject, including the prohibition on joining a trade union or taking strike action. It was recommended that the police should be awarded a substantial pay rise, which recommendation the government accepted, although they decided to phase it in. The Conservative opposition under their barnstorming new leader, Margaret Thatcher, were committed in their manifesto to implement the pay proposals in full immediately.

I can recall the discussions with Bill Pratt in his office during the run up to the 1979 general election. He hated Thatcher and all her works. The government had suffered the indignity of being undermined by its own supporters with the 'winter of discontent' and of course as we know, Margaret Thatcher swept to victory in the 1979 General Election. The Labour Party was split down the middle and, although it could not have been foreseen, had condemned itself to eighteen years in opposition.

CHAPTER 8

Computers

DURING ALL THIS political turmoil, I was reading my way into my new job. I also recall around this time, publishing an article in the *Police Review* on the causes of police corruption. This drew a distinction between fighting ordinary crime and enforcing what I called 'moral' legislation, such as licensing laws, drugs, gambling, prostitution and pornography. Because a large minority of the population saw nothing wrong in breaching these laws, there was a danger of police officers, particularly in specialist squads, becoming too close to the 'service providers'. I had not lost my interest in controversial matters.

In June 1979, the deputy chief constable Mr Henshaw had selected his computer project inspectors and I was told who they were. In addition to myself, there was Stan Hegarty, a slim, bony officer whom I had not served with previously and did not know well; Alan Watson, who I knew very well from my time at Jarrow where we served as constables. Alan was a bright lad who had also done well in his exams and was a graduate of the Special Course at Bramshill; the final inspector was Robin Dodd, a diminutive traffic inspector with whom I got on with well.

I remember that we were all summoned to the chief constable's office at headquarters the on 11 June 1979 and the consensus amongst us was that the team consisted of me (crime), Stan Hegarty (operational) and Robin Dodd (traffic) With Alan Watson heading up the team on promotion to chief inspector, being a fast tracker. It seemed to make sense!

We all stood in a line in front of the chief constable, Peter Puckering, in his office, together with Bill Pratt and Ken Henshaw, the deputy chief. He outlined the purpose of the project and said that we had all been selected for the task ahead. You can imagine our collective surprise when he called me forward and said; 'I am promoting you to chief inspector to head up the project team.' I can honestly say that I had no inkling that it was going to occur. The obvious choice, because of his highflier status from Bramshill, was Alan Watson. Life is full of surprises.

Needless to say I was delighted and set about arranging my promotion 'do' at the Railway Tavern in Shincliffe Village. In those days the licensee was a local 'character' called Harry Lightfoot. He was full of fun and a good friend of the police. I always remember him saying at the party in the private room upstairs, 'Have your next one here as well, and I'll put on a "super" do!' (the rank of superintendent, being the next promotion!). Unfortunately, the Railway Tavern has since been pulled down and flats were built in its place. A shame because it was a village pub with character, built beside the old Shincliffe railway track, likewise no longer there.

Unfortunately in my view, we did not retain the services of Ken Henshaw; he saw the opportunity of advancement and took it. He went to North Yorkshire as the new chief constable. We got a new deputy chief constable with the memorable name of Eldred Boothby. I knew of him only as a result of him being interviewed on Radio Four in relation to some traffic problem or other in the south of England. He was a man who was meticulous about detail. He would read everything that crossed his desk, correcting any grammatical or spelling errors.

In February 1980 I went with Mr Boothby, Mr Henshaw, who was now in North Yorkshire of course and, Bill Pratt as guests of the computer giant IBM, to a 3 day seminar in La Hulpe, Belgium, where they have a training establishment. I remember the trip well, because we were getting picked up to go to the airport at Teesside, and Bill was the last passenger to be collected early in the morning. His alarm did not go off and I had to go and knock him up. I thought to myself, as he stood at the door in his pyjamas, 'he couldn't have chosen to screw up in such exalted company as two chief constables!'

The big players in computing were now starting to take an interest in the police as clients, and the police themselves were waking up to the advantages of information technology in the fight against crime.

On the political front, the Labour Party was in turmoil after the election defeat and although the police are not allowed to be active in politics, as I mentioned earlier my natural inclination, because of my background, was left of centre. So I was a natural Labour voter. I was not happy however with the trade union militancy that seemed to pervade the country around this time. Ever since I was once bullied as a youth I have stood up to people trying to get their way simply by brute force. It may have been one of the reasons why I joined the police service. In any event I was watching the political scene nationally with more and more interest and I continued to be active in the Police Federation.

The work on the computer project was interesting, preparing a feasibility study on the implications of a computerized criminal information system in Durham Constabulary. I was on a steep learning curve.

The Application
During the summer of 1980, I saw an advertisement in the *Police Review*, which is the police publication with the greatest circulation in Britain, and an essential read for any ambitious police officer. When I read the advertisement

for a detective superintendent, I had to blink. If I had been writing the desired qualities of an applicant for promotion, so that they fitted my profile, I could not have done a better job. I read and re-read the advertisement. It was a central service post based in London at the Home Office, attached to the Police Research Services Unit (PRSU) – Crime Group.

The job would involve assisting police forces in the design and implementation of computerized crime information systems and the applicant had to have had police experience, which included the holding of a CID post at not less than that of detective inspector rank. I remember thinking 'how many other ex detective inspectors can there be working on a crime computer system with an honours degree in law?'. I thought about it long and hard. I had only been an inspector for two years; I had only been a chief inspector for twelve months; wasn't I really expecting too much? But then I applied a philosophy, which I have practised for most of my life 'nothing ventured – nothing gained'. In other words, even if I were unsuccessful, I would be exactly where I started, so I had absolutely nothing to lose.

My application went in on 8 July and I got the support of the chief constable, Peter Puckering, who told me I would be promoted temporarily, should I be successful. I was called for interview before a panel chaired by a senior home office official call Ken Dawson. Also on the panel were a Mr Pearce, from the home office and a seconded assistant chief constable called Gerry Openshaw, who I believe was a Sussex officer and who was head of PRSU.

It was the strangest interview I have ever had. The panel did not talk about 'if' I came to London, but 'when'. They told me of the allowances, benefits, leave entitlements and accommodation as though it was a fait accompli. In my heart I knew it was. There was a Durham officer already working in the PRSU, a chief inspector fingerprint expert called Jim Strachan. I had arranged to meet him after the interview and told him I had got the job. I bought him a drink on the strength of it so I must have been fairly certain!

I went back to the force and continued working on the computer project, sharing the same office as Bill Pratt. He was a fascinating man. Superintendents in the force were responsible for investigating complaints against fellow police officers. Most superintendents took it in their stride, but with Bill it was a major problem. He had not been an operational police officer for many years and would probably have found it difficult to deal with a shoplifter, let alone interview a police officer.

The Complaints Department were sympathetic to his plight however and tended to give him the simple jobs. Bill's forte was to drag the enquiry out as long as he possibly could and, they did not usually give him more than one complaint at a time. He would carry the complaint with him for weeks, using the pretence that he could not get an interview with the complainant. When forced to see the complainant, there was such a time lapse that they had usually lost interest. Bill would then sweet-talk them into withdrawing the complaint. It was comical to watch his technique.

I was in the office with Bill Pratt on an afternoon in September when I received the call. It was Gerry Openshaw the assistant chief constable, with whom I had the strangest of telephone conversations. He told me that the panel were still considering the applicants for the post in the PRSU and I was still in the running. He then got personal. 'Can I ask you, Chief Inspector, whether you have a skin complaint?' I thought I had misheard him and asked him to repeat. 'Have you got a problem with your skin?' 'No, why?' 'Well the board thought that was why you perhaps wore a beard.' I went on to tell him that I had grown the beard on attachment to the drug squad and that my wife rather liked it.

He then went on to describe how old fashioned some chief constables were and how, if appointed, I would have to mix in these exalted circles with these non-trendy senior police officers. He was in fact describing himself very accurately! I was now getting the drift and said, 'Mr Openshaw, is there a problem with my beard?' 'Well', he stammered, 'It's just that the board thought...' I didn't let him finish. 'Look, if you want me to shave it off, just tell me'. 'Well would it cause you a problem?' he queried. 'Not at all', I said. I thought to myself that for a superintendent's job, I would show my backside in Harrods shop window! You have to remember that with London allowances this promotion would mean a virtual doubling of my disposable income! 'Thank you', he said and rang off.

I was busy explaining the bizarre conversation to Bill Pratt, when the phone rang again. It was the chief constable's secretary. 'Can you come down, the chief wants to see you.' I knew what it was so I went down smiling, to be told by the chief constable, Peter Puckering, that I had got the job – I was now a detective superintendent at the remarkably young age, in those days, of thirty seven – working in London!

The Home Office

I started work in London with effect from 27 October 1980. The PRSU offices were in Horseferry House in Horseferry Road just beside the Thames in Westminster, near the magistrates' courts. It was bleak compared to the plush surrounds of the new police headquarters at Durham. Plain walls, with blast proof scruffy net curtains. A single desk and chair and, if you were lucky, a coat stand. There were about six or seven of us in the unit and we were all housed in the same building. There was a post delivery run several times a day, when a lady would wheel the mail round the building on a trolley, dropping it off at different offices.

My living accommodation was in Metropolitan Police flats on loan to the Home Office. I shared a flat with two other officers just off the Edgware Road, near Marble Arch. It was a fascinating transition from the northeast to the centre of the capital city of London. I soon settled into my new role and started travelling to forces such as South Yorkshire, the West Midlands, Greater Manchester and Kent in my new advisory role. My flatmates and I were like ships passing in the night, only occasionally, were we all in London together. We had our favourite pubs where we enjoyed a good social life when the machinations of work permitted.

It was whilst staying at the training school at Chester House in Manchester, that I had breakfast with a young up and coming assistant chief constable. We talked about his trips to the United States and I was impressed with his knowledge and experience. He was a wiry, fit looking man with fair, receding hair and, his name was John Stalker, who went on to become deputy chief constable. He became well known for his report into policing in Northern Ireland and was to leave the force prematurely in controversial circumstances. He went on to present a crime programme in the northwest, and I had the pleasure of appearing on his programme when I was President of the Superintendents' Association.

I travelled home every week on the train, pretty much as I do now, planning my work, usually reading, for the three-hour train journey from Durham to Kings Cross. I always carried a small earphone radio so I could catch the news programmes on my cherished Radio 4. It is something I have always done as I look on travelling time as lost time, unless you put it to some use. That is partly why I travel by train rather than fly, because with the latter, the journey is so disjointed on short flights, you don't get time to settle down to work. There is not a great deal of saving with time either, when you take account of commuting to and from the airport and the rigorous checking-in procedures which do not apply on the train.

The boys were now 12 and 9 respectively and settled into the local schools in Durham. The increased salary meant that we could do far more and we went on holidays abroad to the Canary Islands and Spain. I even bought a video camera which, compared to modern ones, was laughable. The camera was enormous and in addition it had to be connected to the recorder, which you carried with you on your back. In 1980 of course it was 'state of the art'. We have some good video footage of the lads growing up, although filming on the move was a major operation.

On the political front things were hotting up. Although a Labour supporter, I had never been a member of the party, not least because of the ban on police officers being 'active' in politics. It seemed that the party was coming apart at the seams. In January 1981 the famous 'Gang of Four' announced their intention of breaking away from the Labour Party. Led by

Roy Jenkins, who had returned from Europe, and supported by Dr David Owen, a former Labour foreign secretary, Shirley Williams, a former education secretary and Bill Rodgers, they made the famous 'Limehouse Declaration', so called because it was outside Dr Owen's Limehouse home in Docklands.

I have to say that all this was having a great effect on me. I found that I was in total sympathy with the 'Gang of Four' and decided to watch progress with interest. It was about this time that I met Fergus Montgomery. I was at a police leaving party, I believe at a military police club in Rochester Row. He was a former teacher from Newcastle and was Tory MP for Altringham and Sale, and I got on very well with him. He would facilitate my admission to the House of Commons to watch Prime Minister's Questions, which was, in my view, pure theatre. I used to sit in the Central Lobby of the Palace of Westminster, 'spotting' well-known faces going about the business of running a parliamentary democracy. Little did I know then, that I would be a central part of it all, two decades later!

On 26 March 1981 the launch took place of the Social Democratic Party (SDP) with its famous yellow logo. The political left seemed to be in disarray, leaving the stage to Mrs Thatcher to do as she wished. In any event I was so interested in what was happening and felt so moved to be part of it, that I actually became a subscribing founder member of the SDP, although for obvious reasons I did not become an activist, nor did I announce it.

It is rather interesting that when I went into parliament in 1998, the 'Gang of Four' had moved from the Commons to the Lords. Although I have spoken to some of them, I have never mentioned my brief conversion from the Labour Party.

My work at the PRSU taught me a lot about the value of technology and one early lesson I learnt was that for police officers to use it, it had to be simple and 'bobby' proof. As a police officer I had learned to type quite quickly with two fingers and soon realized that the information provided by a computer was only as good as the data put in. 'Rubbish in – Rubbish out', was the term.

Each force in the country was developing its own computer system, with different applications and it occurred to me very early on that it might be better if the standard was set centrally so that forces could at least share information. This found little favour at the home office and I was told by Tom Mann, one of the scientists, it 'stifled innovation', as did my suggestion that 'free text retrieval' was by far the most acceptable system as far as police officers were concerned. This was preferable, in my view, to coding all the information first and requiring specialist staff to operate the system.

Since then the service has developed the 'HOLMES' major inquiry system, which is a common kit developed centrally, used in large investigations, enabling different police forces to share information. It was developed on the back of the Yorkshire Ripper Inquiry, which spanned several forces and just about swamped West Yorkshire Police with the sheer volume of information.

Similarly, the most common way of retrieving information from any system now is to search on words or numbers. That requires the proper spelling on input or a skilful knowledge of how to play the system.

The chief constable of Durham, Peter Puckering, used to come down to London for meetings on the use and training of police dogs. He was the ACPO committee chairman, I believe, so I occasionally met him for a drink and he provided a lift in his staff car. He was due to retire shortly and as the anniversary of my first twelve months of secondment was coming up, I took the precaution of ringing his office to have the promotion made substantive before he retired. I was substantively promoted to detective superintendent on 27 October 1981.

Running the help desk at PRSU was a young, bright, Merseyside inspector called Paul Rowlandson. Because he didn't travel the country like the rest of us, he was always good for a pint or a game of squash and we became firm friends. Like all of us he moved on and upwards and recently retired from the police as a superintendent, on being appointed a regional crime reduction director in Bristol.

In my second year in London I had a health problem. You will recall that as a detective in Jarrow, I had lost my voice and had to receive treatment in South Shields General Hospital. Well the problem recurred and I lost my voice again. I went to the hospital and an examination showed that I had a growth on one of my vocal chords. I have to say that whilst I was sick the staff both police and civilians, at the PRSU, were very good, sending cards and gifts. I remember Superintendent Steve Males even visited me in Durham. I had my operation to remove the nodule and was not allowed to speak afterwards for a number of weeks. I obeyed the rules rigorously. When Jean and I went to the pub with friends, I would take a pen and paper and write my contribution to the conversation down. It was quite a novelty at first, but eventually people got tired of waiting and the conversation moved on. Fortunately my voice came back loud and clear, some say deeper, but the experience gave me an insight of what it must be like to be disabled. I have often said since then that you cannot put a price on good health!

Whilst travelling I was still conscious of being a police officer and would enforce the rules on the train. I have had altercations with people smoking, swearing and putting their feet on the seats. It still happens long after my retirement much to the despair of my long suffering wife, who tells me that one of these days someone will turn on me.

On one occasion I admonished two students for putting their shoes on the seats. They looked surprised and at first objected. I started to argue and one youth said, 'Alright, you don't have to shout!' By now the whole train was listening – I had left my radio earphones in ears and was shouting without realizing it!

My experience however is that in the main, people do respond to being told in a civil manner. If more people complained about anti-social behaviour, particularly by the young, I believe we would have a more ordered society.

Indeed, in the summer of 2003 at the time of writing this, I went along to the village pub/restaurant, the Seven Stars for a quiet pint with Nigel Gadd, the former licensee, who now owns the Pump House, another restaurant in the village. It was about 7:00 p.m. when a very large drunken man lurched behind the bar demanding more alcohol. The young barman, who I believe was a student, quite rightly, politely refused to serve him and suggested that he should leave. Two friends of the drunken man tried to pull him back and he got aggressive towards the young barman. In an effort to defuse the situation I went round from the bar and tried to reason with the drunken man. A man in his thirties, his conduct was disgraceful with swearing and alcohol-inspired aggression. I could see that he was determined to have a go at the young barman so I quietly phoned 999 on my mobile.

I knew the police officer in the police control room, PC Bob Mace and asked him to send assistance. Within minutes, PC Andy Davison had arrived on the scene and spoke to the drunken man, who by now was draped over the bonnet of a car. The drunk made a violent lurch towards the officer and tried to strike him, but the officer with a clever body swerve caused him to fall over. The officer kneeled on him and told him to stop struggling. I had gone outside to protect the officer from any untoward interference from the drunk's two friends, who had also been drinking. The officer was obliged to use his CS spray to contain and arrest his prisoner with the help of other officers who by now had arrived.

This type of disgraceful behaviour is now all too common in the streets of our towns and cities and we should not tolerate it. The officer's brave action on that warm evening was commendable and it was interesting that he told me afterwards that whilst holding the man down, he was reassured by seeing my shoes nearby, guarding the scene, to deter the 'jackals' hovering around. It was Edmund Burke who said 'The only thing necessary for the triumph of evil is for good men to do nothing.' [1770] When bad men combine, the good must associate. A healthy interest in politics is essential to a just society as the penalty good men pay for indifference to public affairs is to be ruled by evil men. We have seen examples of this throughout history!

On 25 October 1982 my secondment in London came to an end and I was posted back to Research and Planning Department at police headquarters

Durham on a temporary basis until they found a job for me, as my job on the computer team had been taken by Chief Inspector Eddy Marchant.

The force had changed. Peter Puckering had retired and Eldred Boothby had taken over. We had a new deputy chief constable (DCC) from West Yorkshire called Tom Farmer, whose career had started many years earlier in Durham and he had returned as an assistant chief constable in charge of training. His reputation as a 'character' went before him and he was to have a marked effect on Durham Constabulary. The rumour was that he had never been promoted within his force, except in Durham, to sergeant and DCC. Other than that he had always moved on when he moved up, which can indicate many things.

Sub-divisional Command

Bishop Auckland sub-division was my first operational posting as a superintendent on 15 November 1982, the very station where I had turned down the police house when leaving Harperley Hall, all those years before. Housing was no problem now, as we had our own house in Durham and I drove to and from work. The divisional commander at Bishop Auckland was an ex detective, chief superintendent Russ Peart and his deputy was my old detective inspector from Peterlee, Superintendent Bill Grundy. The CID was commanded by Detective Chief Inspector Brian Turner, who later, along with Ned Lawson, became a Gaming Board inspector.

I got to know my team; most important, in my judgment, was my deputy, Bill Kennedy. He was a great character, with a lovely mild manner and a delightful sense of humour. He and his smashing wife Moira became good friends and we visited each other's houses. It was essential that we got on, because Bill would run the sub-division in my absence.

I recall on one occasion Bill having a near fatal accident. For some reason he did not see a clear glass door in the police station and crashed into it, causing severe lacerations to his legs. It was a wonder he was not more badly injured, but he still walks with a slight limp to this day.

One thing I quickly learned was how to investigate complaints against the police. The regulations were such that this task had to be performed under the supervision of a superintendent. Although the serious complaints were dealt with by a dedicated complaints and discipline department at head-quarters, many were passed out to territorial superintendents to investigate in their 'spare' time. It always intrigued me that many complaints were the result of poor supervision or management, yet all the managers of sub-divisions were leaving their commands to go to other sub-divisions to investigate complaints. This invariably left one's own sub-division unsupervised!

I did not copy Bill Pratt's philosophy of delaying the investigation. All my life I have liked to get on with the things in hand, on the basis that you never know what will happen next. Not a bad philosophy, it seemed to me, in a reactive job like policing. Indeed, I enjoyed carrying out investigations and getting away from the routine paperwork of command.

One of the tasks of a superintendent in those days was to recommend prosecutions for a whole range of relatively minor offences, including traffic accidents and, yet arrests at night, for example, and charges, were authorized by the shift sergeant. So we had well-paid superintendents dealing with the minutiae of criminality, and the constables and sergeants depriving citizens of their liberty and charging them. Such was policing in those days!

On promotion to superintendent, I had automatically become a member of the Police Superintendents' Association and started to receive minutes of branch (force) meetings. It was not until I returned to the force that I could actually physically attend branch meetings, which in our force were usually held four or five times a year, in a local hotel. On attending the meetings it became apparent to me that all was not well in the force. Morale had dipped beyond belief from when I had left on my secondment to London. I did not need to be a detective to discover why. The force was under the iron grip of the new deputy chief constable, Tom Farmer.

Tom Farmer was a round-faced individual, whose name suited him. He talked in staccato outbursts and appeared to delight in humiliating individuals at every opportunity. His leadership style in my opinion was disciplinarian and militaristic.

The whole force, with the apparent exception of the chief constable Eldred Boothby, appeared to be frightened of him. Mr Boothby, in his ivory tower, was either totally unaware of what was going on, or he was indifferent and turned a blind eye. The two assistant chief constables at that time were Fred Wilson, and Percy (Denis) Gatis. Fred was a mild, pleasant ex-CID man, who had served in Durham all his service and had a tremendous knowledge of the county and its people. He had previously been the chairman of the Superintendents' Association in the force. Denis Gatis was a likeable ex-Gateshead Borough officer, with clear-rimmed spectacles and a bald-headed, Germanic appearance. He was not very well known in the force, and as the man who held the purse strings, acquired quite a reputation, for understandable reasons, for being Spartan with the funds.

Like any efficient dictator, the deputy chief constable had his spies and his informers. They became known in the force as 'Farmer's boys' and those in the know would sing or whistle 'to be a farmer's boy' in their presence, to warn others. It sounds unbelievable but it was that bad! It was well known that Tom Farmer would have knowledge of the discussions at our superintendents' meetings before we got back to our respective stations.

The chairman of the superintendents' branch at that time was Alf

Charlton, a fiery chief superintendent of small stature with a great deal of traffic experience, and the secretary was Bill Hills, a pleasant, mild mannered, tall, police cricketer, who had worked as the chief constable's personal assistant, many years before.

It appeared to me that one of Mr Farmer's favourite ways of punishing officers of any rank, without the basic necessity to prove wrongdoing, was to transfer them. He would have officers, including superintendents, passing each other on the roads, travelling miles from one end of the county to the other. The obvious advantage to him was that it saved the trouble of having to adduce evidence and prove a discipline case to a certain standard. A transfer notice was much easier. In fact later on, Her Majesty's Inspectorate of Constabulary highlighted the high number of transfers in his inspection report and the chief constable was asked to explain the reason.

But this was early days, people started to complain at the superintendents' meetings about the number of transfers and I could see that morale was getting lower and lower.

One of the principal tasks of the deputy chief is to manage discipline and complaints in the force, which I believe in Mr Farmer's case was like putting an alcoholic in charge of a brewery! He believed in ruling with a rod of iron and he did. The chief constable of course, was the disciplinary authority and had to be independent of all this so that his judgment was not clouded. It also gave the deputy chief a weapon to hit the superintendents with. It became obvious to me that if a superintendent fell foul of him, for whatever reason, he would be allocated more and more complaints to deal with. Farmer would burden them with long, tortuous inquiries, on top of their normal superintending duties. I could not believe what I was witnessing and used to raise these issues at the branch meetings, to no avail.

On 6th April 1983, I was transferred to my hometown of Darlington as the sub-divisional commander. Darlington was the busiest station in the force and I was quite happy with the transfer. My divisional commander was a chief superintendent with a reputation of his own, Derek Sayers. He would bark and shout, but ran a good ship and socially he was a 'pussy cat' and easy to get on with. My old fellow recruit, Ken Lavery was the detective chief inspector and I felt it was a good team.

The deputy to Derek Sayers was Superintendent David Blakey, who was a Special Course graduate who was clearly going places. In fact he later became the chief constable of West Mercia and at the time of writing is a distinguished member of Her Majesty's Inspectorate of Constabulary. On occasions, duties permitting, because we both lived at Durham, Dave Blakey and I travelled together either in his car or mine. On one memorable occasion I was his passenger when, with both of us in full uniform, David ran into the back of another car on the A167. Fortunately there were no adverse consequences.

On 27 April 1983 I attended the 55th Intermediate Command Course at Bramshill, designed to prepare me for divisional command. The course was for a three-month period and I quickly got into the routine of travelling up and down to Hampshire. I enjoyed the course, did well and looked forward to continuing my command at Darlington sub-division, where I was born and raised.

Politics

Meanwhile on a separate front, at about this time, an aspiring politician was attempting to gain nomination for a seat in the Labour dominated county of Durham. Anthony Charles Lynton Blair, a young barrister, was about to be nominated at the last minute for the constituency of Sedgefield in the south of the county. As we know he became the Labour candidate just before the general election of 1983, which Michael Foot, who had taken over as Labour leader from Jim Callaghan, lost disastrously, with a manifesto famously described by the MP Gerald Kaufman as 'the longest suicide note in history'.

Tony Blair of course was duly elected and entered parliament after the election in June 1983 under the new leadership of Neil Kinnock, who famously said in October of that year 'Remember how you felt on that dreadful morning of 10 June. Just remember how you felt then, and think to yourselves, "June 9 1983: never, ever again will we experience that"'.

Over the ensuing years I had the opportunity of meeting Tony Blair at many functions where either he or I was speaking, also at Downing Street and at police headquarters, when he was invited as a guest to one of the senior officers' guest nights.

I remember that occasion well, and that he was ' shanghaied' by us, i.e. Ned Lawson, Keith Best, Nick Spooner et al, and we bounced political questions off him. He handled it extremely well and listened to our concerns. Eventually, the chief constable came across and said, 'Can I have my guest back!'. The thing that struck me even then was that Tony Blair had a certain presence and charisma! We were being picked up by a friend, Alex Rennie, who was a regular in the New Inn, Nick Spooner's bar in Durham and I remember Alex telling me that when he picked us up at the end of that night, I got into the car, worse for wear, and said, 'That guy Tony Blair is a future Prime Minister!' How about that for vision? Alex still reminds me of those comments.

I returned from Bramshill in the summer of 1983 refreshed, knowledge-able and raring to go. It was certainly a busy sub-division, but I was enjoying it and got on well with Derek Sayers. It was late in 1983 that a horrific murder and rape took place at Sheffield. A solicitor's house was broken into and the family of three were murdered. The chief suspect was a man called Arthur Hutchinson, a big raw-boned man who hailed from Hartlepool. Over the weekend of Saturday 5 November, there were various sighting of Hutchinson in countryside in the Cleveland Police area and the force was conducting a wide sweeping search. Durham Constabulary being adjacent to Cleveland received a request for Police Support Unit (PSU) assistance. This consisted of a trained unit of officers under the command of an inspector and two sergeants.

My sub-division assembled a PSU under the command of Inspector Ray Richardson and joined the sweep of the fields and hedgerows in the Dalton Piercy area of Cleveland. The weather was appalling and my thoughts were with them as they set off to track this dangerous suspect.

Imagine my delight therefore when news came through that Darlington officers, in fields at Dalton Piercy, had arrested Hutchinson without injury to either officers or Hutchinson. I was there to greet them all when they returned on that Saturday and at the debrief, I told them that if any of them called into the police club (most stations in those days had a licensed club in the building), I would buy them all a drink for doing such sterling work and representing the force so well. I then drafted a fax to headquarters, outlining the use of the PSU, the result and, the fact that I had congratulated all officers on a job well done under difficult circumstances. I thought no more of it, but the comments were to come back and bite me!

You will recall that, having been to the Police Staff College, it was normal to have a post-course interview with a member of the executive at head-quarters. In the case of the Intermediate Command Course it was with the chief constable. I had my interview with Mr Boothby at the end of November 1983. It was a positive interview, which took place around 5 p.m. at Aykley Heads in the chief constable's office. I was congratulated on a successful course and report, and after ten minutes left Mr Boothby's office.

The route out of the chief constable's office, takes you through the secretary and PA's office, which separates the chief from the deputy. As I walked past the deputy's open door I heard 'Mackenzie!'. I went back and saw Mr Farmer, the deputy chief constable sitting at his desk. 'Come in and shut the door', he barked. I carried out his instruction.

'I suppose you'll be flying high and quite pleased with yourself now you've seen the chief', he said, with a sarcastic smile on his face.

'Yes, it was quite a good interview, Mr Farmer', I replied proudly.

'Well let me bring you back down to earth. You sent a fax to headquarters a couple of weeks ago about the use of the Police Support Unit!'

'That's right', I said, 'they did a great job.'

'At the end of the message, you commended them?'

'That's right, they were brilliant', I said proudly.

Tom Farmer's face blackened. 'You have no right to commend anyone in this force. Only one man can do that and his office is next door,' indicating the chief constable's office.

'Are you saying that if officers do a good job I can't pat them on the back?' I queried incredulously.

'That's right. You expect people to do a good job. You only intervene when they fall short and then you use the iron fist', he said.

I couldn't believe what I was hearing. 'I've never heard anything so ridiculous in my life, Mr Farmer, what kind of management is that?'

'You will do as you're told', he bellowed, banging his fist on the desk. 'Your problem is, you have been reading too many management books at the College.'

I was getting angry now. 'Mr Farmer, if you didn't want me to read the books, why did you send me to the college in the first place?'

'You could have embarrassed the chief constable with another force, just do as you're told', he bellowed, 'Now get out!'

Many in Durham Constabulary at that time will testify that that conversation gives a flavour of the Tom Farmer style of management. I believe he reduced many people to tears with his autocratic manner. Some even left the job. As a result of my confrontation, I started to get more and more complaints against the police to investigate. I was running the busiest sub-division in the force and at one stage had six uncompleted complaints. The superintendent from the complaints department, Bill Tate, came out to see me one morning and looked apologetic. 'I'm sorry Brian, but here's another one.' I couldn't believe it. 'I told him how many you had, but he insisted.' 'Bill', I said, 'If I get any more after this, I will raise it with the HMI.' I was not allocated any more complaints and ploughed on as best I could.

The Miners' Strike

On the political front Margaret Thatcher was in full control and, following the winter of discontent under Jim Callaghan, she was beefing up the police to take on the trade unions. The new government honoured the Edmund-Davies recommendations in full as they had promised, and police morale nationally was now high in consequence. She had shown sterling leadership qualities by winning the Falklands war and was dubbed the 'Iron Lady' by the Russians.

The police were encouraged to develop strategies for providing mutual aid between forces and to tackle 'flying pickets' when they were used to prevent strike breaking by the use of secondary action or by 'mob violence', such as the mining dispute in 1972 when the police had been forced to surrender to mass pickets at the Saltly coal depot at Birmingham, and the Grunwick printing dispute in 1977.

I remember the effect the confrontations had on police and labour-union relations. My old childhood pal, Tom Sawyer, had risen to deputy general secretary of the National Union of Public Employees (NUPE) and was working in London, during my secondment with PRSU at the home office in the early eighties. I decided to get in touch with my friend and gave Tom a ring. When I spoke to him, I immediately got very cool vibes and did not pursue that particular reunion! This was clearly Tom's 'far left' period, but as we will see later, he would change.

The scene was being set for a confrontation with the unions, and the police were accused of being Maggie Thatcher's 'boot boys'. I reject that suggestion, as the police were simply responding to a new type of threat by having a central control centre at Scotland Yard, which was necessary to take an overview of the national position.

It was one of the natural consequences of not having a national police force and it worked well. The National Union of Miners (NUM) was flexing its muscles over pit closures. Led by its militant leader, Arthur Scargill, they eventually came out on strike in March 1984 and the country entered into one of the bitterest industrial disputes for many years. The main pits in Durham were on the east coast at Easington and Seaham, where mass picketing took place.

There was also mass picketing at Tow Law, where a private opencast mine operated. This was seen as strikebreaking and an attempt was made by picketing to stop the movement of coal, which was being led away from the site by fleets of lorries.

Divisional Command

I must have been doing something right, because around mid April of 1984, I got a personal telephone call from the deputy chief constable, Tom Farmer. 'I'm sending you to Chester-le-Street as deputy divisional commander,' he rattled, 'what do you think?' 'I'm delighted, sir,' I said. It was a promotion. There were a lot of moves in that round. David Blakey transferred to Northumbria as a chief superintendent. Another old pal, Bill Newby became a chief superintendent and took charge of operations at headquarters. Don Moody, who had been instrumental in getting me onto the drug squad, moved to Durham as deputy divisional commander, and my old inspector from Peterlee, Ray Brammer took my job at Darlington as superintendent.

I moved to Chester-le-Street on 1 May 1984 under the command of chief superintendent Jack Passmore, a tall slim, quiet man who kept himself to himself. In all my time working for Jack Passmore, I had never been made to feel that I was welcome. We did not 'share' command in the true sense of the word, which is what should happen. I had my job dealing with juvenile panels and the like and he did the rest. The problem was, that when the divisional commander was on leave, I was in charge with only half of the information required to really be effective. Again, I just got on as best I could.

I recall one night being called from home by the shift inspector, Vic Errington. The chief superintendent was on leave. There had been a serious riot on the Drum Lane Estate, near Birtley, and the youths had scattered. When I got to the office I set a team up to investigate the disturbance and I attached a detective constable, a young keen officer called Alan Watson, to the team. They did a good job and it got back to Tom Farmer, who to his credit, rang me and complimented my good work.

On the Superintendents' Association front, I was quite active and on 8 May 1984 I was nominated and elected treasurer of the Durham branch. Although I had not sought it, I was on the political ladder!

The Summer of Discontent

Throughout the summer of 1984, morale amongst superintendents got progressively worse. The deputy chief constable Tom Farmer was using force inspections to find evidence of negligent supervision. For example, if lost or found property records were not accurate, he would order discipline notices to be served on the sub-divisional commander. There would then be a formal investigation by a chief superintendent or an assistant chief constable.

My turn came when an inspection at Darlington some months before, had revealed that a notice had not been put on the front of a found property book, a purely administrative matter. On 19 July 1984, I was summoned to Police Headquarters at Aykley Heads, to be interviewed by the assistant chief constable, Fred Wilson. He said to me 'I'm sorry I've got to do this, but we have to go through this as long as we've got that silly bugger next door,' indicating the deputy chief, Tom Farmer's office, adjacent to his. I told Fred that I understood. I was then served with forms alleging neglect of duty. I denied the charges and stated 'although accepting command responsibilities, I cannot not be held vicariously liable for every minor infringement by anyone under my command. Otherwise,' I said, 'I would have to examine every line of every officer's pocket book, every day, an impossibility.'

Some officers had been disciplined on the instructions of Mr Farmer for failing to underline certain entries in their pocket books, which is technically contrary to standing orders, and my former command was the largest sub-division in the force. Needless to say nothing came of the ridiculous allegations although Tom Farmer did tell me that he had discussed the matter with the office of the director of public prosecutions and that such actions could amount to the common law crime of malfeasance, i.e. neglect of duty whilst holding public office. What the DPP must have thought, I cannot imagine.

My old divisional commander from Darlington, Derek Sayers, came under the spotlight also, as the result of a divisional inspection, and of course the press got to know about it. There then began a war of words that was in danger of making the force a laughing stock. Trivial book-keeping errors were used as a pretext for investigating senior officers, and Chief Superintendent Derek Sayers was quoted in the *Northern Echo* as saying, 'The inquiry is administrative and internal. It's a question of book-keeping at a very junior level... I would prefer to say no more about it.'

The miners' strike went on for twelve months, almost to the day, and it was a very difficult time for the mining communities and the police. Families were divided with some sons in the police and some down the pit. It took years after the strike for the police to rebuild trust in some mining communities. Having said that, my attitude towards bullies was such that such mob violence had to be confronted.

During this time I commanded PSUs at Easington and at Tow Law and on occasions there was extreme violence by some of the pickets. Police officers are human of course and are entitled to defend themselves and, I have little doubt that there was violence from this quarter in return. It was a bitter dispute, not helped by police officers, on overtime, being bussed in from London and elsewhere to mining communities in the north where they had neither knowledge of the area, or allegiance and commitment to the community. It was the local police who had to pick up the pieces and I was always aware of that.

In later years when after-dinner speaking to local and national audiences, I used to lighten my description of that period by telling this story:

As a superintendent, I was in command of a police support unit at Easington Colliery one winter's morning around 7 a.m. The bricks and bottles started to fly and a young officer at the front got hit. He struggled back and sat in a shop doorway in Seaside Lane. Being a good commander, having been to the Police College, I walked over to where he was sitting. His head was in his hands and blood was running down his face. 'Come on,' I said, 'Pull yourself together, get back to the front, your colleagues need your assistance', trying to raise his morale. He looked at me, no higher than my knees, through his blood-marked fingers and said, 'I'm sorry Sarge, I've had enough and, I can't go on.' 'Sarge?' I cried, 'I'm your superintendent!' 'Bloody hell,' he exclaimed, 'I didn't think I'd run that far back!'

I often found that putting yourself down in humour could be quite effective!

In the summer of 1984 the chief constable, Eldred Boothby, asked me if I was interested in entering a competition to attend a course at the FBI Academy in Quantico, Virginia. It was a three-month postgraduate course and there was a place for a British officer. He said, 'Go home and think about it over the weekend.' I told him that I did not need to think about it, I would be delighted to attend. I discussed it with Jean and she gave me her full support.

The interviews were to be held at the Police Staff College at Bramshill House in Hampshire and I was short listed, along with around twenty other officers. I travelled for my interview on 4 September 1984 and was interviewed by the commandant at the time, former Chief Constable Price, and the dean of studies John Watt. After the wide-ranging interview I felt I had given a good account of myself and was delighted to find a few weeks later that I had been successful. Once again my law degree and CID experience had combined successfully. The course was not due to start until the summer of 1985, so I had plenty of time to prepare.

Meanwhile, back at the coalface, if you'll pardon the phrase, I remember on one occasion in October 1984, when a particularly serious incident occurred at the Inkerman Road coal depot near Tow Law. As I mentioned earlier this is an opencast pit owned by Banks Ltd. We had a nominal group of six police officers on the site, when 700 people descended on the site one Tuesday night. There was violence in the air and police vehicles were overturned. Even after reinforcements arrived there was less than thirty officers at the scene.

The police were forced to retreat under a hail of missiles and after trying to rescue a police dog from an overturned police van, they were driven back again. An acting inspector re-grouped the officers for a charge, with officers and dogs and the crowd dispersed. Twelve officers were hurt that night and five, suffering from broken bones to concussion, were treated in hospital. I recall PC Andy Summerbell with a badly damaged helmet, which probably saved him from serious injury. I went public and pointed out ' this incident gave the lie to the claim that violence only occurs when there is a big police presence'. I added, 'This was not a picket. The premises were locked and shut up when these people arrived and I hope that people in mining communities will condemn what has happened because it does their cause no good at all. The sad thing is that someone is eventually going to be killed if this goes on.'

My prediction was of course proven right when two 'picketers' in Wales were later convicted of killing a taxi driver by dropping a concrete slab from a motorway bridge.

The superintendents in Durham were still having their problems and I raised the suggestion of going as a branch to the chief constable, pointing out how poor executive management practices were ruining the morale of the force. I submitted a paper setting out my concerns. I remember Superintendent Alan Miller telling me 'You've described the problem exactly, it's an excellent paper.' It was agreed that an approach be made to Mr Boothby, the chief constable. The ructions that this caused can only be imagined and I was asked to do a 'presentation' of our concerns to the executive officers, which I duly did. Everyone knew what the problem was, but not a great deal changed, other than the resignation of Alf Charlton as the chairman of the Durham Branch. Alf had had enough of being abused by the deputy chief.

Then an interesting thing occurred. You have to understand that hitherto, the Superintendents' Association, both nationally and locally, tended to be led by the most senior superintendents who were coming to the end of their service. It was not a radical organization, indeed many people never knew of its existence. Because of the problems in the Durham force, none of the chief superintendents wanted the job. It had previously been unheard of for a superintendent, as opposed to a chief superintendent, to take over the chair.

I was approached to stand, by Don Moody, my former chief inspector from headquarters CID. He represented one faction. Another group supported Superintendent Bill Hills, the former chief constable's personal assistant. I was the treasurer and Bill was the secretary. The significant point is that neither of us was a chief superintendent. The electorate in Durham was only about 22 strong, 21 men and one woman. There was a secret ballot on 15 January 1985 and I won by about five votes. That democratic election was instrumental in shaping the rest of my life. In fact I remember pulling Bill Hills' leg some time later, 'Do you realize Bill that if you had won that election, you might have been in the House of Lords now!' There was no bitterness and Bill and I remain firm friends.

Matters got worse when the chief constable was away on leave and Tom Farmer was acting chief constable. Reports started to appear in the local press about Tom Farmer's alleged misuse of police transport and that he had had a police alarm fitted to his private house in Peterlee. The force was in turmoil at a senior level and the police authority became involved. Tom Farmer couldn't seem to understand that his autocratic, inquisitorial style was ruining a police force with a reputation second to none in the country. In the end, another chief constable was brought in from Norfolk, to inquire into the allegations against him, and the result was that Tom Farmer retired shortly after that.

It was a period of time of which Durham Constabulary should not be proud. Careers were destroyed and good police officers left the service as broken men. That particular period taught me a lot about management skills, or lack of them, and I was strengthened in my determination to take on bullies, whether on the streets or within organizations.

My maiden speech in the House of Lords fourteen years later was to be on the subject of bullying, but more of that later.

In those days I had got into the habit, from my CID days at Jarrow, of using a dictaphone for reports and letters. I got very adept at using this new-

Good Conduct and Long Service reception, 1985.

fangled technology, as it was then, and I recall the arrest of the solicitor at Peterlee in the Benny Mottram case mentioned earlier, where the typist could not keep pace with the interrogation. This was instrumental in the prosecution failing and I believe if we had recorded the interview it would have made a difference. It is standard practice now of course. On one occasion I was describing crime trends as reaching 'peaks' and 'troughs'. I could not help but laugh when, by a perfectly understandable association of words, it came back from the typing pool as 'pigs' and 'troughs'!

It was about this time that I received my Long Service and Good Conduct Medal from the Lord Lieutenant of County Durham. A reception was held at police headquarters and of course all my contemporaries with whom I joined attended. We were all still good friends and of course, different ranks from constable to superintendent.

Social Life
Our social life at this time was good. We were upwardly mobile and relatively affluent and we had kept in touch with a lot of the 'newcomers' from our old street on the estate. We used to have house parties and invite twenty or thirty couples. In those days I would record 'Top of the Pops', play

it back through the large television with amplified speakers and we would dance the night away. I had converted the single garage into a study, built a double-garage on the opposite side of the detached house, and at the back of the garage, constructed a stone clad bar. I acquired some bar fittings from friends in the licensing trade and would have 'beer spheres' of homebrew, piped through from the garage into the bar. We all had great nights.

Two of our friends from Chillingham Road were Elsie and Brian Longstaff who owned a general dealers shop at Meadowfield just outside the city. I was always amazed at married people who could spend every waking, and sleeping, hour with their partner and not get under each other's feet. Elsie and Brian seemed to manage it, and got on very well. Elsie has a brother called Keith Best, who at that time was going through a very difficult divorce and was quite depressed. He would come through for a drink with his brother in law and stay at their house on a Friday night.

Friday tends to be a 'guys'' night out and we would all meet at the Newton Hall public house, which in those days was the focal point of the estate. It was there that I got to know Keith and we became, and still are, firm friends.

Keith was coming out of his period in the 'blues' and when he heard about me going to the United States on the FBI course, he said he might come over for a holiday whilst I was attending the course. I told him that there were plenty of cheap motels and we could meet up at weekends. He then started making the necessary arrangements to come out to visit towards the end of the course, for a couple of weeks.

CHAPTER 9

The FBI
(Federal Bureau of Investigation)

BEFORE TRAVELLING to Washington at attend the course in June 1985, I had to go through some preliminary matters with the American legal attaché in London. He was an all-American guy called Darrell Mills. Darrell was a tall, slim, good-looking FBI agent, attached to the US Embassy in Grosvenor Square, and his task was liaising with my police force, and me, explaining the arrangements for the course. I travelled down to see him and got to his office around 2 p.m. He immediately offered me a drink of bourbon, which is a sweet whisky made mainly from maize. I liked it and had another, and another. We became good buddies that afternoon and, unusually for an American in my experience, he liked a drink!

Not all Americans drink liquor, in fact some positively look down on it, but Darrell was more in the culture of the British police officer. He worked hard and played hard. He was a brilliant 'people' person. Indeed he still is, even though he is retired from the FBI. He still turns up at re-training conventions and has hardly changed at all. I remember that as part of his liaison function, he came up to Durham with his wife and another agent, and took the chief constable Eldred Boothby and his wife, together with Jean and me, out for a very pleasant dinner at West Auckland. A truly remarkable man, he was sorely missed when he retired. Darrell's son is a fiction writer and doing very well. I still keep in touch by e-mail and count Darrell Mills as a close friend.

I travelled to America on 29 June 1985. It took some preparing for, as I had never been away so far, for so long!

I was to fly to Washington on the Saturday and was not required to muster with other attendees at the FBI Headquarters, the Hoover building, in the capital until the Sunday. Darrell had kindly fixed me up with a room on the Saturday night at a 5-star hotel in the centre of the city. It was first class and I found I had been allocated a suite with a king-sized bed and the most enormous basket of fruit and chocolates you have ever seen. I had an evening to kill so I went down to the bar and had a drink. I got chatting to the girl behind the bar who was very friendly. I realized quite soon that we are very similar countries divided by a common language when she said, 'but you'll miss your family and friends,' and I replied innocently, 'Oh, I should think I'll manage to keep my pecker up!' The term 'pecker' of course, has a totally different meaning in the States, to the nasal reference in the UK.

I assembled with other course members, the next day at 2:00 p.m. at the Hoover building for transportation (I'm starting to revert to US speak), to the FBI Academy at Quantico, where, a few years later, the film about the serial killer Hannibal Lecter, *The Silence of the Lambs*, would be partly filmed.

Law enforcement in the United States is diverse. There are literally thousands of different agencies with varying powers, many armed, policing the towns, cities, villages, states, waterways, highways, universities, housing projects, subways, railways and many other utilities. Superimposed on all this are the Federal law enforcement agencies. The law enforcement arm of the US Department of Justice is the FBI. The law enforcement arm of the US Treasury Department is the Alcohol, Tobacco and Firearms Agency (the ATF). It will be recalled that Elliot Ness, of the Untouchables fame, was often described as an FBI Agent when stories of his arrest of Al Capone are related. He was a 'G' (government) man of course, but an agent of the ATF, as Capone was eventually convicted of tax evasion.

The FBI, like New Scotland Yard, had a formidable reputation of which they were rightly proud. The original director of course was the controversial J Edgar Hoover who allegedly had files on all the politicians! At the time of my visit the director was a former judge, William H Webster, a clean-cut, smart individual. He left some years later under a cloud of alleged expenses discrepancies, but was later rehabilitated to high office by a different administration. Law enforcement gets mixed with politics far more in the States.

The accommodation was first class. It was like a university campus set in woods near the massive Quantico Marine Base, where we would occasionally go shopping. Food was exceptional. The catering was privatized and at that time the Marriott Hotel group held the contract. I recall that there were at least seven, 'creamy' ice cream machines in the dining hall. I can fully understand why there is the large number of obese people in the United States.

Sleeping was in rooms of two, with shared ablutions, very modern and acceptable. I shared with a police chief from a small town in New York State, called Suffern. His name was John Morris and he had a hard time on the course and worried about his studies. The other two, with whom we shared the bathroom, were Marshall Newman, an aptly named police captain from Hobbs, New Mexico and the unfortunately named Mike Looney, a sergeant from Louisiana.

The programme itself was called the FBI National Academy and had been running since 1935. Although we were not FBI agents, the course was principally aimed at raising the standards of law enforcement in the United

FBI course, 1985.

States. Eventually however, they threw it open to foreign nationals as well, one from each selected country. I was on Course 142, which happened to be the 50th anniversary of the inception of the course. Every state in America was represented on the course, with a handful of foreign nationals from Europe, Asia, Africa and the Antipodes. It has produced a number of British chief constables as well as at least three chief inspectors of constabulary, Sir Trefor Morris, Sir David O'Dowd and the present incumbent, the pleasant former chief constable, Sir Keith Povey, all of whom I know and admire.

The course was divided into manageable sections and the leader of our section was a larger-than-life supervisory special agent, a New Yorker called Tom Colombell, whose dad had been a New York Cop. Each group had a counsellor to look after our domestic needs, and in our case it was another New Yorker, Linda Fusina, who eventually married a graduate in the class from California, Lieutenant Tom Freeman.

The bar at Quantico was known as the Boardroom and as you can imagine, a lot of the leisure time on the campus was spent there. We would at first drink 'Bud' and 'Miller Lite' out of small plastic cups, but those of us used to drinking pints, soon graduated to 'pitchers', (a large jug) which probably held a couple of pints. That was another language problem I encountered, when I went to the bar on one occasion and caused embarrassment by requesting 'a pair of jugs', but I soon learned what was appropriate and what was not.

Physical fitness was a major part of the programme and we spent a lot of time in the gymnasium working out. We also went swimming and running. By the end of the course I was probably as fit as I had ever been all my life. I even took the 'Potomac River' challenge, which involved swimming the equivalent of the length of the river Potomac, (about 57 miles, I believe) in the swimming baths, over the length of the course. I used to skip lunch and go swimming, notching up the miles, week by week. My very good pal from Pomona, California, Lieutenant Brian Lee Schubert, brought me a salad sandwich from the dining room every day to eat when I had finished swimming. I was determined to rise to the challenge, I did it and I have, literally, got the tee shirt to prove it! Brian Schubert is an Anglophile, having spent a spell in Europe when he was in the military. He used to laugh when I asked him if he fancied a 'jar' and we got on extremely well.

Down to Studies

Being a postgraduate course, the standards expected were high. A choice of subjects was available and I chose; Crime Scene Search; Inter-personal Violence; Managing Marginal and Unsatisfactory Performance; Mass Media and the Police; and Effective Communication. It is ironic that I got straight

A's in every subject except Mass Media, where I was awarded B, and yet this was the vehicle which, later on in life, was to put me on the political map!

The most interesting and consuming module was 'Inter-personal Violence', which was really a synonym for deviant sexual behaviour, in particular, the sexual exploitation of children. The FBI was undoubtedly expert in this field of investigation. For some years they had been methodically interviewing convicted serial murderers and rapists, analysing the data at a special unit at Quantico to find out what made serial offenders 'tick'. This was the first time I had come across criminal personality profiling as a tool for the criminal investigator. It was absolutely fascinating. It was not simply an academic exercise either, because, when police forces in the States, investigating murder, had exhausted their inquiries and the offence was thought to be the work of a serial offender, that is someone who repeats the offence, often in the same manner in different areas, they would call in the Behavioural Science Unit from Quantico.

The experts who ran my course were hardened FBI agents, Roy Hazelwood and Kenneth Lanning, who powerfully argued that a person's personality, leading to certain behavioural patterns, was as important in terms of identifying a criminal as, say, his fingerprints. I have to say that I was sceptical about this at first, but as the course developed, I became impressed with the academy's professional approach.

The rationale was to study all the information available, the crime scene, and the victims, with a view to determining the type of person who might have been responsible. They would then match this information to common patterns of behaviour by offenders with similar personality traits held on their database.

How does this help the investigating officer faced with a number of unsolved murders or rapes, apparently committed by the same offender? Perhaps this is best illustrated by example.

During the summer of 1979 a woman in a city on the east coast reported to police that she had been raped. After learning the facts of this case the investigating officer realized that this was the seventh rape in two years, by a man using the same modus operandi (MO). There were no investigative leads left open in any of the incidents and there were no suspects.

The incident reports and transcripts of the interviews with the victims were sent to Quantico with a request from the police for a psychological profile of the suspect. After careful examination of the submitted materials, the FBI constructed a profile and provided it to the police. In essence it was as follows; the rapes were probably committed by the same person; he was described as a white male, 25-35 years of age (most likely late 20s or early 30s); divorced or separated; working probably as a labourer; high school education; poor self-image; living in the immediate area of the rapes and being involved in crimes of voyeurism (peeping tom).

It was also suggested that there was the likelihood that the police had already interviewed him, as he was certainly on the streets in the early morning.

Three days after receiving the profile the police identified around forty suspects in the neighbourhood who met the criteria. Using additional information in the profile they narrowed their investigation to one individual and focussed on him. He was arrested and charged within a week.

During the course, several examples were given like this of the ways that profiling can help. It was stressed that it is simply another tool, more an art than a science and is nothing more than understanding current principles of behavioural science, such as psychology, sociology, criminology and political science. In other words the crime scene can reflect the personality of the perpetrator, pretty much the way we decorate the home reflects our personality. A fascinating course, the principles of which, have been used with some success in recent years, in the United Kingdom. The important lesson is that it is an aid to investigation and not a panacea.

Another fascinating experience, was when one of the instructors asked the class how long it would take to commit a forcible rape, from identifying the victim, to fleeing the scene. There were varying estimates, none of them less than ten minutes.

We were then played a horrific tape of a woman in an apartment in New York, making an emergency (911) call to the police. She was in a state of panic and was screaming down the phone reporting a man breaking into her flat. The sergeant receiving the call was trying to calm her down and assured her that a squad car was on the way to assist. We could hear the man battering down the front door as the householder screamed. We then heard her drop the phone and she came on again and said she had run into the bedroom and had barricaded the bedroom door. 'He's in the apartment! He's in!" she screamed as the sergeant continued to try and pacify her.

Listening to this tape was unnerving, as though we were witnessing the assault without being able to intervene. We could here the man battering down the bedroom door and the woman screamed as she dropped the phone. There was then a lot of shouting and screaming and then silence.

When the police arrived, the man had fled (although he was later arrested). The point of the story is that whilst we were all listening in chilling silence, the instructor had started the clock. The whole incident ran for no longer than two and half minutes. Quite extraordinary!

Ted Bundy

One of the most graphic case studies in that course in 1985 was the notorious serial killer, Ted Bundy. He vented his rage on women, mostly college girls, all the while maintaining the façade of a perfectly normal, intelligent, model citizen. His travelling ways, clever tactics and thorough body disposal methods make it difficult to say how many women Bundy killed during his reign of terror (some put the number at 150), but he was one of the most prolific and frightening serial killers of all time.

Bundy's rampage most likely began with Kathy Devine, 15-year-old hitchhiker who disappeared on 25 November 1973 and was found on December 6. She had been sodomized, strangled and her throat was cut. Linda Ann Healy soon disappeared from her basement bedroom. In fact women were disappearing throughout the upper Northwest of America, some abducted from their homes and some vanishing right off the street. Other women had been attacked in their beds and, most often, left to die.

Investigators where most of the abductions and attacks were centred, could not help but notice the similarities. In most cases there were no bodies, just missing women, so no true evidence was available. That all changed when a man identified as 'Ted' by witnesses, abducted two women from Lake Sammamish State Park on the same day. Police finally had a name and witnesses to put with a disappearance. The discovery of two women's remains about a month later, mixed in with the bones of other women, confirmed the fact that a serial killer was on the loose. The hunt for Ted Bundy was on.

The unknown murderer continued killing, despite the best efforts of law enforcement, and women soon began disappearing in Colorado also. Bundy had moved to Colorado to attend law school. It was not long before the abductions increased there, whilst those in the Northwest ended. But Bundy's luck finally ran out on August 16 1975 when he was 'spooked' and fled from police in a squad car, around Salt Lake. Arrested for possession of burglary tools and released, it wasn't long before police noticed similarities between Bundy and a man who had attempted to abduct a girl called Carol DeRonch previously. Bundy was soon arrested for the attack and convicted.

It was fairly obvious at this point that Bundy was responsible for the killings in the north and when he was transferred to the Garfield County jail in Colorado to await trial for the murder of Caryn Campbell, to the embarrassment of the police, he escaped out of a second floor library window. Bundy took to the woods until he was recaptured, only to escape again from the Garfield jail on December 30 with much more drastic consequences. He made his way to Tallahassee, Florida, settled near the Florida State Campus, and whilst there killed several more women, including a horrifying blitz-style attack in a residence on the campus that killed two young women. He then abducted Kimberly Ann Leach from her school and her body was found two months later in a nearby state park.

Bundy's horrifying hallmarks were mutilation and in some cases decapitation, the heads being taken as 'trophies', the trademark of many serial killers.

Leach would be the final victim when Bundy was arrested for the final time in Pensacola, Florida, following a routine check by a traffic cop. There was a violent struggle, but he was taken into custody and despite Bundy's attempts to draw out his trials and appeals, acting as his own attorney at times, he was sentenced to death and executed in the electric chair on 24 January 1989.

That case is one of a number which prove the value of routine police patrol work, whether on foot or patrol car. The most sophisticated detective work can gather evidence in many of these high profile cases, but it is often the uniformed patrol which picks up the suspect. The man responsible for the bombing of the federal building in Okalahoma City was arrested fleeing the area by traffic cops. If we think of notorious cases in this country, such as the 'Yorkshire Ripper' (Peter Sutcliffe) convicted of 13 murders and 7 attempts, arrested by a uniformed sergeant following a routine check in Sheffield on 2 January 1981. Multiple murderer Robert Black arrested by a traffic officer, with his next victim trussed up in the boot of his van in the Scottish borders. DNA testing is producing even more spectacular results. For example, Colin Jackson arrested in 1999 for drink driving, was connected by DNA from his blood sample to multiple rapes ten years earlier in Washington (Tyne and Wear) and Nottingham.

It is for that reason that we should be very careful before we take action, or comment in parliament or elsewhere, in such a way that makes police officers fearful of carrying out their legitimate powers of stop and search. Of course such stops and searches must be based on objective evidence and carried out sensitively, without bias against any minority interests, but to discourage such police activities is to increase danger for all decent members of society. I have always believed that the temporary interference with my liberty at a police check point or in the street, is a small price to pay for vigilance against those who would seriously harm our society.

The Visitor
Keith Best, my pal you will recall, had decided to take a holiday and join me in the United States. He came out on the appointed date and the guys on the course, whom I had now got to know very well, treated him proudly. We met Keith's plane at JFK Airport, and when I wanted to go to the bathroom, the counsellor Linda Fusina, said, 'How will I know him if he arrives before you get back?' It was a hot summer in Washington and I said, 'He'll be the only one wearing a collar and tie,' jokingly. Sure enough, along came Keith, collar and tie on, dragging his suitcase. He had been 'well looked after' on the

flight, but still fancied a welcome drink so we went to a nearby Irish bar where we toasted his arrival. The staff at Quantico even provided him with accommodation on the campus and he was allowed to sit in on lessons. It was quite extraordinary hospitality, which Keith and I will never forget.

We spent the most wonderful summer, travelling at weekends to the Blue Ridge Mountains of Virginia, visiting New York and generally keeping fit and working out, as well as 'partying' at barbecues and on boating trips. Our transatlantic cousins certainly know how to enjoy themselves!

Jean had arranged to come over for the graduation ceremony at the end of the course and Keith was to fly home. We then planned to have a holiday with Brian Schubert from Pomona, California at the end of the summer. I have to say that Keith was reluctant to go home and nearly missed his flight. He would have quite readily joined us in California had the offer been made. We still talk fondly about the summer of '85.

The graduation ceremony went well and there was a fine display of 'special forces' from the marine base. We then went to California where, needless to say, the weather was superb. The Schuberts (Brian has since parted from his wife Joanne) had a swimming pool at the back with a hot tub. There was a fine view of the San Bernardino Mountains from the pool. It was a joy to sit in the hot tub at night with a Mexican coffee.

Back to the Real World
Following the training at the FBI Academy I returned in the autumn of 1985 to Chester-le-Street as deputy divisional commander. Before I had left for Quantico, the incumbent chief superintendent, Jack Passmore, had retired and a new divisional commander was appointed. He was Ray Dinning, a time served detective of long standing, from the regional crime squad. Ray was a mild mannered gentleman, of the old school, who was clever at pulling strings behind the scenes. I felt that I got on well with him and we socialized at the police club in the police station.

When Tom Farmer retired we were very fortunate indeed to have a man from Lincolnshire appointed as deputy chief constable. He was a Mancunian called Frank Taylor and was a remarkable character. On returning from Quantico I made a point of seeing him, in my capacity as the chairman of the superintendents' branch. He was a mild, avuncular gentleman with a shy smile, which belied his tough early life as a sub-mariner. I fully briefed him on the problems of the force under the previous regime and advised him to mend some bridges with the staff associations and individual commanders. I believe he listened and took my advice. Frank Taylor and his wife Sylvia even came to one of our parties in Etherley Close, although what he made of my home brewed beer, I never knew.

One day I was invited through to see Mr Taylor at the Aykley Heads police headquarters. He told me that he was planning to do a full review of the management structures and procedures of the force and he would like me to head it up. I told him that I was an operational officer and enjoying my present posting at Chester-le Street. He was very persuasive however and had clearly made his mind up. It was the second time that, being the chairman of a staff association; I was being brought into headquarters to perform a reviewing role. It gave me an insight into the workings of the force and the character of Frank Taylor, but I would be less than honest if I said that I enjoyed the experience.

One of my difficulties was getting decisions on policy. My task was to assume nothing and produce options, including the status quo, for running the force. It was a mammoth task, but I had excellent, bright staff, who have all moved onward and upward. For example, I went to Frank Taylor and asked him what the chief's policy was in relation to the mounted branch based at the training school at Harperley Hall. Cost effectiveness told me that it would be far better to hire them in from another force for specific purposes, rather than keep a standing mounted branch, with all the maintenance and training implications, but there was not much point in recommending disbandment, if the chief constable Mr Boothby was determined to keep the branch. 'I don't know what his policy is?' he replied laconically. I remember thinking, 'Well why don't you go and ask him?' In the end we produced mountains of paper and reports, but I am not at all sure how useful they were in restructuring the force. I have always taken the view that 'if it ain't broke – don't fix it'! Yet I have seen numerous examples in the police service of people taking over commands and changing everything just for the sake of it

In January 1986 I published an article in the *Police Review* on my course at Quantico, with particular reference to psychological profiling. One of the beneficial spin-offs of attending the National Academy is that you get to attend re-trainers in various parts of Europe and in consequence I have been to most of the European major cities. That October, I went to Wolfsberg in Switzerland.

I was now a regular after dinner speaker, normally at official dinners through the staff associations. The Durham superintendents' branch hosted a dinner every year with chief officers as guests and my speech became a regular feature. One of the difficulties as I rose up the staff association ladder, was to acquire new material, because the same audience, (of super-intendents and their wives) was following me around the country! But I was enjoying it and found that timing was the trick of comedy. My old skill of learning by rote paid off, as I found that I could pluck a humorous story out of the air, to fit any situation. Indeed, I have dined out on the strength of it on many occasions since, although I have detected Jean getting a little weary from time to time, from having to listen to the repeats!

Eldred Boothby retired, and everybody was pleased when Frank Taylor got the well-deserved promotion to chief constable.

It was whilst at Chester-le-Street that a retired superintendent, Alan Campbell, approached me and asked me if I was interested in joining the local Rotary Club. I new nothing about Rotary, but when he explained, I decided to give it a go. I had known Alan, and his wife June, for a number of years. There was a group of us who used have small gatherings in each other's houses, telling jokes and drinking beer. They included Tom Cundall and his dear wife Vera and Harry and Jean Rogers, all of whom we knew from Harperley Hall.

I used to attend Rotary meetings on Friday lunchtimes whenever I could and have spoken at regional and local meeting on several occasions. As I moved up in the Superintendents' Association it became increasingly difficult to attend Rotary, but I went when I could. Eventually, when I became a member of the Lords, I felt I should allow somebody else to have my place and offered my resignation, but they very kindly invited me to become an honorary member and I still attend infrequently as and when I can.

Promotion

I was also at this time, applying for chief superintendents' posts outside the force, because I had a sense of having been overlooked within. People like Eddy Marchant and Bill Hills, who were extremely competent superintendents, were promoted ahead of me, even though I had been a superintendent for longer. I am pleased in retrospect that none of those applications was successful, as my turn came in Durham Constabulary. When Ray Dinning retired, Frank Taylor promoted me to chief superintendent in charge of the north division based at Chester-le-Street, on 24 June 1989. This command covered the whole of the north of the county, from Peterlee in the east, to Consett in the west and I was happy with my lot. My new deputy was a quiet, no-nonsense former detective and chief constable's Personal Assistant, Tom Whitton, and we worked very well together.

It was during this period that the force was inspected by Her Majesty's Inspector (HMI), Colin Smith. Mr Smith had a reputation for not suffering fools gladly. A former chief constable he was ruthlessly ambitious and a stickler for protocol. The inspection details were circulated and he was due to visit my divisional office for a round table discussion with senior officers, including the chief constable and senior divisional officers.

We had just adopted a new system of administrative support units in the division, devolving the decision on prosecutions, down to local level. The divisional model was too remote from the police officers in the case.

On the day of the inspection, the HMI arrived with his staff officer and the entourage, including Frank Taylor the chief constable. We had tea and biscuits in my office and sat round my large table. We were all in full uniform apart from the civilian admin officer and the detective chief inspector Dave Gill. Mr Smith asked me about the new restructured admin support units and how they were working. He made it clear that he preferred the divisional, larger, model, on the grounds of economy. I begged to differ and told him. He was clearly not happy and accused me of impertinence, amongst other things. I pointed out that he had asked me a question and I had simply answered it. He then shocked the whole meeting by picking up his hat, gloves and cane and simply strode out of the office without a word, his staff officer running after him. We were all left looking at each other.

I thought I had blown it, not so much for me, but for the chief constable, Frank Taylor, who had promoted me. The visit of the HMI went on in my absence as I thought there was little point in me taking the risk of upsetting the temperamental Colin Smith again. I went home that night around 6:30 p.m., with no idea of how the inspection had gone. The telephone rang about 7:00 p.m. It was the chief constable Frank Taylor. Now for the rocket! But no, he said 'Brian, I just want to thank you for your support today. You were quite correct to stand up to the HMI, who was out of order in the manner he spoke to you. You've got nothing to worry about.' He then went on to describe how Colin Smith had, in his waspish way, criticized the chief constable in the presence of the police authority and belittled his efforts. Clearly there was no love lost between them. I did not see Colin Smith until some years later when as president of the Superintendents' Association, I went to a meeting with Her Majesty's Inspectorate and he was there. He could not have been more pleasant and charming, as though the incident at Chester-le-Street all those years before had never happened. As they say, it's a funny old world!

When Tom Whitton retired, my new deputy divisional commander was Sunderland born Ned Lawson, a blunt, florid faced officer who was one of Durham Constabulary's characters. He had built a reputation as the sub-divisional commander at Sedgefield where he developed a first class relationship with the local council.

I was of course delighted to have him on board and for the next two years, we worked as a good team. Ned had served with the National Drugs Intelligence Unit at Scotland Yard and, like me was at one time head of the Durham Constabulary Drug Squad. As a very dedicated former detective, he had spent his early years in Darlington, where he met and married the love of his life, Ann, a former policewoman, who came from Cumbria. Ned loved cooking and sampling his handiwork and I have spent many happy hours with him drinking beer and tasting the cuisine at barbecues where he has been cooking.

One story, which I still smile about, occurred when I was on leave and Ned was acting divisional commander. He had gone to the town hall in Durham City in uniform, to a meeting with the councillors, and had parked his car in the market place nearby. On returning to the car he saw that he had received a parking ticket and was absolutely furious. He had been on police business and technically could give himself permission to park. He saw the traffic warden across the street and called her over. Ned was a relatively small, rotund officer and he told me afterwards, 'She hadn't a clue who I was.' In fact, it transpired that she thought he was a fireman!

Ned was volatile and exploded. He told her to report to him at the Durham police station. She duly arrived and there was a confrontation, which unfortunately reduced her to tears. I know I shouldn't have, but I burst out laughing when he told me, as I could picture the scene. Ned saw the funny side too. Unfortunately, she made an official complaint against him and the chief constable was not too happy with the way he had handled the incident. Ned believed and I suspect he was right, that this incident cost him promotion.

He retired in 1991 and joined the Gaming Board for Great Britain, where he carved out a distinguished second career. One of the best presents that I got at my retirement 'do' at Scotland Yard in 1998, was the surprise of Ned walking in with his new boss, Graham White, head of the Gaming Board.

You will understand my devastation when a close friend of his, former detective Michael Wood rang me on Boxing Day 1998 to tell me of his sudden death at home. Ned was in his mid fifties and it was a great honour when his widow Ann invited me to pay tribute to Ned's life, at the funeral on 4 January. It brought home to me yet again, the vulnerability of us all!

Billet Master

One of the consequences of being the divisional commander covering Durham City was that I was appointed the honorary Billet Master for the city. This is an historical appointment, military in origin and referred to as a responsibility in the Army and Air Force Acts 1955. It requires the chief officer of police for any area to provide billets (accommodation) for personnel and vehicles on the issue of a billeting requisition during hostilities.

In Durham City, the first borough police force was formed on 5 January 1836, comprising five constables. On its amalgamation with Durham County Constabulary in 1839, the force consisted of one chief constable, five superintendents and sixty constables. The mayor and his council appointed the superintendent covering Durham City as the Billet Master, and the first reference to this was under Mayor William Henderson in 1848.

With the passing of time the post became a more ceremonial appointment and today the incumbent leads the mayoral bodyguard during official processions in the cathedral and through the city. I used to lead the procession, in best superintendent's uniform, with brown gloves and my superintendent's baton in my hand. The two principal occasions were the annual remembrance service and the annual service for the courts, with the judiciary in all their splendour.

CHAPTER 10

The Superintendents' Association

I WAS NOW BECOMING more active in the Superintendents' Association and was attending the annual conference as a delegate. I reacted with incredulity when I found that we were debating such hot political topics as the protection of wild flowers, the issue of uniforms, and demanding increases in motor car allowances! I used to intervene in debates, raise points of order and generally became a bit of a thorn in the side of those who wished for a quiet life. I would always announce myself 'Mackenzie, Durham' and this became a bit of a joke and was adopted as my title.

The conference in 1986 at Harrogate was looming so I decided to liven the proceedings up with a resolution from Durham. (Individual force branches could forward motions for debate at conference.) I believed that arming the police was a 'sexy' topic and moved the following motion on behalf of Durham, 'that this conference disagrees with the open display of guns at airports as a matter of routine'. Well it certainly rocked the boat. The national secretary at that time was a chief superintendent, the late Ken Smith from Nottingham, and he opposed the motion on behalf of the national executive. That was neither here nor there, in my view, it mattered not which side won the vote (in the event the motion was lost). The objective of the exercise was to put the Association on the map.

Ken Smith was a volatile man with an explosive temper who had difficulty handling all the consequential press interviews and interest. In the end he shouted to me, 'You put the bloody motion down, you talk to the press!' So I did. I held a press conference and got a lot of publicity for the Super-intendents' Association – we were on the way.

I was never one to toe the party line, and when a London superintendent argued for the re-introduction of the death penalty for the murder of a police officer, I argued powerfully against. Not because of any sentimental reason about the sanctity of human life, but on the practical, common-sense ground, that juries would be less likely to convict if they believed they were condemning a man to his death. I was becoming a very active delegate.

What you have to understand is that the Superintendents' Association of England and Wales is the meat between the massive Police Federation, which represents rank and file police officers up to, and including, chief inspector, and the Association of Chief Police Officers (ACPO), who are the board of directors and policy wonks. Like the Federation, the Police Superintendents' Association was born following the police strike in 1919.

The Association's secretariat operates from Pangbourne in Berkshire, and was to some extent a one-man band in those days, with a typist thrown in. The national executive was made up of ten superintendents, two appointed by each of the various districts (A to E). It was usually the district chairman and secretary. 'A' District was the largest district and stretched from Cumbria and Northumbria in the north to Humberside and Staffordshire in the south, covering 13 forces in all.

Around the end of 1990, the then chairman of 'A' District retired, his deputy, Trevor Davey took over and I was invited to fill the vacancy as vice chairman. I have to say that I was not looking for the position, as I had a busy life as divisional commander at Chester-le-Street. I was advised however that it was not onerous and simply involved attending executive meetings of the Association from time to time. So I reluctantly agreed and, took a decision that would change the course of my life yet again.

As mentioned, the new chairman of 'A' District was Chief Superintendent Trevor Davey from West Yorkshire police. A blunt, pleasant and friendly character, he was the one who invited me to stand as his deputy. What he had omitted to tell me was that he was planning to retire himself from the service in the near future. To be fair, he probably didn't know at the time, but following a good job offer at a local golf club, it was too good to be true, so he retired in June 1991.

That of course left yours truly holding the baby. I remember chairing my first 'A' District meeting. Anyone who knows me knows that I am a stickler for good timekeeping. Having sat through meetings all my life, I used to despair at weak chairmanship, long-winded speeches about nothing, and meetings being allowed to over-run. Not on my watch! After my first meeting in the chair, I recall one of the delegates, who was also about to retire, came across and said, 'That's the best chaired meeting I've ever attended.' I thanked him and realized I had talked myself into another job!

I got to know a great number of fine men and women whilst an active member of 'A' District. A lovely, quiet, unimposing man was a super-intendent from Nottingham, Nigel Spencer. He would announce himself as 'Nigel Spencer, Notts'. I remember later on at national conference the confusion that was caused by another delegate from London who had a hyphenated name, you've guessed it, 'Nigel Spencer-Knott'. When he retired, Nigel Spencer booked me to speak at his Rotary Presidents' night and put me up for the evening. We had a great time.

I was now publishing articles on police corruption, teamwork and other policing issues in *Police Review* and the Federation's *Police* magazine, and I was really getting into police politics.

The National Executive

So I found myself on the National Executive of the Police Superintendents' Association of England and Wales, more by accident than by design. The national secretary at that time was a large imposing man with whom I became a firm friend, called Peter Wall, from Hampshire. We quite often breakfasted together when staying in hotels, as, like me, Peter was an early riser.

I used to travel around the 13 various forces in 'A' District, chairing the meetings, as well as attending the national executive meetings, which were held at the Association offices in Pangbourne.

Not everything was going well. Brian, our eldest son had gone to Sheffield University and I went to bring him back one Saturday in my car, which was a large Peugeot saloon. We travelled back through West Yorkshire and I remember seeing the blue lights of a police car behind me and, actually commented to Brian junior that someone was in for trouble, never dreaming that it was me! You've guessed it, the police car signalled for me to stop, which I duly did. I got out of the car and was invited to sit in the back of the police patrol vehicle.

'We have recorded your speed over the last two miles and you have been exceeding the limit. You can have a fixed penalty ticket or contest the matter in court.'

I told them that I understood and they started to write out the ticket. When he came to occupation, I was a little embarrassed.

'I am a police superintendent from Durham,' I said.

Both police officers looked up. 'Why didn't you say earlier?' he queried.

'It will teach me not to speed,' I said. I got my ticket and went back to my car.

'What happened, Dad?' enquired Brian. I told him that I had got a speeding ticket, which made it an expensive pick-up for him. His response was interesting. 'I'm impressed.' He chortled.

Things were also heating up on the political front with regard to policing. Margaret Thatcher was said to be disillusioned with lack of delivery by the police. Despite the large increase in monies being allocated to police budgets, crime continued to rise under the home secretary Kenneth Baker. It was said that the prime minister favoured direct entry of ex-military leaders into the force. In November 1990, the rebels in the Tory Party moved against Margaret Thatcher. Despite her high stature throughout the world and, her unquestioned leadership skills in the Falklands war a decade earlier, she did not have the foresight to defend her position at home. Whilst attending a meeting in Paris she was overthrown, not by the people of Britain, but by her own party in parliament.

Much to the surprise of everyone, not least the 'big beasts' of the Tory

Party, Margaret Thatcher's Chancellor of the Exchequer, a quiet, unassuming, relatively unknown, grey man, called John Major, replaced her. He had little impact on the nation and was tipped as a one-term prime minister. However, following a surprise win in the 1992 General Election, often attributed to the first Gulf War in the early nineties, John Major appointed Kenneth Clarke as home secretary.

Clarke was a smoking, beer drinking, and rotund former health and education secretary with a no-nonsense reputation for taking on the vested interests. The police love affair with the Conservatives was coming to an end. Following abolition of the rent allowance, which was replaced by a housing allowance worth far less, the police staff associations were becoming angry.

At the same time the Labour Party was changing its leader and changing its spots! Following the resignation of Neil Kinnock after his surprise defeat by Major, the dour lawyer from north of the border, John Smith, was elected leader, with 91% of the vote and, inspirationally, appointed the upwardly mobile, Tony Blair as shadow home secretary, where he undoubtedly made his name as a possible future leader. His slogan 'Tough on Crime, Tough on the Causes of Crime' still resonates in any discussion on crime. The police realized that this was a man they could do business with and as the debate on law and order progressed, Tony Blair's position went from strength to strength.

Meanwhile Kenneth Clarke launched a full frontal attack on the police service by appointing Sir Patrick Sheehy, chairman of British American Tobacco (BAT) Industries, to head a committee of businessmen and academics to inquire into police responsibilities and rewards. Kenneth Clarke was later to take an executive position with BAT on his retirement from government. The police service generally welcomed the Sheehy Inquiry in principle, albeit the Superintendents' Association had pressed for a Royal Commission. However, the welcome changed to dismay and outrage, once we detected the way that the inquiry was moving. I published articles on police accountability, appraisal related pay and countered other leaks from the Sheehy deliberations, which appeared to us to be bringing the application of alien business principles and performance measures to the police service.

Precious achievements from the Edmund-Davies Report a decade earlier, such as the indexed pay formula, housing allowance, overtime and pension entitlements came under attack, so we had no choice but to retaliate. Meetings and conferences were held, but the home secretary, Kenneth Clarke, who had a history of belligerence with other public services, was adamant that we needed a dose of private sector efficiency.

I remember, under Ken Clarke's stewardship at the home office, strong rumours of amalgamations of police forces. This was seen as a threat to the independence of chief officers. Regional or even a national structure was contemplated and the home office did nothing to dispel the gossip. I remember putting out press statements asking the home secretary to come clean, and if he had such plans, to conduct an open and full debate.

Things were also happening on the National Executive of the Super-intendents' Association. We had discussed how best we could raise our profile to be more politically effective. I had made the point that the nature of the president's one-year appointment meant that it came round like 'Buggin's turn', with the president's main preoccupation being with planning to retire, after his or her year in office. This meant that there was very little incentive to be radical, as the first six months were spent learning the ropes, making the contacts and networking, and the second winding down to retirement. There was a feeling amongst certain members of the executive at that time, that in terms of the best man for the job, the senior superintendent in line was not always the best person. It was a very sensitive time, as a struggle for power took place. A longer presidential tenure of office was suggested and three years seemed reasonable. This constitutional change was agreed and the then president, Chief Superintendent David Golding of the Metropolitan Police, agreed to stay on. Then the bombshell occurred. I was invited to jump the queue and be the vice-president. Again it was totally unsolicited on my part, but although I had thirty years service, I was enjoying the cut and thrust of police politics and agreed.

It was in March 1992 that I had a long weekend away in New York with my good pal Nick Spooner to re-charge my batteries. Nick took his video camera and we filmed each other on the plane and stayed at a hotel near Maddison Square Gardens. When Nick went into his room he got the shock of his life when he discovered a dead mouse on its back with its legs pointing skyward. Needless to say, he changed rooms. It was a memorable weekend, which I will always treasure. I recall that there was a bar underneath the hotel at which there was karaoke entertainment. Needless to say I did a rendition of 'Always on My Mind', with Nick videoing me in the half-light. After that I could always proudly boast that I had sung on Broadway!

I suggested that my role as vice-president should include raising the profile of our Association, by writing press articles, appearing on television and radio and, most important, cultivating and lobbying politicians (much of which I had been doing in 'A' District). This was accepted and I set about the task with gusto!

The sudden withdrawal by Britain from the Exchange Rate Mechanism (ERM), caused the rather swift departure of John Major's Chancellor of the Exchequer, Norman Lamont, from the government and fortunately for us in my view, Kenneth Clarke got the job. This left a vacancy in the home office and in May 1993, Michael Howard was appointed. In a sense, he was left with a poison chalice, in that the Sheehy Report was due to be published in the summer.

Michael Howard was a no nonsense QC, with a fine mind, clarity of vision and excellent political instincts and antennae.

Wembley Arena

The police staff associations were meanwhile campaigning vigorously against the Sheehy proposals and in a remarkable display of solidarity, unprecedented in police history, chief officers, superintendents and the federated ranks combined to oppose what was seen as a real threat to a police service, respected throughout the world. It was decided to have a mass rally of 20,000 police officers at the Wembley Arena in the summer of 1993.

It was a tremendous event with speeches by representatives of all ranks and front bench spokesmen from the Labour Party and from the Liberal Democrats. Tony Blair gave a rousing speech, as shadow home secretary, but, in my view, the star of the night, was undoubtedly, the normally quiet, and relatively unknown Liberal Democrat spokesman, Robert (now Lord) McLennan MP. It was a tremendous rallying performance. He pressed all the right buttons, spoke with great passion and literally brought the house down (well, to its feet!), receiving a standing ovation. I have since seen him in the Lords and reminded him of that impressive performance. The Conservative government declined to send a representative to the rally.

Michael Howard's fine political antennae must have been working overtime as he watched that rally from afar and even then, I believe, he was starting to have second thoughts about implementing many of the controversial proposals of Sir Patrick Sheehy and his cohorts. I remember spending my summer holiday that year in Canada with Jean. We stayed with a fellow FBI graduate from Ontario Police, Ron Kendrick and his wife Mary. They kindly looked after us, and I spent virtually the whole time ploughing through the Sheehy report and its appendices. What really amazed me was that it contained proposals which even undermined the traditional eminence and role of the police staff associations, which had stood the test of time with little industrial unrest since 1919.

The campaign against the Sheehy proposals represented what was perhaps a turning point in the profile and activities of the Superintendents' Association. Besides representing the interests of its members in matters of pay and conditions of service, the Association had always concerned itself with the quality and efficiency of policing. But, as a 1980 rulebook noted, 'successes have been obtained quietly and with the decorum expected of their rank'.

This low-key approach had, as I described earlier, started to change at the beginning of the 1990s. For example, it was decided to make the annual conference more professional. Instead of delegates simply listening to presentations, proper debates were introduced, with motions being voted on. This produced conference decisions on such important issues as the criminal justice system, crime and punishment and the role of the police in a modern society, so as to inform the national executive in making policy.

The Media

My agreement with the executive committee was to raise the profile of the Association, on the understanding that I had the power to make public statements and react to events, without having to get authority from the executive committee each time. I told them that I might occasionally get it wrong in which case I would take the consequences, but in the event, chairing conferences and speaking regularly to members, meant that I was usually 'tuned in' to grass roots thinking.

I have to say that throughout my work with the Superintendents' Association, I always had the full support of my chief constable, the late Frank Taylor, even though I was absent from the force and he still had to pay my salary. He always told me my position brought credit to the force.

There is little doubt that this new approach worked. Press and public interest in what the Association was saying was aroused, and it was realized that media and political skills were necessary if members' interests were to be represented properly. The higher profile became even more evident as the opposition to Sheehy gathered pace. A one-off levy on members during the campaign financed a 'fighting fund' to buy professional public relations advice, together with video and conferencing expertise. At the same time, with the help of retained consultants from both Houses of Parliament, intense lobbying of politicians and other influential players was undertaken with some success.

As I said in a newspaper article as we campaigned against the proposals, 'It is an accountant's attempt to reduce the public sector deficit without regards to the culture, service ethic, loyalty and commitment of a police service second to none in the world.'

I remember undertaking a mission on behalf of the executive committee to penetrate deepest Penrith, in the Lake District; to lobby the former distinguished home secretary and 'grandee' of the Tory Party, Lord 'Willie' Whitelaw. As Margaret Thatcher once famously said, 'Every Prime Minister should have a Willie'.

I arranged to see him at his country home in the beautiful Cumbrian countryside, and organizing it was like a military operation. Special branch officers, who escorted me in, met me about three miles from his home. Lord Whitelaw opened the front door on my arrival and invited me in. He was just like someone's elderly grandfather, with baggy trousers and an old shirt and slippers. He took me through to what appeared to be a sitting room, strewn with papers and books, and invited me to sit on the settee with him, which I did.

I then went through our principal concerns with him and he nodded in agreement. 'We had the same problem with Ken Clarke in health and education', he said, 'the trouble is he implements his changes, buggers off, and isn't there to pick up the pieces'. I thought to myself, 'we have a potential powerful ally here!'

I left Willie Whitelaw that day, happy, having been well supplied with tea and biscuits, and reported back to my executive committee. True to his word, Lord Whitelaw adopted many of our concerns when he spoke on the Sheehy proposals in the House of Lords. There is little doubt, in my view, that the combined efforts of all the staff associations helped to dissuade the government from implementing the worst excesses of Sheehy, although inevitably the police service was obliged to accept some changes, including new pay arrangements and the abolition of the chief superintendent rank, although, ironically, this has recently been brought back.

The way in which the Sheehy campaign was conducted marked a watershed in the Association's affairs. The positive, professional, high profile approach confirmed the Association as more effective and influential than at any time in its history. The Superintendents' Association had come of age and was becoming the leading Police Association in the country!

My first conference at Torquay as vice president was looming and we started what was to be a long, and continuing, campaign for the reform of the criminal justice system, to make it more 'victim' centred, and less sympathetic to the criminal. To use a phrase I have used many times since I coined it then, 'The criminal is a volunteer in the system, the victim has no choice!' We tabled motions demanding a reform of bail legislation and a change in the rules relating to the criminal's right to silence. These were controversial areas and the usual libertarian suspects lined up to oppose us. But I said then, and I repeat now, it is important to judge people as you find them and in my view, we had now got a listening home secretary.

The theme of that modernized, 1993 conference was *Justice on Trial*, and we got massive publicity, with headline features and articles. 'POLICE SAY THAT JUSTICE SYSTEM IS COLLAPSING', screamed the *Times*. In my speech proposing the motion 'THAT THIS CONFERENCE BELIEVES THAT THE CRIMINAL JUSTICE SYSTEM HAS FAILED THE PEOPLE OF THIS COUNTRY!' I talked of law-abiding people being 'tired of being bullied, burgled, beaten, battered and butchered in their homes' and all the headline writers picked up this blatant alliteration. My very able colleague and friend, Des Parkinson, seconded the motion, and we firmed up a very productive relationship for years to come. We continued to use humour to good effect and I can always remember Des in his speech, following a Welsh Rugby defeat at the hands of Western Samoa, saying, 'It's a good job we weren't playing the whole of Samoa!'

All 200 delegates at Torquay passed the motion unanimously.

After my morning speech, I remember going to my room at lunchtime for some fruit, as I did not normally have lunch. I switched on the radio and heard my own voice on the 'World at One', at the top of the programme 'beaten, battered and butchered in…' The policy had worked and we had put the Superintendents on the map.

I was doing the rounds of television and radio studios, as were my colleagues regionally, and as we were to discover, the politicians were starting to sit up and listen. That conference changed the way the Superintendents' Association were looked upon throughout the country, with editorials in most of the popular newspapers supporting our campaign.

The assistant secretary of the Association at that time was a quiet, workmanlike Thames Valley superintendent called David Clarke, who eventually became the national secretary and a good friend. He has now retired to rural Scotland where he quite rightly enjoys a different world from the Police Negotiating Board, organizing national conferences and all the other work that goes on with running a national representative body.

David was methodical in his work, and was the right man at that time, when we were re-organizing and raising our profile. An important facet of our approach was to connect with the membership through improvements to *The Superintendent*, the Association magazine. We also sent faxes to each branch explaining the 'party line' on policy issues, which meant that we all spoke with one voice.

I well remember a minister saying to me, 'Well Brian, I know that what you are telling me is a real concern because I am getting the same message from your operational colleagues as I go round the country.' Of course he was – we were telling them what to say!

Michael Howard

I believe that the appointment of Michael Howard to the home office was a critical and positive factor as far as our Association was concerned. I described him earlier as a man who listened, and he did. My strategy had been to turn the usual argument of the 'civil liberties' lobby around. I was arguing passionately for the restoration of civil liberties:

The liberty to park your car without it being vandalized.

The liberty to leave your house without it being broken into.

The liberty to travel on a train or go to a town centre late at night without being bullied, sworn at or assaulted by mindless gangs of young men who seem to know no rules of behaviour.

It was no coincidence, I argued, that, as more liberal methods of 'treatment' had been introduced; with prison being a last resort, crime had increased fivefold.

I have to say that the more I got to know Michael Howard, the higher regard I had for his ability to see through the Home Office, liberal fog. He knew what was wanted, persuaded his cabinet colleagues and implemented the policies. Crime had been increasing remorselessly for years and Michael Howard's tough approach, supported by the police, reversed that trend quite dramatically, causing a record massive reversal in increasing crime levels and therefore, importantly, fewer victims. I knew exactly what he meant when he told Conservative delegates at his conference that 'prison works!', he meant that at least when they were in prison they could not be preying on more innocent members of the public!

Although he wears different political colours from me, I am pleased to have advised and supported him in his difficult role. Examples of how we contributed will be seen later. Indeed whenever I heard Michael Howard's detractors condemning him (and he had plenty – including, it appears, his colleague Anne Widdecombe), I would wade in to defend him by simply pointing out his achievements!*

Because of the burden on a small force of supporting a vice-president of the Association, which was becoming a full time role, we approached the home secretary for financial assistance from the home office and I was delighted when the government agreed to carry the financial burden thereafter. We were really moving forward now.

In November of 1993 I was honoured by being invited to speak at the Durham University Union, the motion being 'this house believes that the police force is in urgent need of reform'. Needless to say I opposed the motion against such a noble protagonist as Lord Fraser of Carmyllie QC, and Richard Wells QPM, the then chief constable of South Yorkshire. Supported by the Rev John Bach JP, I am delighted to report that we won the argument and the vote which followed. I was particularly pleased because in the audience that night was a young Rotary Exchange student from North Carolina's Duke University. As a Rotarian I had volunteered to take Patrick Brooks Jordan under my wing, and I was looking after him as a counsellor. We became firm friends and we still keep in touch. Patrick had the clean cut good looks of a John F Kennedy, and I often used to predict, having heard him speak, that here was a future president of the United States!

It was about that time that I was invited to speak at a conference organized by EPIC [Ex Police in Industry and Commerce]. They were meeting in a hotel at Wetherby in North Yorkshire and I was pleased to go along and bang

---

*This was written before the demise of Iain Duncan Smith and my comments are reinforced by Michael Howard's election as Tory leader in November 2003.

the drum amongst friends, on behalf of the Superintendents' Association. I was delighted to see that my old friend Ray Basham, who was then working for ICI on Teesside, was there and the chairman was a man who I grew to respect a great deal, Barry Wells.

It is an important organization in my view, because at a time when the security industry was unregulated, here was a group which could guarantee the bona fides of its membership. It came with its own 'kite' mark of high standards and I liked that. Later, as a member of the House of Lords I was invited to become a vice-president of EPIC, and still hold that position at the time of writing. The organization has a wealth of police experience to call on. The president is Sir Stanley Bailey, the former distinguished chief constable of Northumbria, who has a veritable wealth of police knowledge and historical detail. Lord (Peter) Imbert, the highly respected former Commissioner of the Metropolitan Police, is a fellow vice-president. The national executive boasted such stalwarts of policing as Bob Hancock, Harry Atkinson, Tony Miller, Chris Flint, Trevor Barton, Barry Davis (the hardworking secretary), John Kennard (the frugal and 'senior' treasurer), Barry Watters and Brian Sturman. Few organizations could boast such an array of policing skills, working in the security sector.

A former executive member, Harry Atkinson, asked me when I was in the Lords if I would donate a prize for a charity raffle he was involved in. I was happy to provide a tour of parliament, followed by lunch in the Peers Dining Room. I have done that on several occasions since and it is always a pleasure to see the looks of amazement on the winners' faces as we walk round the historical building or dine with political heavyweights of yesteryear.

Indeed, at the beginning of 2003, I suggested that the constitution of EPIC had some anomalies in it, so they gave me the task of re-writing it, which I did. I never learn!

CHAPTER 11

Becoming President

ALTHOUGH I WAS extremely busy with Association business during the week, I generally managed to get home on a Friday for the weekend. Jean and I had a good circle of friends and we usually went out for a meal or a drink on a Saturday night. Friday was usually a boys' night out and I would go out with Keith Best to Nick Spooner's New Inn, in the city, or the Rose Tree to see Arthur Walsh, or Dougie Urquart in the Railway Tavern, in Shincliffe Village. I would often swim and play squash on a Saturday morning. The weekend would often be interrupted by media calls of course, when I flew to London to do the *Dimbleby Programme* or *Friday Live* in Manchester or Birmingham.

Indeed, I was and still am, a news fanatic and a regular listener to the *Today* programme, even at Christmas time. It was December 1993 that I heard the home secretary Michael Howard being interviewed on Radio 4. He was asked what he would do about a paedophile who had declared that on his release from prison he intended to continue to practice his sexual preference for children. The home secretary, in exasperation said, 'I can't do anything about it. He's served his sentence. The courts should impose a life sentence in the first place and then the prison authorities could recall him or stop his release.'

I remember thinking that the imposition of a life sentence might be regarded as 'using a sledgehammer to crack a nut'. There must be other improvements to the criminal justice system that we could make? My experience from the FBI Academy told me that police intelligence records on paedophiles were at best patchy and, at worst speculative and in some cases downright inaccurate. What we needed was a true record of the identity and whereabouts of child molesters long after they left prison, and the offenders could only provide this themselves! We also required a new sentence in such cases, one that, like a life sentence, was indeterminate, so that if any early signs of re-offending behaviour were seen, the offender could be detained before the life of a child was put at risk again.

I knew, having been a working detective for many years, that child molesters were a very special type of offender. They were compulsive, determined and secretive. There was also a medical view that, rather like an alcoholic, their offending behaviour could not be treated; only controlled. It was evident to me that such offenders were, in a sense, aliens in our midst and we should, therefore, treat them as such. All police forces keep an aliens' register and there is a requirement on such people to report to the police and provide information on movements and changing circumstances.

That was the answer with paedophiles, I thought. It was a requirement, which could be imposed by the trial judge on conviction. Being the vice-president of the Superintendents' Association, I put my thoughts down on paper and submitted them to the national executive committee for consideration. But more of that later…

Licensees and Pubs

In January 1994 I was invited to present the prizes to the Rose Tree cricket team, which I was happy to do. It became an annual event and it gave me another speaking opportunity to entertain people present with a few jokes. It was a very enjoyable time. Quite often in the eighties, after playing squash Keith Best and I would call at the Rose Tree or the Railway Tavern, in Shincliffe Village for a pint.

On one occasion we went to the Railway Tavern after a game of squash at police headquarters, and Keith was driving. We left our squash gear in the back of his car and when we went back to the car to go home, found that it had been broken into. Our squash equipment had been nicked! I rang the police to report the theft, but to no avail, the property was not recovered. It was only later that the landlord, Dougie Urquart, told me that his customers were up in arms after the theft. Because of who I was the police, unknown to me, had sealed off the village on a few occasions, to check cars going in and out. The customers at the Tavern were concerned of course, in case they had drunk one or two over the eight.

I got to know a lot of interesting people in and about Shincliffe, including Peter Bromley, a retired bank manager and his wife Jackie, a lady full of personality and verve. They now run a little stall in Durham Market. Another lad I became friendly with was Gerry Breslin, a bluff Yorkshire man who liked a drink. Gerry was a very successful businessman, who had an extremely good degree from Durham University in business administration. He had come back from the United States where he was the vice president of a successful company and I regularly played squash with him, until we lost touch when he moved away from the area.

In country pubs of course, the rules are not usually enforced to the limit. My view was that if people stopped back a little after time, and there was no nuisance caused to people living nearby, it would not shake the fabric of society if the police ignored such minor infringements. The Tavern was a popular spot for locals to have a drink in the afternoon when, legally, the pub should have closed at 3:00 p.m. I remember being in the Tavern one afternoon after the licensing laws were liberalized and customers were allowed to drink all afternoon. One of the regulars stood by the window with a pint in his hand, twitched open the curtain, sighed and said, 'Ah! It's not the same having a drink in the afternoon, now that it's legal.' The forbidden fruit syndrome!

Drinking in the Rose Tree brought its humorous occasions as well. I picked up on the 'grapevine' that Arthur Walsh, the landlord, had allowed a party to take place for a Durham University ladies rugby team, trained by a local Scots lad called Cameron, one Sunday afternoon. Things apparently got out of hand, and some of the young ladies, having had a few drinks, took off their tops and displayed all. Arthur was embarrassed when his wife Jan told him what was happening, but took no action.

When I found out I decided to be a little mischievous. I took Arthur to one side and told him (untruthfully) that I had seen a very disturbing video at police headquarters recently. It was taken secretly, I told him, by special branch officers who were monitoring the security and welfare of students from important political families. The topless antics were clear on the video and discussions had taken place at a high level, I told him, with a view to closing down the pub. I told him that I had argued, successfully, that the Rose Tree should be given another chance. Arthur was shocked and admitted what had happened and thanked me for my support.

The story was repeated for months after that and became part of the folk law of the pub. In fact it ran for so long that it reached the point of no return, and I could not bring myself to tell Arthur and Jan that the story of the video was a joke. In April 2003 they left the Rose Tree and therefore I can now reveal the truth, and knowing Arthur and Jan, they will enjoy this humorous economy with the truth.

I was still regularly speaking on a variety of occasions, Rotary meetings, police dinners and licensed victuallers' functions, and thoroughly enjoyed it. Crime was now starting to fall and I found myself being called to debate crime issues increasingly on television. *Panorama*, *Newsnight*, *This Week*, *Jonathan Dimbleby*, and *Kilroy*, in addition to special programmes chaired by the likes of John Humphrys and Jeremy Paxman. I was also becoming a regular on the *Today* programme, *The World at One*, the *PM* programme and the *World Tonight*.

I wrote articles for the *Daily Mail*, *Express*, *The Times* and others. We were using every means possible to get the message across. I still make people smile when I tell them I often did important, incisive telephone interviews with John Humphrys or James Naughtie, whilst sitting naked on the edge of the bed, much to the despair of my wife! That is the beauty of radio of course, compared to television; you don't have to dress up!

1993 and 1994 were grooming years for the top job in the Association. I was learning quickly and, as well as trying to influence the government, we

The author with Jack Straw.

had our eye on the opposition too. Jack Straw was now the shadow home secretary and I had developed a workmanlike relationship with him and his shadow minister Alun Michael. We would invite them to participate in our conferences and it was a useful bridge-building exercise, following the damage caused by the coal strike a decade earlier.

David Golding had announced that he intended to stand down as president in the spring of 1995, and I had a good festive season that year, as we entered what was to be a momentous and defining time of my life. It was about this time that I realized that there was not a definitive history of the Superintendents' Association available, for new members. I decided therefore to research the topic and write a brief history. This I did and it was published by the Association in 1995 – my presidential year!

We had just got down to business after New Year and I was attending a national executive meeting in London when Jean rang me in the early hours of 24 January. I was half asleep and I could hear that she was distressed. I asked her what the problem was and she said, 'It's Nick, he's dead.' You will recall that Nick Spooner was one of my oldest friends, the licensee from the New Inn with whom I had spent time in New York. I could not believe my ears! She said, 'Alex (Rennie) is here.' I then spoke to Alex Rennie, a regular in the New Inn with his wife Claire, who told me that Lesley, who was Nick's partner, had rung him to say that Nick had passed away in bed. Alex was distraught. 'I don't know how to tell Nick's mam and dad, Brian', he said, 'and thought of you, so I came straight round.' I told him that the best thing to do was to contact the local catholic priest at Shotton Colliery, and he would perform the difficult task. I did not sleep for the rest of the night.

I have to say that I was absolutely devastated the next morning. Nick was undoubtedly my best pal and we went back many years. He had joined me in Switzerland when we stayed with his cousin near Zurich. He was only in his early forties for God's sake. It was unbelievable! I told Jean I would be coming home the next day.

I attended the executive meeting next morning and could not concentrate at all. I made my apologies and caught an early train home. It was the only time I can recall quietly shedding tears on the way home and was slightly embarrassed. It transpired that Nick had had a massive heart attack, and the whole community were devastated by his death.

I was invited to give the eulogy at his funeral, in his home village in Shotton Colliery, and paid tribute to his life, humour and loyalty. It was a packed occasion and a fitting tribute to a man who had touched the lives of so many and brought them fun and happiness. In my case he was irreplaceable and his early death has left a great void. Jean and I still keep in touch with his mother and father, Nichol and Sarah, who still live in Shotton Colliery and are in their eighties.

President

In March of 1995, I was unanimously elected as president of the Superintendents' Association of England and Wales. Needless to say I was delighted and it was one of the proudest moments of my life. Crime was also falling dramatically in the United States at that time too, and I had been talking to the deputy director of the FBI at a re-training session in Europe. I asked him what the most effective crime fighting measure introduced recently in the States was. 'That's easy, Brian, three strikes and you're out. It has had a salutary effect on criminals and is proving to be a real deterrent.'

In my first presidential speech, I therefore asked for consideration to be given to introducing similar sentencing provisions in this country. We had already persuaded Michael Howard to change the law relating to a suspect's right to silence – much against the wishes of the legal profession. It had always seemed anomalous to me that when, as a detective, I asked a suspected rapist where he was at the material time and he refused to tell me, that fact could not be brought to the attention of the jury. This was particularly galling, if subsequently he sought to prove an alibi placing him somewhere else at the time of the rape.

I am a firm believer in placing trust in the hands of juries, who are in the main an intelligent cross section of the public. I consider therefore, that unless there is an overwhelming reason for not telling them, juries should be given all the facts, including, in some cases, evidence of previous misconduct.

The whole thrust of my presidential term was to try and achieve a better deal for the victims of crime. It seemed to me that unless the general public out there was satisfied that the criminal justice system was providing justice in an even-handed way, there would be a continuing trend for members of the public to take the law into their own hands. Vigilantism was to become an important debating topic in the months and years to come.

My election as president was marked with a number of high profile interviews in newspapers and on the broadcast media, particularly in the northeast.

The Heart of the Matter

1995 was a hot summer and I was doing a lot of reading in the garden, with an eye on my first annual conference as president of the Association in September that year. In August, there was to be a remembrance service in Coventry Cathedral to commemorate victory in Japan (VJ Day) and those former police officers who lost their lives. It was agreed that I would attend in uniform on behalf of the Association and I decided to drive to Coventry from Durham. I had recently bought a new Peugeot Saloon, which fortuitously, as you will find, had air conditioning.

The ceremony in Coventry was to take place on Sunday 13 August and I rose early that day leaving Jean in bed, donned my best uniform and prepared to travel. A number of dignitaries were attending, including the home secretary, Michael Howard, Fred Broughton, chairman of the Federation and the president of ACPO.

The following day, 14 August, was my wife's fiftieth birthday, and unknown to Jean, I had planned a surprise karaoke party on the following Saturday, at the Salutation pub in Durham. I had invited a whole range of family and friends, and Jean new nothing about it.

As I set off driving south that morning I was not feeling well. I couldn't put my finger on what was wrong; it was just a general malaise. But I was representing the Association at a very important event, had rarely taken sick leave in the past, so started my journey. As I drove, I gradually felt worse. There was something wrong and I remember at one stage thinking that I should turn back. However, determination was one of my guiding values, so I ploughed on with the clear blue sky above and the sun blazing down.

The ceremony was due to start at 3 p.m. with a lunch provided before then. Des Parkinson, the assistant national secretary was meeting me at the luncheon venue and I arrived still feeling unwell. Having parked my car in the blazing sunshine, I took off my tunic and walked into the dining venue. Everyone else was smartly dressed in jackets and ties. By now I was perspiring profusely and told Des that I was unwell. He suggested that I go home before the lunch. In the event, I decided to stay for the lunch, to see if my condition improved. It didn't.

It was one of the worst lunches I have ever attended. I must have been miserable company. I ate nothing, was still sweating, and left the table for a walk outside to get some air. I had a word with Fred Broughton, who was outside for a smoke, and we passed pleasantries.

There was a march past at which those of us in uniform were to take the salute. I stood with the others in the blazing sun and wondered if I was going to collapse. I managed to remain standing and had a quick look round an exhibition with Michael Howard, and told him that I was not going into the cathedral, as I was unwell. I then went back to the car park.

My car, which had been standing in the mid-day sun for hours, was absolutely boiling inside. The lifesaver was the air conditioning, which I switched on and brought the temperature down. I then set off to drive home, feeling worse with every mile. I rang Jean on my hands free mobile and told her what was happening. As I journeyed north my condition worsened, I felt pains in my chest and pains shooting down both arms. My thoughts went back to the premature death of Nick Spooner in January and I had thoughts of joining him.

As I passed milestone after milestone, Jean was screaming down the phone that I should go to a hospital. I did toy with going off to the Pinderfield hospital, at Wakefield, but when you are ill, like an elephant, you seem to get a powerful homing instinct, so I continued driving. The pain was getting so bad that I remember being hunched over the wheel to try and reduce the pain. I am convinced to this day that the air conditioning in the car saved my life. I honestly believe that without that I would have collapsed at the wheel.

The rest is history. I eventually arrived home, Jean had arranged for the doctor to meet me. He examined me and arranged for an ambulance immediately to take me to Dryburn Hospital in Durham where I was placed into intensive care. Following tests, the specialist told me that I had, indeed, had a heart attack and would be off work for some months.

I could not believe it had happened to me. Here I was, a swimmer, squash player, reasonably slim and yet I have heart disease. Nobody could really give me a satisfactory explanation of what caused it. Stress might have been a factor, but I had been going at the same pace for a few years. One thing the doctor did tell me. If I hadn't been as fit as I was – I might not have made it!

I was in Dryburn hospital for a couple of weeks and was told that the convalescent period was a few months. I got scores of visitors, with letters and cards from numerous well-wishers, including the home secretary who wrote in his own hand, as follows:

Dear Brian

I have *just* learned (on my way to the airport to resume my holiday which I had interrupted for VJ Day) about your illness. I am so *very* sorry. It comes as a great shock to me as it also must have also to you.

Please accept my most sincere good wishes for the fullest and speediest recovery. We cannot afford to be without you. I look to you as one of my most effective partners in the war in which we are engaged and I do hope you will be back in harness very soon.

With warmest good wishes to you and yours,

Yours ever

Michael

I read all the material provided by the hospital on convalescing and diet and the only thing that I considered I might have been doing wrong perhaps, was overdosing on cheese. I used to love it. So I cut it out and have never eaten it since. When I got home I continued to have a stream of visitors, and went back to see the specialist from time to time. I was told that the normal convalescent period was around 3 months.

I was not allowed to go upstairs at first, and going for walks was recommended, so I gradually started increasing the distance. I remember having a visit from Des Parkinson and a colleague from the Association. They gently broached the subject of my future and the fact that I now had over thirty years service, and could medically retire with an indexed linked pension, with immediate effect. 'Retire! Retire?' I retorted, 'I'm half way through my first presidential speech.' And I was. I had been giving some thought to important topics for inclusion, and was looking forward, as the home secretary had put it in his encouraging letter, to 'getting back into harness'. Retirement had never entered my head!

It occurs to me now that if I had heeded the very well meaning advice being proffered, I would not be where I am now. In fact I believe that I may well have thrown the towel in altogether, for what is life without a challenge, goals and achievement. It never ceases to amaze me how these tricks of fate operate, one thing connects to another, a decision here, a delay there, put you in a certain place and your future is mapped out. Or is it? I am sure that individual personalities have a great part to play in there own destiny.

After a few weeks, I was not sure how to handle the heart specialist at the hospital, who was a formidable lady called Dr Pearce. With Jean at my side, I told the doctor that I was feeling a lot better and, as I had an important conference coming up in a few weeks at the beginning of October, I was hoping to start work before then. She looked at my records and said, 'Mr

Mackenzie, you go back to work. I think you will suffer more stress watching the conference take place without you, than if you were there! But don't stay up too late!' Arrangements were then made for me to do a monitored 'treadmill' test, which I took and passed with flying colours.

Since then I have been on a range of pills, including aspirin, and can honestly say that I have never felt better in my life. Brian, my eldest boy, bought me a home blood pressure testing kit, which I still use regularly and my blood pressure has remained within the proper limits.

I have to say that the experience of having a life-threatening illness, such as a heart attack, concentrates the mind tremendously. As a direct result of that Jean and I decided to buy a place in the sun and went to Tenerife, the following January. I contacted a British estate agent and bought a delightful property in Los Cristianos, with a balcony as long as a cricket pitch. Having looked at one or two apartments, we fell in love with this one immediately. An English lady, Mrs Pears, who was moving to the north of the island, owned it. We had been looking at one-bedroom properties, which were more within our price range, and this one had two bedrooms. I was determined to have it however, left the Princessa Dacil Hotel, where we were staying, and went to a phone kiosk. I rang then my financial advisor in England and asked him to sell all the unit trusts that I had invested in since joining the police. I also took out a small top-up mortgage and we bought the property. It was a compulsive decision, but it was a good one. The property has trebled in price in seven years, and we have also had some wonderful holidays.

Whilst on the topic of Tenerife, Jean and I were very fortunate in choosing a complex where the president of the Los Diamantes community, is an Englishman from London called Clive Rollinson. He lives on the complex, overlooking the pool, with his nice partner Wendy, who is also English. They had met in Tenerife after Clive moved there on retirement from running his own highway maintenance business. He is a Rolf Harris look-alike, and we all get on extremely well. Having been in amateur dramatics, Clive likes to sing. He has an extremely good voice and we always go out for a meal on each visit, ending up at a local bar singing karaoke.

The apartment was my post-cardiac therapy, and I had visions of spending long periods of my retirement in the Canary Islands. Little did I know then that I would not exactly be retiring.

The 1995 Conference
My first conference as president was at Leicester, at the beginning of October 1995. Throughout my convalescence I had been giving thought to the 'big idea' for my first conference. One innovation we had introduced in our 'New Superintendents' Association', was to replicate the various committees run by ACPO, such as crime, traffic, communications and so on.

You will recall that I had submitted a policy paper for consideration by the executive committee on the question of monitoring child molesters, as I had been exercised about it after hearing Michael Howard on the radio.

As I have mentioned, paedophiles by their very nature are a very special type of criminal. They are manipulative and deceitful and can spend considerable time 'grooming' their young victims, or indeed the victim's families. They also continue to offend, unlike most criminals, well into old age.

The policy paper was received with interest and passed to the newly formed 'Crime Committee' for consideration. To my astonishment it received a negative reception from senior detectives. The response from Detective Chief Superintendent Michael Cox stated, 'On the face of it I find the proposals initially attractive... Further consideration... does however give me some cause for concern.' He then went on to describe how in his view it would not work.

In spite of that (or perhaps because of it!) I was determined to push the matter forward in my speech at our forthcoming conference and set about my task with determination. One thing I found when I came into the top job, was that my predecessor's speeches were written by a sub-committee. A number of the executive members contributed to the writing of the speech for the president to deliver. I decided from the outset that what I said in addressing the home secretary and conference was my responsibility. I would get the credit or the blame, and therefore I would write it personally. I applied that rule throughout my three years at the helm, and it still holds good in the House of Lords.

I was of course still briefing Jack Straw and his team, as well as meeting Michael Howard, to further the Association's aims. I remember shortly after my return to work following my heart attack, sitting round a table in Jack's office at No 1 Parliament Street. As well as Jack, Alun Michael, special adviser Ed Owen, and a couple of others were there. I remember Jack Straw asking me to describe in great detail the symptoms of the heart attack on that fateful Sunday. The concern was clear. They were all coming up to the optimum age for such problems!

During the run up to the conference I got myself back to the rudest of health. I bought myself a 'Nordic Ski' machine, to work out at home, as the heart needs to be exercised vigorously, and I take the view that road running damages the knee joints.

I drafted my presidential address to the home secretary, including one or two humorous stories, but the main thrust was my suggestion for the setting up of a national paedophile register. I remember listing the advantages of such a scheme:

• It would meet our policy of satisfying the needs of victims;

- It would act as a deterrence to potential offenders;
- It would provide hard, accurate intelligence;
- It would provide an alternative to a long (possibly life) sentence in appropriate cases
- It would protect children.

I went to Leicester in October with a spring in my step and my controversial speech in my briefcase.

The national executive had approved this approach and we had decided that rather than just have sterile presentations, we would have a proper debate, which resulted in a vote, thereby informing policy.

I drafted a straightforward motion to the effect 'that this conference supports tighter legal control on the activities of known paedophiles'. Interest in the debate was stimulated as a result of a few high profile child sex murders, committed by convicted paedophiles, together with emerging evidence of offenders' working, often for many years, in positions of trust and power, in children's homes and other institutions.

In the debate we involved Bob McLaughlin, then head of New Scotland Yard's Paedophile Squad, together with Michelle Elliott, the dedicated and committed director of the children's charity 'Kidscape'. Michelle is an American lady, long time resident and fully at home in Britain, who brought along a victim of child molestation, who very bravely agreed to speak about her experiences and give media interviews.

Needless to say the motion was passed unanimously and I was able to emphasize to Michael Howard the need for government action, both privately and in my conference address.

I took it easy at the conference, and as David Clarke and Des Parkinson had acquired several sponsors, for the wine or the meal, I found myself making thank you speeches each day at receptions, before dinner.

I recall some time later, showing an American FBI visitor round the newly renovated quay at the old Hartlepool docks where there is an attractive maritime museum. I received a call on my mobile phone from a senior civil servant at the home office, Jonathan Duke-Evans (who could forget a name like that?). He said that the home secretary had asked him to contact me to get me to flesh out my proposals for a paedophile register. I knew then that something was happening and that we had hit the jackpot!

As an association we continued to campaign up and down the country whenever we could, and the issue became more and more topical as new cases, both here and abroad, hit the headlines. Michael Howard is a very industrious politician and in 1996 the Sexual Offenders Bill was published, requiring not only paedophiles, but also other sexual offenders, to register their name and address, and any subsequent change, with the police.

This started another public debate, which is still going on, about who

Superintendent's Conference with Home Secretary, Michael Howard, 1995.

should have access to the register. This centred round a case in the United States involving the murder of a little girl called Megan. Following widespread public protest that the convicted murderer, a paedophile, was living anonymously in the community, 'Megan's Law' was passed. This allowed publication of the paedophile's whereabouts to the community in which he resided. The police service and the government in this country opposed such blanket disclosure on the grounds that it would drive offenders underground and could lead to vigilantism.

As a matter of record, the Tory government was defeated in May 1997, but because of our continuing dialogue with Her Majesty's Loyal Opposition, Jack Straw, the new home secretary brought the Act into force on 1 September 1997, some four years after the Christmas broadcast by Michael Howard had planted the idea for a register and indeterminate sentences for paedophiles into my head.

Of all the things I have done over a long and interesting career, it is this achievement above all else of which I am proudest. Both Michael Howard and Jack Straw have since commented publicly on the contribution by the Superintendents' Association in this regard, for which I am very grateful, and the Sexual Offenders Act 1997 stands as public testimony to our accomplishment!

In that first year of the New Labour government, all was not well with the Crown Prosecution Service and I recall bemoaning the lack of cooperation between the CPS and the police to Jack Straw. In any event I received a pager message asking me to ring the Prime Minister's Policy Unit in Downing Street, which I duly did. It was an unusual request for a serving police officer. I was invited to go along and talk with a senior policy advisor about my thoughts on restructuring the CPS. My views were clear. There was a lack of coordination with the police, and I described how well the prosecution system worked when each police force had its own chief prosecuting solicitor based at force headquarters. Eventually, the CPS was restructured into 43 divisions, each matching the 43 police forces in England and Wales. The prosecuting system has worked a lot better since, and prosecuting solicitors are now consulted on a whole range of issues at a far earlier stage in the prosecution process. They will eventually take over the charging decision. I hope I contributed to that reform.

I remember being approached by Ed Owen, Jack Straw's very capable and hardworking special adviser. Jack wanted to know if I was prepared to speak on crime at the September 1996 Labour Party conference in uniform. As the outgoing president of the Superintendents' Association, I was naturally flattered. Fortunately, I sought the advice of the then Chief Inspector of Constabulary, Sir David O'Dowd, who is also a good friend through my FBI connections. He cautioned against it and he was, in hindsight, absolutely right. I will always be grateful for his wise counsel. In the event, I did get to speak at conference the following year – but as a new Labour Peer!

CHAPTER 12

Continued Campaigning

IN ADDITION TO PAEDOPHILES, I was also campaigning for a three strikes rule, in relation to persistent offenders, simply on the grounds that the judiciary was not protecting victims by using to the full the powers that parliament had provided. I argued that for conviction for a third serious or violent offence, there should be a minimum period of imprisonment to act as a deterrent. Lawyers and civil libertarians again saw this as an attack on the independence of the judiciary. I regarded this, and still do, as nonsense, as under our constitution parliament is sovereign and the government accountable through parliament. It is parliament which set the rules on behalf of the people, and the judges are required to interpret and apply them.

Again, Michael Howard acted and parliament brought in the Crime (Sentences) Act 1997, against a background of howls from the usual suspects! It provides for a mandatory life sentence on conviction for the second time, of a serious violent or sexual offence. A mandatory minimum seven years imprisonment for a third conviction of drug trafficking and a minimum of three years for a third conviction of domestic burglary.

The Act was phased in with Michael Howard bringing in the first two provisions and Jack Straw finishing the job, following the May 1997 election.

There was only one problem – parliament left a loophole with a provision that the judge could give less if he felt there were exceptional circumstances, which had to be stated in open court. Although the Act is applied on occasions, judges are reluctant to apply it and the let out clause is exploited. Still, we did well to get the provision onto the statute book – another lobbying success.

Complaints Against the Police

As superintendents, my members were the main investigators of complaints from members of the public against police officers. The system on the whole worked well and was overseen by the Police Complaints Authority (PCA), but there were areas of concern. One was the length of time some complaints were taking to investigate. It came to a head in a case on Humberside where allegations of wrongdoing were alleged against the police. The details aren't important but it took over six years to finalize, during which one officer had died and several others had retired. In the event there were no criminal or disciplinary proceedings and the costs were huge.

The members of the Association have a great deal of experience in complaints and discipline investigations and we set up a 'panel of friends' to assist superintendents who were subject to investigations themselves. A 'friend' is a non-lawyer who can assist, counsel and accompany an officer subject to discipline. Following the Humberside case, the 'panel of friends' suggested that long investigations should be more professional, rather like a major criminal inquiry, with a policy book being kept, proper terms of reference set, and a review by an independent senior investigating officer after a set period of time.

We took this to government and we took it to the Police Complaints Authority. The chairman of the PCA at that time was Peter Moorhouse, who listened patiently but took no action.

As an organization, we were satisfied that complaints were generally dealt with properly, but because of continuous sniping in the press about cover-ups and whitewashes we decided to announce our policy that all complaints against police officers should be investigated by people independent of the police. Although I knew that this was impossible from a practical viewpoint, it provided good ammunition when debating these issues on television and radio.

I was really enjoying my non-party, political activities now and whenever I went to The Palace of Westminster I used to love sitting in the Central Lobby of Parliament, thinking what it must be like to work in such an historical setting. I would try and recognize the faces of well-known politicians, past and present, as they went about their business in that cauldron of political activity.

On 7 February 1996 I paid my first of many visits to a social function at 10 Downing Street to a reception hosted by John Major.

One thing I found when becoming involved in politics was that the thing that thwarted the best of intentions and political ambitions was, as Harold Macmillan so accurately put it, 'Events, dear boy, events'!

On 13th March 1996 an event occurred in Scotland, which was to change the political landscape, the Dunblane Massacre. Thomas Hamilton shocked the world by gunning down 16 children and their teacher in Scotland, and this started a campaign to ban the carrying of handguns in Britain. The Executive of the Police Superintendents' Association considered its position and we quickly decided that there was a good case for banning handguns altogether.

This position brought some criticism from some of our 'shooting' members but we stuck to our 'guns', if you'll pardon the pun, and I spent considerable time writing articles and broadcasting in an effort to influence the politicians in general and the ministers in particular.

We found however that we were at odds with chief officers. The

Meeting John Major at Downing Street.

Association of Chief Police Officers (ACPO) considered that there was no justification for such a ban and simply suggested more police powers were required to enable them to refuse a firearms certificate. I gave evidence to the Commons Home Affairs Select Committee and made it clear that we felt that there was no justification for people to keep handguns at home.

In September of 1996, my second conference as president of the Association, at Stratford upon Avon, provided a unique opportunity to seize the high ground and we devoted a large part of the programme to debating the whole issue of firearms control. Chief superintendent Dai Davies, who was then the head of the Royalty Protection Department, at New Scotland Yard, led this debate superbly. Our purpose, yet again, was to persuade Michael Howard of the need for tough new firearms laws. Even my local regional newspaper, the campaigning *Northern Echo*, launched its own campaign in favour of a ban.

Robo Cop

During my presidency I had become aware of the growing prominence of a detective chief inspector at Hartlepool, in Cleveland Constabulary, one Ray Mallon. He was a detective with a mission. A non-drinking, non-smoking, keep-fit fanatic, Ray set himself targets and goals which appeared to be unattainable. He was a disciple of zero tolerance policing, which was being pioneered in New York by Mayor Giuliano and his hard-nosed police chief William Bratton. I liked Ray Mallon and got on well with him. I admired his determination and single-minded focus on getting on with the job. I could see that like me, his forthrightness could risk rubbing people up the wrong way, but with Ray, what you saw is what you got!

The philosophy was based on a pamphlet called 'Broken Windows' by two American academics. Put simply it means that if you allow neighbourhoods to become run-down and don't remove graffiti or repair broken windows, things will get worse. By the same token, people who commit minor infringements and are allowed to get away with it, are more likely to go on to more serious offending.

Another way of putting it is, that if people are prepared to commit serious crime, they are hardly likely to obey minor rules about dropping litter, paying fares on public transport and the like. It follows that the enforcement of minor infringements will result in law enforcement getting its hands on serious criminals. Police commanders on the ground were also made to account for what was happening on their patch, by the use of computerized crime statistics at daily meetings with their bosses.

Ray Mallon started to apply this controversial philosophy to Hartlepool. There were those who said that it was confrontational policing, which went against our system of policing by consent and likely to stir up conflict in communities. The public however seemed to like it, crime started to come down and Ray talked of 'taking back the streets'.

Certainly, in the run up to the 1997 general election, he was visited by Michael Howard, Jack Straw and Tony Blair to be photographed and applauded for his crime fighting techniques. His chief constable, Barry Shaw, a quiet, publicity-shy Scotsman, was basking in Ray Mallon's glory. Ray was eventually promoted to superintendent and was posted to Middlesbrough, which had Cleveland's heaviest crime problem.

I liked his controversial style and thought it would make a good debate at our conference, so I invited him to speak in a debate on policing styles. He is a straight talking, no nonsense, northerner and he gave it to us straight. I recall that his main theme was that chief constables were continually demanding more resources, when really all that was required was for them to police in a 'smarter' way and, do the jobs they were paid by the public to do i.e. enforce the law!

Now I know that this ruffled a lot of feathers at senior levels in the police service and, I suspect that Barry Shaw was advised to rein in Mr Mallon, who was applying his 'zero tolerance' policies at his new command in Middlesbrough.

At our conference I recall at one stage, with me in the chair for the debate, Ray Mallon, in his own inimitable style, starting to tell me what I should put to the vote and when I should put it. Having chaired conferences and meetings for many years, I was having none of it. In front of the delegates, I simply said firmly, 'Ray, *you* talk about zero tolerance and *I*'ll preside over the conference!' We remain good friends and we have laughed about that since.

Suspension

Whether it was connected to his comments at our conference or not, I do not know for certain, but on 1st December 1997, the then deputy chief constable of Cleveland Police, Robert Turnbull, a dour Scotsman, suspended Superintendent Ray Mallon, for, amongst other things, 'matters which could be construed as criminal'.

Now I know Ray Mallon and I for one, do not believe he was corrupt. As I watched events develop in the Mallon investigation, which became known as 'Operation Lancet', I committed myself to do whatever I could to fight what to me was a monumental miscarriage of justice against one of my members.

Without going into detail, which would take a separate book, Ray Mallon was to be investigated by Cleveland Police for nearly five years at public expense, estimated to be between five and seven million pounds. He was alleged to have covered up drug supplying, his expenses claims were combed through, and his personal relationships with female colleagues checked. His relationships with the media were examined in fine detail and in all these matters he was exonerated.

I have said in public previously that not many people could have their lives and activities examined in such fine detail over such a long period of time and not be found wanting. Ray Mallon was such a person, and I was delighted to support him during this period when his life was on hold.

The case was jinxed and has had dire effects on others involved in 'Lancet'.

Robert Turnbull, the deputy chief constable who suspended Mallon, mysteriously announced his retirement at short notice in late January 1999, shortly after it became public knowledge that a 999 call had been made from his home following a disturbance. He was then appointed to a senior police post in the Turks and Caicos Islands, much to the surprise of everybody, including the then chairman of the Cleveland Police Authority, Ken Walker, who stated publicly that 'Turnbull has misled the Authority as to the reasons for his retirement'.

When asked about the matter from his haven in the sun, Mr Turnbull was quoted as saying that 'it has nothing to do with the people of Cleveland', even though they had funded his lump sum of over £100k and his pension, out of local taxes!

Heading the 'Lancet' inquiry was Andrew Timpson, the then chief constable of Warwickshire who, in September 1999, also went on sick leave after being accused of inappropriate conduct with staff in his own force. He was subsequently retired medically.

In late March 2001, the home office announced that Sir John Hoddinott, the highly respected former chief constable of Hampshire, would conduct a review of the 'Lancet' investigation, with regard to its strategic and operational management, cost, timescales and resources used.

I knew John Hoddinott well, as a former president of ACPO. He was a larger than life personality, well liked by all. An excellent detective, he had helped to root out corruption in the Metropolitan Police and was described as 'untouchable'. On one of his early visits to Middlesbrough, he tragically died of natural causes in his hotel bedroom.

Ray Mallon meanwhile, had developed political ambitions of his own, and spoke of standing as a candidate for the newly introduced post of elected mayor of Middlesbrough. There was one problem however, he could not become actively involved in politics whilst still serving as a police officer, which although suspended, he still was. His offer to resign was myopically refused by Barry Shaw, thereby prolonging the agony and the cost to the Cleveland ratepayers.

Ray and I had been meeting throughout the investigation, to keep me abreast of developments and also for me to advise him on political tactics. He would drive across to the Rose Tree in Shincliffe Village, usually on a Saturday lunchtime, and the licensee Arthur Walsh and his staff got quite used to seeing me huddled in the corner with my well known guest.

Although cleared of all criminal activity, 'Lancet' had thrown up possible breaches of discipline, such as oppressive conduct to junior ranks. As I said earlier, in any fishing expedition of this nature, it would be impossible, rather like driving a car, not to find some minor breach of the rules. With the deadline for the mayoral elections rapidly approaching, Ray Mallon knew that he had to terminate the whole sorry business, so he reluctantly decided to plead guilty to the discipline charges and take the consequences and I supported him in that, even though it brought a lot of criticism from some quarters.

In my judgement he was vindicated by the subsequent sentence of the tribunal headed by a chief constable. He could have been fined, reduced in rank, reduced in pay, or dismissed. In the event he was required to resign, which was something he had offered to do many months earlier, and been refused permission by his chief constable, Barry Shaw. That in my view speaks volumes!

The rest is good news for Ray. He won the mayoral election in Middlesbrough in 2002 by a massive majority and is still in post doing an excellent job of work. I wish him continued success.

Double Jeopardy

With the New Labour government installed, we were looking for headline-grabbing material, for what would be my last annual conference as president of the Police Superintendents' Association. Something which had always concerned me was the ancient rule of double jeopardy, which in essence means that you cannot be tried again if you have already been tried and convicted (autrefois convict) or acquitted (autrefois acquit). This was based on the simple premise that justice should have finality and suspects needed protecting from the oppressive state in the days when the rule was developed, as death or transportation were the order of the day.

I recalled a case I had read in a Sunday tabloid in the 1950s, I think it was the *Sunday Pictorial*, about a man called Stanley Setty who had disappeared. A man called Donald Hume had been arrested and tried for Setty's murder and was acquitted as there was no body. He then wrote a newspaper article, no doubt for payment, describing how he had murdered Setty and then cut his body into pieces, hired a small aircraft and dropped the body parts into the North Sea. That seemed to me to be a monumental miscarriage of justice! It was compounded by Hume's later murder of a taxi driver during a robbery in Switzerland, where eventually he died in prison. Little did I know then that I would be expressing similar concerns some four years later in the House of Lords!

I thought that the time had come to campaign to change the law in Britain. We had seen a number of miscarriages of justice, which, quite rightly, had resulted in the quashing of the convictions. My simple philosophy was that it was just as important to correct wrongful acquittals, where there was new compelling evidence, as it was to correct wrongful convictions. The advent of DNA evidence and other scientific advances would assist in these serious cases.

I suggested a launch of this new policy initiative at Jack Straw's first, and my last, Superintendents' Conference in September 1997. I suppose what triggered the matter off in my mind, was the murder of black teenager, Stephen Lawrence by racist thugs in Eltham, south east London, some four years earlier. Three men were later, misguidedly in my view, privately prosecuted and acquitted, which effectively, as the law stood, provided immunity forever from future trial on the same issue.

I gave my speech and it received a lot of media interest, not least by the mass circulation *Daily Mail*, which had been campaigning on justice for Stephen Lawrence for some time. There was an unprecedented outcry from the civil liberties lobby, the Law Society and the Bar Council who brought their big guns out, to point to the police having several bites at the cherry and the likely harassment of acquitted defendants.

I recall well at the joint press conference with Jack Straw after my speech, nearly all the questions being around this topic. Again I had chosen my topic well! Mr Straw's position was extremely guarded and he stated that it would be difficult to change such an ancient rule. I did not hold out much hope therefore, but none the less did the rounds of television and radio studios debating the issue with the great and the good.

It has been fascinating in the following years, since my retirement, to see the Stephen Lawrence Report, the Lord Justice Auld Report, the Law Commission and even the Commons Home Affairs Select Committee, following in the footsteps of the Superintendents' Association and recommending the abolition of double jeopardy!

My determination was compounded by the local case of Julie Hogg who disappeared from her home in Billingham on Teesside in 1989. But more of that case later.

In my final address to conference I did my version of the 'I have a Dream' speech of Martin Luther King, and I quote,

> As I approach retirement, I have been reflecting on my hopes and aspirations for the greatest police service in the world. I have the following vision:
>
> I see a society in which the police service respects and treats its personnel as its greatest asset and calls them people and not human resources.
>
> I see a society where PC stands for police constable and not for political correctness.
>
> I see a society with a police service where patrolling officers are valued as much by the service as they are by the public.
>
> I see a society where clergymen do not advocate shoplifting as a means of distributing wealth.
>
> I see a society where violent football supporters from this country are not given media time to whine about the justice meted out by our European colleagues, when they often ask for everything they get.
>
> I see a society where children don't commit rape or murder.
>
> And, I see a society where politicians don't accept as normal, the receipt of brown paper envelopes stuffed with 20 pound notes!

So my final conference passed off and we had a splendid time on the final night with me singing Al Jolson songs with the live band.

After the conference things were good during my final festive season as a police officer too; both boys were now settled into their own homes with steady girlfriends, Brian in Manchester and Andrew locally. Jean was still working as a part-time receptionist at a local medical surgery, which she enjoyed. As an organization it was important for us to visit the main party conferences to lobby on the various concerns which we had. I recall in 1997, attending the 'Northern Night' of the Labour Party conference, which was a social event at which the Prime Minister Tony Blair traditionally was putting in an appearance. I bumped in to my old pal Tom Sawyer, then General

Secretary of the Labour Party and he said, 'Come over and say Hello to Tony.' We waited patiently as all the television cameras followed the Prime Minister round the room to cheers and laughter. As he approached Tom and me, Tony Blair stopped and said, 'Brian, it's good to see you. I was watching you only the other night on television.' I said, 'Tony, I watch you every night on the telly.' We all laughed as Tony and Cherie continued their whistle-stop tour.

The OBE

I was delighted towards the end of 1997, to be informed confidentially that I was to be appointed an Officer of the Most Excellent Order of the British Empire (OBE) in the Queen's New Year honours to be announced on New Year's Day of 1998. What I did not anticipate was the volume of letters of congratulation I would receive, all of which I might add, I answered personally.

I recall, over the Christmas break, the son of Jack Straw being splashed all over the newspapers following 'entrapment' by a newspaper concerning drugs. Jack, to his credit, marched the boy to the police station to face up to the consequences. My view was crystal clear; you were not, and never could be, your son's keeper. So I quickly put out a statement from the Superintendents' Association on 2 January 1998, making it clear that we had every confidence in the Home Secretary. He was extremely grateful for the support and wrote me a very nice personal note of thanks.

One of my final official engagements as the president of the Superintendents' Association was to speak against the legalization of cannabis at the Oxford Union on 12 February. The national secretary, Des Parkinson accompanied me and I have to say it was a very enjoyable debate even though, as you might expect, we lost the vote!

My plan was to retire in May 1998 and spend more time writing and reading. I thought that perhaps I might stand in the local council elections in an effort to continue to satisfy my political interests. I also still had my after-dinner speaking engagements, for which a fee could now be charged.

In the spring of 1998, Jean and I went to Buckingham Palace, me in full uniform, to receive the OBE, and we had a splendid day. It really was the icing on the cake! I have a video of the ceremony and when I show it, people invariably ask what conversation did I have with the Her Majesty? I can never resist telling them that it went as follows. 'Good afternoon Ma'am, are you going to the FA Cup Final this year?' Her Majesty replying, 'No I am not, Chief Superintendent, why do you ask?' 'Well, Ma'am, I was wondering if I could have your tickets!'

I decided to have a retirement party at Scotland Yard in the 'Peelers' bar and invited a lot of my old pals and associates from policing and politics. Jack

Investiture at Buckingham Palace, 1998.

Straw the Home Secretary came, as did Michael Howard MP and his former deputy David MacLean MP, the Police Commissioner, Sir Paul Condon and my good friend John Stevens, the Deputy Commissioner.

It was a splendid night with fulsome tributes all round. My colleagues on the Executive Committee had really pulled out the stops and I was extremely grateful to everyone. I was particularly pleased at the comment by the Home Secretary Jack Straw, that I had raised the profile of the Association and gone about my duties impartially and not shown any bias towards any Party.

Indeed, in his speech to the assembled throng, he said this,

What I really want to say is, and I say it on behalf of my colleagues and on behalf of everybody who has been involved in Home Affairs, you really have put the Superintendents' Association on the map and you have done it Brian, in an extremely skilful way. One of the ways you have done it is by making yourself ever available to the press. Now there is always a danger in that. And there are some of us who have colleagues on both sides of the house, who make themselves available to the press and in doing so, make themselves risible. You have managed to do that – always been available, and absolutely right to do so because that has put the Association on the map – but you have done it in a sensitive, calibrated way so people have listened to what you have got to say and what your Association has got to say and it has made a great difference to the understanding of the British people about the police service. It is not a knee-jerk reaction, but a sensitive, intelligent reaction to the problems that are often put before you

Another thing that I would like to pick up on is the personal impact you have had on the Home Affairs agenda. Again it is not just beating a drum about something that was said or done, ten or 12 years ago, it is an agenda where you have sought to identify what needed to be changed and then gone forward with proposals for change, and you have been skilful enough to get that change and at the same time to preserve the independence of the police. You have to work with both sides of the house and I think the way in which you did that was in absolutely straight ways, so we never got the sense that we were in any way being used and that you were saying one thing to us and another to the other side, and I think that both sides as a result came very gradually to respect you and the work of the Association.

What I would like to say on behalf of the government and on behalf of my colleagues who worked with you in the Association is to thank you for the way you have conducted yourself as an executive office holder and as the President of the Police Superintendents' Association. Thank you for what you have done for your members. Thank you for what you have done for the police service, but above all, thank you for what you have done to make this country a safer place.

I could not have asked for a finer tribute from a man whom I hold in very high regard and who was a reforming and innovative Home Secretary for over four years. The Association kindly videoed all the speeches and I retain it with fond memories.

Thinking back now of that period, I was completely taken up with the media. Writing articles in broadsheets and tabloids alike, television appearances on *Panorama*, *This Week*, *Dimbleby*, *Newsnight*, *Kilroy*, *Richard and Judy* and all the news slots on every channel. As for radio, the *Today Programme* was a regular. I went to the studio in London and did interviews with the veteran broadcasters, John Humphrys, who told me his grandfather was a policeman, Sue MacGregor and James Naughtie. Eventually, I had declined to get up early and travel to the studio and negotiated better arrangements. A sign of your importance to the programme was their willingness to send a radio car to your house early in morning in order to make your contribution. *The World at One* and *The World Tonight* were also favourites. The one programme which eluded me was *The Jimmy Young Programme* which I enjoyed listening to. I am pleased to say that this was put right later and I did it twice as a member of the House of Lords before Jimmy retired!

Having so much exposure on the media had its humorous side too. I was frequently recognized, usually at airports for some reason. People would come over and say, 'You're that policeman aren't you?' Quite often they would mistake me for someone else. On a flight to Tenerife, a lady sat next to Jean and said, 'I think I recognize your husband'. Jean was used to this and said, 'You probably do'. Whereat the friendly enquirer said, 'Does he stack the shelves at Sainsbury's?' Another man on a flight said that his wife thought I read the sports results on television, and when people tell me that they saw me last night on the box, I always test them and ask what I was talking about and they can rarely remember. What an impact I must have!

It was a strange feeling after 35 years, coming up to retirement. I can only describe it as approaching a void. I had not made any firm plans but I was certainly not intending to be idle. I always recalled a retired officer saying to me that the biggest crisis he ever endured now was if the newspaper did not arrive on time in the morning! That, I could not face. I believe I was lucky in that my health had held up and I was still taking vigorous exercise with my Nordic Ski machine, which I had in the spare bedroom. I would peddle on there for thirty minutes, with perspiration dripping off my nose. Jean thought that I was overdoing it but I felt good and was determined to keep in shape.

So on 6 May 1998 my long association with Durham Constabulary and the Police Superintendents' Association came to an end and I looked forward to a somewhat uncertain future.

I also had a retirement 'do' in the police club at Chester-le-Street, where friends and family gathered. It was superb and again, the then deputy chief constable, Eddy Marchant, made the tribute speech. In my response, I commented on my high media profile and said, 'I can share with you tonight for the first time, that only yesterday I signed a television contract with Granada and, if I keep the payments up, the set will be mine in three years!' The timing was absolutely critical and it brought the house down. We had a great night and I recall finishing with a rendition on the stage of the late, great, Frank Sinatra's 'My Way'!

When I retired from the police in 1998, having served as Billet Master for nine years, because of force reorganization, coupled with drastic reductions in the number of police superintendents, a trend which was happening nationally, the new chief constable, George Hedges declined to appoint a serving superintendent as the new Billet Master and I was asked to continue in post as a retired officer, to which I agreed. I was given permission to continue wearing my superintendent's uniform, with the exception of my cap badge, which was replaced with the Durham City coat of arms. I even continued when I became a Peer, and became the only member of the Lords to perform such an honorary duty. I stood down as Billet Master in 2003 on reaching sixty years of age, having served for a record fourteen years in the post.

It seemed natural for me to join the National Association of Retired Police Officers (NARPO), which was chaired then in Durham, by a bluff, no-nonsense, ex superintendent, Derek Harrison, who also has an LL.B degree. Derek became a very distinguished national President of the Association and is now the branch secretary in Durham. Alan Watson, my old pal from Jarrow and the computer project team is now the branch chairman and they jointly edit the branch magazine to which I contribute the odd article now and again.

The present national president of NARPO is a delightful Welshman, with the fine name of Idwal Jones. I occasionally have lunch with Idwal and his delightful wife Audrey, when they are in London, and we discuss national issues and generally put the world to rights. Idwal is just about to retire and intends, I believe, to settle in the United States. I wish him and his family well.

On the domestic front, one achievement I am really proud of during my thirty-five years in the police, was to teach my wife Jean and two boys, Brian and Andrew, to drive. I taught them the 'police system' of driving, just as I was taught as a probationer constable, and I am proud to say that each one of them passed the driving test on the first sitting. I recall that we had one or two altercations in the process, but they now probably drive better than me!

CHAPTER 13

The House of Lords

IF I COULD HAVE chosen a retirement gift myself, I could not have chosen better than the letter, which dropped through my door at Etherley Close in the middle of June 1998. The envelope said 'From the Prime Minister – Personal, in Confidence'.

When I opened it you could have knocked me over with a feather. It was from the Prime Minister, Tony Blair and said,

Dear Brian

I am writing to let you know that I have recommended to The Queen that a Barony of the United Kingdom for life be conferred upon you.

Should The Queen approve this recommendation, your Life Peerage will be announced on Saturday 20 June in a supplement to the London Gazette; details of the Working Peer List will be released to the press on Friday 19 June, under embargo until midnight.

Your title will be settled on a recommendation from Garter King of Arms, who will get in touch with you in due course.

Yours ever

Tony

I called to my wife Jean in the kitchen and told her that I had received a letter from the Prime Minister. She came through and said, 'What about?' 'Well,' I said, 'I think the best thing is to read it to you.' I then read the letter out loud. Jean looked stunned and said, 'A Barony of what?' I repeated, 'a Barony of the United Kingdom for life.' She then made a comment that only a wife could make, 'Well what will you do after that?'

I then swore Jean to secrecy until the announcement was made public. This was the most difficult part of all as I was returning to my beloved Palace of Westminster again, not just to watch this time, but also to participate!

It did not dawn on Jean at first that it affected her, as she acquired the title of 'Lady' and was no longer Mrs Mackenzie. When I explained the implications of changing passports, driving licences and the like, she decided there and then that she would resign from her job as a receptionist. I said there was no need – but I understand how she felt. It is often said that behind every successful man is a very surprised woman! Jean had started courting a young apprentice, all those years ago, and could not have possibly had any idea where it was going to lead.

The following days passed extremely quickly and the media published all

PERSONAL IN CONFIDENCE

1O DOWNING STREET
LONDON SW1A 2AA

THE PRIME MINISTER   12 June 1998

Dear Brian,

  I am writing to let you know that I have recommended to The Queen that a Barony of the United Kingdom for life be conferred upon you.

  Should The Queen approve this recommendation, your Life Peerage will be announced on Saturday 20 June in a supplement to the London Gazette; details of the Working Peer List will be released to the press on Friday 19 June, under embargo until midnight.

  Your title would be settled on a recommendation from Garter King of Arms, who will get in touch with you in due course.

yours ever

Tony

Brian Mackenzie Esq OBE

PERSONAL IN CONFIDENCE

Letter from the Prime Minister.

the details on Saturday 20 June 1998. *The Times* had a small article giving details of all the new Peers and under my name it had a short piece as follows; 'Brian Mackenzie, ex-policeman, recently retired former president of the Police Superintendents' Association. Close to Jack Straw and Michael Howard his Tory predecessor. Has influenced crime policy'. This was a short, balanced piece, which reflected my endeavours as a police officer not to be party political in my campaigning on crime issues. Indeed, as stated previously, Jack Straw had referred to it at my leaving party at Scotland Yard as had Michael Howard at my birthday party.

That Saturday evening was momentous for Jean and myself. We were entertaining some American visitors with FBI connections and took them to a Rotary Ladies' night at the Waldridge Tavern at Chester-le-Street. After the dinner I made a short speech and an announcement about the Peerage and the majority of the audience thought I was joking! That's what happens when you have a style of humour which involves a straight face until the punch line. In any event that was my first public announcement of my appointment. Because of the difficulty of attending meetings, I later offered my resignation from the Rotary Club, thinking that I may well be depriving some other law enforcement official in the community of Rotary membership. I was most pleasantly surprised when the secretary wrote to me and told me that I had been made an honorary member. It seemed that on retirement there was no end to the honours being bestowed upon me!

Other names which appeared on the list of new Peers in the *Times* article were Melvyn Bragg, the author and broadcaster, Toby Harris, now chairman of the Metropolitan Police Authority but, the most special of all, which gave me much pleasure and not a little amusement to read –was Tom Sawyer! So after growing up together in the back streets of Darlington and parting ways so dramatically when I decided to join the police, here we were, thrown back together again in, of all places, the House of Lords. Tom was retiring as the General Secretary of the Labour Party and it was a remarkable quirk of fate, but I was delighted by the coincidence. We often chat about old times in the Lords and have even performed a very pleasant duty together, as you will see later.

Again, I was inundated with letters of congratulation, all of which I again replied to personally. There was also a great deal of media interest, particularly in the northeast. I recall giving an interview and saying that after a lifetime in the police service and having been promoted on five occasions, this was the mother and father of all promotions! The only downside to this honour on a personal level was the fact that I became disenfranchized in national elections, along with prisoners and lunatics! Perhaps I need say no more.

Choosing a Title

As the Prime Minister explained in his letter, the Garter King of Arms, Peter Gwynne-Jones, LVO, did indeed write to me and invited me to the College of Arms in Queen Victoria Street, London to choose the date of my introduction into the Lords and, not least, to choose my title. My mind went back to my days in the Police Federation and the Superintendents' Association. You will recall that I had acquired the habit of standing up at conferences and introducing myself as 'Mackenzie, Durham', so I thought perhaps Lord Mackenzie of Durham might be appropriate.

It was not to be. 'Garter', as he was known, was meticulous about such things and pointed out that Durham was a county, as well as a city. But another more important obstacle was the fact that there was an existing Earldom of Durham. The former Tory minister, Tony Lambton had disclaimed his Earldom in 1970 in order to remain as MP for Berwick-upon-Tweed. His son the Honourable Edward Richard (styled Baron Durham), will succeed to the Earldom on his father's death. So it was a complicated business.

At that time I was living in the Framwellgate area to the north of Durham City. I thought that it had a nice ring to it and therefore decided to become Brian, Lord Mackenzie of Framwellgate. I mentioned earlier that Jim Punshon, the brother of my former superintendent at Jarrow, John, had done some research in the local library and kindly copied documents which showed that the ancient city of Durham had a number of gates, primarily to keep out the marauding Scots. (Clearly some of the Mackenzie Clan got through!) Indeed there are streets in the city called 'Walkergate', 'Gilesgate', 'Owengate' and 'Milburngate', all named after various ancient gates. I discovered that Framwellgate was situated near the 'Fram Well', which supplied water to the city. So the title became even more interesting and I am indebted to Jim Punshon for his efforts on my behalf. It is interesting that some of the nameplates in the city spell the word with only one letter 'l', This however seems to be a modern mistake, as in the historical works I have researched in the Lords library, they always refer to Framwellgate with a double 'l', which is to be expected when it is the name of a water well.

Coat of Arms

After the interview had finished, Garter, who works in the College of Arms and deals with all matters to do with heraldry, invited me to design my family coat of arms. I was intrigued and he discussed what was involved and although it was quite expensive, I felt it was such an honour to be in the Lords, that cost was irrelevant. Another factor was that whereas my Barony was for life only, the family coat of arms would be passed to my sons and would be there in perpetuity.

Coat of Arms.

So I gave it some thought and chose as a centrepiece the cross from the Durham City coat of arms, with a set of handcuffs in the centre, fastened to the bars of the cross. On the crest sits a prairie dog, keeping watch, holding a police truncheon and the sides are supported by two colourful great crested newts, to remind me of my youth, around the ponds and streams of Darlington. Then there was the family motto to consider. I remembered the inspiration given to me by my old headmaster, George Welford and the values he instilled in me, of – '*strength, humour* and *determination*'. I translated these into Latin, as well as I could, and so I had the legend '*Firmitas, Lepos, Constantia*', which adorns the Mackenzie of Framwellgate coat of arms and of which I am very proud.

The Introduction

My official summons to parliament by Her Majesty was on 17 July 1998 so I chose to be introduced into the House of Lords on Monday 20 July. It was a momentous occasion. My first task was to select two supporters, who would, like me, don the ermine robes and process into the chamber from the Monarch's Robing Room, through the splendid Royal Gallery, down the Division Lobby and into the Moses Room, to await the call to be sworn. I asked the former Easington MP, Lord (Jack) Dormand and the former senior Metropolitan Police officer, Baroness (Jenny) Hilton if they would do me the honour and they both agreed. I was saddened by the news that Lord Dormand had passed away during the 2003 Christmas recess.

I recall that I was filmed that day for the local TV channel going into the Lords and interviewed by the political reporter Gerry Foley, who I have often worked with since, on his 'Round the House' late night political programme.

There were two of us being 'introduced' that day, Lord Clement Jones, the Liberal Democrat, and myself. The rules allow a new Peer to host a luncheon before the ceremony in the Peers' Dining Room with up to fourteen guests. Prior to that we had champagne in the Peers' Guest Room. The luncheon party consisted of Jean, Brian and Andrew, my sister Sylvia and her husband Rick, my pal Keith Best, Arthur and Jan Walsh from the Rose Tree, Eileen and Alan Finlay and my former colleague Des Parkinson, the Secretary of the Police Superintendents' Association. I also invited my two sponsors to dine with us.

It was a splendid occasion and as I recall it, an extremely hot day. I was whisked away after the meal to get robed, and my guests watched the Lord Chancellor's procession and then were shown to prime seats in the upstairs gallery of the chamber to watch the proceedings. The ceremony used to be quite protracted, with the doffing of hats and walking backwards, but it has recently been streamlined and is now simply a matter of processing in between the two 'introducers', bowing to the throne, taking the oath of office, processing out and shaking hands with the Lord Chancellor, Derry Irvine. The procedure lasts for no more than about seven minutes.

I was told that the ceremony was being filmed for training purposes and would be shown to future candidates. Tim Clement-Jones was the first to go and I watched him on the monitor. He is an articulate, professional man, who often speaks on health matters for the Liberal Democrats. This occasion however, was a bit too much for him, because when he came to take the oath, which is read from a card, he spoke of 'Her Majesty's Heirs and Successors ', but he inadvertently pronounced the H in Heirs!

When it came to my turn I was wondering what sin I would commit? In the event it went off all right and I disrobed afterwards and then took my seat for the first time in the chamber. I was now a true member of the House of Lords!

Mine was an early introduction to the House, amongst the group of Peers appointed at the same time as me, and I realized that the House authorities were using the video of my introduction as a training aid, when Lord (Melvyn) Bragg stopped me in the corridor on the day of his introduction sometime later and said 'I've just seen you on television!'

After I had taken my seat in the chamber for a few minutes and watched proceedings, I went to rejoin my family and friends on the Lords' Terrace where we had a drink. It was, as I said, an extremely hot day and my shirt was wet with perspiration. During that hot afternoon I got my first taste of the whips. I heard the division bell ring and decided to ignore it, as it was my first day. Some hope! A man suddenly ran on to the terrace and said, 'Are you Lord Mackenzie?' When I nodded he grabbed my hand and pulled me up from the chair. We then ran to the chamber to vote. It was one of the whips, Lord Simon Haskel and, I hadn't a clue what I was voting on, or whether I was content or not content – I was learning already why I was there!

I have since checked *Hansard*, the official record of proceedings in parliament, and find that my first vote in the Lords was cast at 4:05 p.m. 'not content' against an opposition amendment in the Report Stage of the National Minimum Wage Bill. Incidentally, the government lost by 58 votes, so I can understand why every vote was vital!

The big task ahead now was finding my way round the Lords. I did not have an office or a desk and had to use whatever telephone or table I could find to lead a very basic existence. I have to say that everybody was magnificent. For example I was walking just outside the library one day when a tall, smart man stopped me in the corridor and said, 'I watched your introduction into the chamber the other day. If there is anything I can do to assist you, please ask.' I thought that this was a very nice gesture, thanked him and just as he walked away, he said, 'Oh by the way, my name is Colin Cowdrey.' It was the late former test cricketer, ennobled in 1997 by Prime Minister John Major. That incident is indicative of the friendliness of the Lords, across party lines, regardless of rank or background, and my affection for the second chamber and the people in it, has increased pro rata to the years I have spent there.

It is not the combative, confrontational, argumentative, chamber that the Members of the House of Commons portray. Business is carried on very effectively in a courteous and civilized manner, it seems to me, without the cross-party rancour, and belligerence of the 'other place', to use the parliamentary term. The great advantage of this in my view, is that the whips are not all powerful, as they are 'down the corridor'. Members on all sides in the Lords often rebel against the 'party line' and indeed although generally, I am a strong supporter of New Labour, there have been occasions on the Police Reform legislation and on issues like legalizing gay sex in public toilets, where I have voted against the government. That is why the Lords is invaluable and is very effective in carrying out its function of scrutinizing and calling to account the government of the day. I have also voted against the ban on hunting with hounds, as I firmly believe that people's freedoms should not be curtailed without extremely good reasons and with all the problems in the world, this is an irrelevance!

I spent that couple of weeks in the summer of '98, before the recess, listening, watching and learning the procedures and customs of the House. My best tutors were undoubtedly the staff, the bar workers, waiters and particularly the door-keepers who are the 'keepers of good order', working directly for the Queen's representative in the Lords, the 'Gentleman Usher of the Black Rod', commonly called simply 'Black Rod'.

Black Rod is invariably a retired military general and the incumbent in July 1998 was General Sir Edward Jones, a man of great presence, both physically and in terms of his personality. Part of the induction process is to meet on a 'one to one' basis, the main players in the Lords, and I took an immediate liking to Sir Edward. He was an ebullient, commanding figure in his tights and buckled shoes. The clerk of the Parliaments, who controls the administration and proper procedures, was Sir Michael Davies, by contrast a shy, quiet man, who recently retired in the summer of 2003.

The doorkeepers were led at that time by the inimitable principal doorkeeper Mick (Richard) Skelton. His family call him Richard, whereas everyone else knows him as 'Mick', which can be quite confusing. Nearly all the doorkeepers are former military personnel, although one or two former police officers have recently been appointed. Mick was a flight sergeant in the Royal Air Force, although he has a southern accent, his roots are in the northeast, in the Whickham area of Tyne and Wear, which used to be part of County Durham and was policed by my force, when I joined in the sixties.

I hit it off immediately with Mick and on quiet days I would meet him for a pint in the HOP Inn, just below the Lords chamber. Indeed the friendship blossomed and I discovered that he had married Edith, a nurse born and bred on Tyneside. Keith Best from Hartlepool came to stay with me in London over one weekend and we went to visit Mick and Edith at their home in Epsom, not far from the racecourse. We visited Mick's 'gentlemen's club' of which he is now the proud president and were made extremely welcome by the members.

Indeed we have reciprocated and Mick and Edith have visited us in Durham on more than one occasion and, we have been out for meals on their regular trips to see relatives in the northeast. It is often said that it is a small world, and Mick's cousin's husband Trevor Brown, had asked Mick if he knew a Lord Mackenzie and it turned out that it was the same Trevor Brown who had joined the police with me in 1963. Indeed Trevor and his wife Pierret joined us for lunch with Mick and Edith on one occasion at the Rose Tree in Shincliffe Village, where we now live.

Peter Tate ran the HOP Inn in the Palace of Westminster at that time. He was another exiled 'Geordie' from Newcastle. Peter's mother and father Hazel and Des, who used to be licensees, would come in and help out behind the bar. I got to know all the bar staff, Theresa, a lovely, nice natured Irish lady, who worked on reception in the Central Lobby, Jim Herring, the young jack-the-lad from Hartlepool, who eventually took over the bar when Peter retired and Nicola, a delightful, fun-loving girl with a permanent smile, who works there in her spare time from her main job as a Westminster switchboard operator.

My penchant for story telling soon spread and I found myself becoming a source of jokes and anecdotes for various acquaintances, usually doorkeepers I have to say, who were officiating at dinners, retirements and weddings. I was more than happy to oblige, as I have built up quite a fund of humorous material over the years.

I must say again that one of the enduring qualities of the House of Lords is the friendliness of the staff. From Biagio, the restaurant manager in the Peers Dining Room to Alistair and Jan in the Barry Room, the men and women, too numerous to name, provide their Lordships with service and attention of a quality, which cannot be praised too highly.

One delightful waiter shall not escape individual mention. Luciano Conti, who has since retired, was the delightful barman in the Peers' Guest Room and, as with everyone else, was very easy to get on with. He was reaching retirement age then, but had a wry sense of humour which he teased people with. A good friend of mine, Lord Gerry Fitt, the former leader of the SDLP in Northern Ireland whom I mentioned earlier, was taken ill in Belfast and was in hospital. I knew they were very friendly, so I asked Luciano if he had the telephone number of the hospital where Gerry Fitt was detained and he gave me it. I duly rang the hospital to speak to Gerry and a protection officer answered the phone and asked who wanted to speak to Lord Fitt. I heard him say to Gerry 'It's Lord Mackenzie.' Lord Fitt was still felt to be at risk from terrorism at that time.

I mentioned this to Luciano, when I saw him next, and the story he told illustrated the humour of Gerry Fitt, recovering as he was in hospital. Luciano said that he had rung the hospital and asked to speak to Lord Fitt. A man answered and said, 'Who wants to speak to him?' 'Luciano!' came the reply. After they had had their conversation, the curious detective said to his Lordship 'Who is Luciano?' As quick as a flash Gerry Fitt responded 'Why Luciano Pavarotti, who do you think? He always rings me if he knows I'm not feeling too well.' For all I know that detective still believes that Gerry is a great friend of the Italian tenor!

Gerry is a delight to be with for a man in his eighties and still makes passionate, anti-IRA speeches in the Lords, which are a pleasure to see and hear. Talking of Gerry's protection officer, Gerry told me of a new appointee to the job who came back to his flat with him and, Gerry being Gerry, said to him, 'I hope you like a drink?' Not wishing to offend his new charge, the detective, who shall remain nameless, nodded his head; Whereupon Lord Fitt poured him a large gin and tonic. They then proceeded to drink for England (or perhaps Ireland!) to celebrate the officer's new appointment. Each time the drinks were down, Gerry would ask the officer to pour another one.

After a good few of these 'nightcaps', the officer left and Gerry went to bed. It was next day that he discovered that his new man was ill and had to go to the doctors. Gerry thought it was an unusual detective who could not take a drink and raised it with him when he eventually surfaced from his sick bed. It transpired that the officer, being quite rightly conscious of his new responsibilities, had decided to keep a clear head that night, so whilst pouring a gin and tonic for his master, he had been omitting the gin from his own drink. When he told the doctor this, he smiled and said, 'I know exactly what is wrong with you – you have quinine poisoning!'

'So there is a lesson there', says Gerry when he is telling the tale with a gin and tonic in his hand, 'you should never take your tonics undiluted!' A wonderful story which, I often repeat with affection in after dinner speeches.

One of the first contacts I made in the chamber was with James Callaghan, the former Prime Minister, Home Secretary and adviser to the Federation. His daughter Margaret Jay of course was made Leader in the Lords following the sacking of Lord Ivor Richards shortly after my arrival. I spotted Jim sitting on the front bench, to the right of the gangway, where former ministers usually sit. I bounded down and sat beside him and shook his hand. 'You won't remember me,' I said, and told him about my Federation days and my presidency of the Superintendents' Association. He listened with great interest and was very knowledgeable about the role of the police staff associations which he had played such an important part in developing.

One interesting fact which I discovered was that the House of Lords has an average lifespan which is 10 years higher that the population at large throughout the country. Looking around in that place I can well believe it and I put it down to the fact that if the brain is kept active, the body is maintained to service it. Once the computer stops, there is little reason to continue and it closes down the peripherals. I think of remarkable contributions from the likes of the late Lord Longford, Jim Callaghan and Lord (David) Renton, who at the age of ninety-five years is still making a meaningful, valuable and often humorous contribution to the second chamber.

Jack Straw

The home secretary at the time of my appointment to the Lords was Jack Straw, with whom I had been working in opposition as the president of the Association. He wrote to me on 6 July inviting me to 'be a member of my wider team.' I was delighted therefore to be asked to attend Jack's policy meetings each Monday lunchtime to examine the week's business in both houses and discuss important policy issues of which there were many. There was always a splendid buffet lunch with tea or orange juice and I got to know ministers and MPs very well. People such as Alun Michael, Charles Clarke, Paul Boateng, Tom Levitt, Barbara Roache, together with officials and special advisers. I continued in this unpaid capacity throughout Jack's period of office and I have to say it was an extremely interesting time of my life.

After a while one or two security companies approached me to become a consultant, no doubt because of my previous background. As I have to maintain an office and home in London, and as the Lords do not get paid a salary, any additional income is welcome, so I accepted these positions and registered them with the Registrar of Interests. I was also invited to sit on the board of a couple of companies, as well as being invited to be the honorary president of the Joint Security Industry Council [JSIC] and president of the Association of Police and Public Security Suppliers [APPSS]. So I was still being kept busy.

I became quite friendly with Lord Montague of Oxford, a slight, dapper man with a bushy moustache. He was extremely helpful about becoming a non-executive director and advised me to set up my own independent company through which to channel my financial interests, such as speaking fees, writing and consultancies. I did just that, and set up Framwellgate Resources Limited. I wrote to him later thanking him for his advice and said if he ever wanted advice about investigating murders – I was his man! He liked that and telephoned me to thank me for the humorous letter. Unfortunately Lord Montague collapsed in the chamber shortly after that and died on the way to hospital.

Whilst I was still attending Jack Straw's ministerial meetings, the chief whip in the Lords, Dennis Carter, invited me to see him. He wanted me to become what is called a Liaison Peer at the Home Office. This was a first rung on the ladder, acting as a go-between with ministers and backbench peers. Other similar appointees are now ministers in the Lords. Lords Willie Bach and Steve Bassam spring to mind. My personal whip, Josie Farrington, also asked me to broaden my questions and speeches to other than home affairs, so I got the distinct impression I was being groomed for greater things. I gave it long and hard consideration but on balance decided against accepting the offer, not least because at my age I did not want the hard grind of late sittings and preparation for long debates, although to be fair, there is the back up of officials, which I do not have at the moment. But I was extremely happy as a one-man band and did not want to give up my other financially rewarding positions.

An early mentor of mine was the late Lord (Joe) Dean of Beswick, a bluff, stocky, no-nonsense Yorkshire man, who took me under his wing. I usually sat near him on the Labour backbenches and he was the Labour peers' 'shop steward'. He was always reminding me to put my claim in for this, and explaining my rights to that. Joe was in his late seventies and was a former leader of Manchester City Council. As MP for Leeds West he had been a parliamentary private secretary in the Civil Service Department and represented Labour peers on the on the Parliamentary Committee which met with the Prime Minister on a weekly basis. I was greatly saddened by his death not long after I entered the Lords.

CHAPTER 14

Learning the Ropes

THE TWO WEEKS before the summer recess in 1998 were important to the government legislatively. I would sit in the chamber watching the Crime and Disorder Bill, a government flagship measure, being steered through the House by the late Lord (Gareth) Williams of Mostyn, and what struck me was how few were in the chamber during the passage of the bill. Only those Peers with a specific interest, or who are speaking to an amendment will attend and it can get very quiet later in the evening. I could not speak of course because I had not made my maiden speech. I had considered that there was not a lot of advantage in making my maiden speech too soon after being introduced, as I needed to understand the rules and procedures in the House. So I watched, listened and hopefully learned.

I have to say that I became frustrated watching the Crime and Disorder Bill being debated, as it was a measure to which I could have made a meaningful contribution, having advised Jack Straw on the usefulness of anti-social behaviour orders and other matters.

I often relate how I could never understand why the house was so quiet when debating important issues like robbery, burglary and car crime. Then the government decided to tack on the end of the Bill, a provision reducing the age of homosexual consent from 18 years to 16 years. Well, the chamber may have been empty before, but this was a subject which brought out the backwoodsmen and women. The chamber was absolutely packed for the debate on this provision. I then go on to relate how I said to an elderly colleague sitting beside me on the red benches, 'Why is it, when this place debates important issues of crime like burglary, the benches are almost empty! Yet, when the question of buggery is discussed, there isn't a seat in the house, even Maggie Thatcher turns up?' 'Well Brian', he replied wistfully, 'perhaps there aren't many burglars in here!' The *Times* Diary column got wind of my remarks and ran an item on it on February 20th 1999.

I have to say that I have collected more material for my after dinner speeches since being in the House of Lords, than anywhere during my eventful life so far. On one of my first visits to the House in that hot July, I went into the Peers Entrance and saw an elderly hereditary Peer sitting on one of the large chairs near the revolving doors, apparently waiting for a taxi. Being a friendly lad from the north I went across to him and said, 'Good afternoon, do you know who I am?' Thinking he might have seen me on

Royal snub

PRINCE EDWARD and Sophie Rhys-Jones intend to leave Princess Beatrice and Princess Eugenie off their list of bridesmaids. The snub would highlight the rift between the couple and the Duchess of York, and the lack of enthusiasm in the Royal Family for the duchess.

The pair have given no hint that the Queen's granddaughters will be invited to accompany Sophie. Edward and the duchess worked memorably on *It's A Royal Knock-out* in 1987, but their friendship has cooled. Their paths rarely cross.

This has not been helped by Sophie. She asked the duchess to pose in a swimsuit and have water jets sprayed on her for a PR stunt. The duchess was "astonished".

● *IT SEEMS buggery has moved a Labour peer, Lord Mackenzie of Framwellgate, to moan: "Why is it that when we discuss buggers, this place is full, but when we discuss burglars there is no one here?" To which a perpetual Being croaked: "Well, we've not got any burglars in the House."*

Times *Diary.*

158

television. 'No', he said helpfully, 'but if you ask the attendant at the desk he will tell you!'

Another one from my repertoire is when I was standing behind the coat pegs in the Peers Entrance and I heard an elderly hereditary Earl talking to an equally mature Baroness. 'Hello', she said, 'I don't think we've met before.' 'I am surprised', he said, 'I've been here for thirty-five years!' Her Ladyship continued, 'I'm very good at predicting what age people are', she said. 'Will you allow me to tell how old you are?' The old man perked up excitedly. 'Go on then', he cried. I was listening intently now behind the hat pegs as she said, 'Well pull down your zip'. I listened and heard the sound of a zip being pulled down. I strained to see what was happening between the coats and umbrellas and saw the elderly Baroness put her hand into his trousers and fondle him. 'You're eighty-six!' she said confidently. 'Good heavens you're absolutely right, how on earth did you know that?' He asked quizzically. Straining my ears, by now, I saw her lean towards him and whisper, 'You told me yesterday...'

What can you say – it's priceless!

So the House of Lords rose at the end of July for the summer recess and I decided then to get my maiden speech over and done with as soon as possible when the House returned in October.

During the recess I had another important engagement. You will recall that I had been invited to speak at the Labour Party Conference in 1997, whilst still a serving police officer; well now as a Labour Peer, I could fulfil that obligation. I went to Blackpool in September as proud as punch, gave a brief, humorous speech on policing and the rule of law, with an intimate knowledge of government thinking on these issues as I had been part of their development. I spoke just before Jack Straw, with the Prime Minister and Tom Sawyer sitting on the platform. It was a momentous occasion for me, with former colleagues, including Des Parkinson, from the Superintendents' Association, watching from the public gallery.

A maiden speech in any parliament is a special occasion. No less so in the mother of all parliaments. It is usual for a member making a maiden speech, to speak uninterrupted and to be congratulated by the next speaker on behalf of the whole House. It is therefore expected that a member will make his or her debut in a debate with a speakers' list, so that the House in general and, the next speaker in particular, may know that the conventional courtesies apply.

In return, the maiden speech is expected to be short, less than ten minutes, and also uncontroversial. When a maiden speech is being made and during the following speaker's congratulations, Members of the House are expected to remain in their seats and not leave the chamber. A rule encouraged diplomatically by the doorkeepers.

As I scanned the business coming up, I saw that there was a debate on bullying in schools, set down for Tuesday 6 October. I gingerly wrote my name on the speakers' list hanging in the Whips Office and put (m) beside my name, indicating to one and all that I was taking the plunge.

The doorkeepers have told me of odd (in every sense of the word) hereditary Peers, who have attended the House for years and who have never, ever, got round to speaking in the chamber. I suppose that is another reason for removing the hereditary principle, although I have to say they did bring colour and character to the place.

In any event, having made my choice I set about writing the notes for my speech. Although you are not allowed to read in the course of a speech, it is permissible to refer to notes, a very fine dividing line, which when crossed will result in cries of 'reading, reading!' from across the chamber.

I intended to start as I meant to finish. I decided to make my first words in the House of Lords humorous so I started with a joke!

I got to my feet at 7.43 p.m. that October evening with the chamber a quarter full. I repeat the text from *Hansard* for 6 October 1998, although I have to say, it is indelibly imprinted on my mind and I repeat it often. I always carry with me a copy of the *Hansard* page as evidence that I am not making the story up! These were my opening words:

> My Lords,
>   It is with some humility and not a little trepidation that I rise to address your Lordships' House for the first time. Perhaps all I can hope for is to emulate the performance of the one-eyed javelin thrower at the last Olympics in as much as I shall probably not win any prizes but at least retain your Lordships' attention! [*Hansard* 6 Oct 1998: Column 325]

It was then that I looked across the chamber to the Tory benches and saw an elderly Peer with a walrus moustache and the biggest patch over his right eye that you could imagine. It was Lord Mowbray, a 26th Baron, one of the oldest titles in the place. I couldn't believe that I had told that joke and did not see him sitting there! But I had not. A titter ran round the house and I got on with my full oration on the serious topic of bullying.

I then concluded on a lighter note yet again, quoting a visit to a nursery school in my area, where a youngster had asked me what it was like to be a Lord. I explained my response to their Lordships, 'I said that although it is nice to be important, it is far more important to be nice.'

I finished, 'I read recently that in the Middle Ages, many Members [of the Lords] had to be bullied and fined to attend. I hope that has stopped! – and, as I say that I look at the Whip...'

The Right Reverend Prelate, the Bishop of Ely, continued the humorous theme, when he rose to follow me, saying warmly 'My Lords I am happy to be the first to congratulate the noble Lord, Lord Mackenzie on a delightful speech and welcome him to the House. I was a resident of County Durham for 11 years and I am pleased to say that we never met...' [*Hansard* 6 October 1998: Column 326]

I have to say that since that night in the autumn of 1998 I have spoken on numerous occasions on serious matters of crime and justice, but always find, as I have throughout life, that a little well placed humour helps to get the message across. I have found the House to be courteous and helpful, with a wealth of knowledge on a whole range of disciplines and long may it continue in that vein.

It is interesting that a few days after my maiden speech I was telling a colleague the story and the fact that I had not seen Lord Mowbray sitting in the chamber. 'You didn't say that?' he said, 'I'm afraid so,' I said apologetically. 'Did he say anything to you?' Without thinking I said, 'No he didn't bat an eyelid!' As they say – you couldn't write it!

Talking of maiden speeches, some time later I had the honour of following the distinguished former Commissioner of the Metropolitan Police, Peter, Lord Imbert. During his speech he spoke of the memorable Irish terrorist siege in London when he was the principal negotiator, which ended peacefully. In paying tribute to his very popular commissionership and welcoming him to the House, I took the opportunity to pull his leg by reminding the House that as the former president of the Superintendents' Association, I could reveal the difference between a chief officer of police and a terrorist. The answer of course is that you can negotiate with a terrorist!

Whistle-blowing

An interesting coincidence arose from my maiden speech on bullying, when a short time later, an ex-police colleague, Alan Long, rang me. Alan had retired from the Regional Crime Squad, which used to work out of Chester-le-Street police station where I was the divisional commander. I had known him as a fellow CID officer and we were quite friendly. He asked if he could come to see me in London and I invited him to the Lords.

We met just after lunch early in 1999 and I took him onto the Lords' Terrace where we had a drink. He started to tell me about this idea he had, following a conversation on a train with Bill Cleghorn, a forensic accountant, who I later got to know quite well. Bill had asked Alan what he thought about the Public Interest Immunity Act, which protected 'whistleblowers', who spoke out in the public interest. Alan told him that what was required was the equivalent of a 'Crime-stoppers' programme, with an independent hotline to report wrongdoing in the workplace, such as discrimination, fraud and health and safety matters. I listened with great interest and said, 'You've obviously read my maiden speech.' Alan looked perplexed and it was clear he did not know what I was talking about! 'Well it was about bullying and I mentioned the importance of whistle-blowing,' I said. He was as astonished as I was. Talk about a meeting of minds. I took out my maiden speech and showed him the relevant text.

> One of the difficulties of those in command, whether it be school teachers or supervisors, is finding out that bullying is taking place. There is a fear, which I have experienced in my 35 years in the force, of being labelled as a 'grass' or a 'snitch'. People are frightened of being intimidated because they have told the authorities what is going on. It needs to be made much easier to 'whistle-blow', anonymously if necessary, and such information needs to be taken seriously by those in authority. [*Hansard* 6 Oct 1998: Column 325]

The rest as they say is history. Alan set up his whistle-blowing company 'Safecall' and I was invited, and accepted, a seat on the board of directors. Since then it had gone from strength to strength, with a number of fire brigades, British Nuclear Fuels and the Police Service of Northern Ireland amongst those joining our list of clients.

Being in London I was ideally placed to keep in touch with former police colleagues in the Police Federation, the Superintendents' Association and ACPO. I also had a good working relationship with Sir David O'Dowd, Her Majesty's Chief Inspector of Constabulary, with whom I lunched from time to time. I retained my friendship with Sir John Stevens, who I actively supported for appointment as Commissioner of the Metropolitan Police when Sir Paul Condon retired. I had seen him transform the Northumbria force and I was delighted when Jack Straw eventually offered him the post.

Tony Blair

The prime minister, Tony Blair was still enjoying a remarkable honeymoon in 1998. The Tories, who were in disarray following their massive defeat in 1997, had chosen the young William Hague as leader with the 'big beasts', Kenneth Clarke, Michael Heseltine and Michael Howard retiring to the backbenches and, licking their wounds in the jungle!

It was expected that Gordon Brown would be appointed Chancellor of the Exchequer and, by popular acclaim, he was making an excellent fist of it. One of his first decisions was to give the power of changing interest rates to a committee chaired by the Governor of the Bank of England, Eddie George. This took the politics out of the decision and the committee made the judgment on economic rather than political grounds. It was a masterstroke, and even became a policy adopted by the Tories.

The economy generally seemed to be working well with reasonable productivity; low unemployment, interest rates and inflation and, the government had a massive majority in the House of Commons to do with whatever it wished. Tony Blair remained popular in the opinion polls and could almost walk on water.

William Hague however had an image problem and although an excellent debater in the Commons, he remained constantly low in the polls. He was given bad advice when he tried to be 'one of the lads' by wearing a baseball cap at an amusement park and, by bragging about having drunk seven pints of beer when he was working as a drayman! Having said all that, I rated William Hague quite highly. I would regularly sit in the Peers' Gallery in the Commons and watch Prime Minister's Questions and often saw him knock spots off Tony Blair by employing a deadly weapon treasured by me – a delightful and incisive sense of humour!

The Prime Minister is not often given credit for the remarkable trans-formation from Old to New Labour. The removal of Clause Four from the constitution, the commitment to low income tax and the divorce from the big barons of the trade unions, signalled a new dawn. The race was on for a record achievement, the election of a Labour government in two consecutive terms for the very first time!

I regularly attended the parliamentary Labour Party meetings, which the Prime Minister addressed from time to time, and I was captivated by his great knowledge of detail and his ability to speak on a range of detailed policy matters without a note. He was evangelical in his approach, with even old left-wingers, if not applauding, at least showing indications of admiration. Tony Blair displayed a passion about the subject about which he was talking, which left you in no doubt that he believed he was on a crusade, and you wanted to be part of it. His inclusive approach well and truly captured the middle ground of the political landscape in Britain and I felt, and still feel, very proud to be at the heart of it.

What the critics forget, or care not to remember, is that the old party was the face of unelectable Labour, and staying the same was not an option. That is what saddens me when I hear the likes of Roy Hattersley, Lord Hattersley no less, constantly sniping from the sidelines. This was a man who was a failed shadow home secretary, and a failed deputy leader of the party. I do however give credit to Neil Kinnock who I believe tried valiantly to take on the subversive forces within the party with his attack on Derek Hatton and others. The country was ready for a change and with Tony Blair 'Cometh the hour, Cometh the man.'

The Palace of Westminster

The Palace of Westminster fascinates me even now and, in those early days, I took it upon myself to research and learn about this magnificent building, that I was destined now to work in on a daily basis. I am indebted to one of the doorkeepers in the House, Tim Healy, who put me onto a fascinating book by a former Clerk to the Parliaments, Sir Barnett Cocks, called *A Mid Victorian Masterpiece*.

The spot where parliament stands has been the site of a royal palace for over nine centuries and still remains a royal palace. Nothing remains of the original palace, which Edward the Confessor built – only the name Old Palace Yard, by which the space around the statue of Richard Coeur de Lion (Richard the Lionheart) is called, survives to remind us where it once stood.

William Rufus, the son of The Conqueror, built Westminster Hall in 1099 as the great hall of his new palace, which gave its name to the yard between the hall and Big Ben (New Palace Yard). The Palace continued to be the principal royal residence until 1512, when in consequence of a fire, Henry VIII acquired York Place from Cardinal Wolsey and renamed it the Palace of Whitehall.

In 1834 another fire, which broke out in the furnaces where two men were burning wooden tally sticks, destroyed many of the ancient buildings, including the old House of Lords and St Stephen's Chapel, where the Commons sat. Following the fire, two architects, Charles Barry and Augustus Welby Pugin, were commissioned to rebuild the Palace. The Commons first sat in their new chamber in 1850 and the new Palace of Westminster is a sight to behold. Built to a Gothic design, the fine detail both inside and on the outside of the building is truly amazing. Charles Barry, who was later knighted, was the main architect, but his colleague, Pugin, was an amazingly creative character, a workaholic whose efforts eventually led him to an early grave. Married three times, he had an attack of 'nervous fever' in the spring of 1852, was straight-jacketed and then confined to Bedlam, a psychiatric institution, where he died at the age of only forty. As his doctor was to record, 'He had done a hundred years' work!'

The Clock Tower was finished in 1852, but it was not until 1859 that the clock, the hour bell and the chimes, came into use.

During the Second World War, on 10 May 1941, incendiary bombs dropped by the Luftwaffe destroyed the chamber of the House of Commons. Sir Giles Gilbert Scott designed the present Commons chamber and, Members first sat in it on 26 October 1950.

From the moment I went into the Lords, I took the decision that if people asked to look around the Palace, it was my duty to facilitate that, particularly if they were from the northeast! One of the first people to contact me for a visit was Alan Booth from The Dunelm Club in Durham, where I am a member. He came with his wife Edith and the joy on their faces when they entered the magnificent structure was a delight to behold.

When showing visitors around the Palace of Westminster, I usually start at the Peers Entrance and point out the peg allocated to Baroness Thatcher. I then take them up to the Prince's Chamber, with pictures of the Stuarts and the Tudors and centrally, a statue of Queen Victoria. We then go down to the Sovereign's Robing Room, where Her Majesty prepares and puts on the Imperial Crown before processing through the Royal Gallery during the State Opening. The Sovereign's Robing Room has an ornately decorated ceiling and a large fireplace, designed by Barry, who used stone from all parts of Britain to construct it.

The Royal Gallery is on the ceremonial route of the royal procession. It is used also for receptions and I had the honour of being invited by her Majesty to attend a reception with other Peers to celebrate Her Golden Jubilee. It is also used for visiting Statesmen to address members of the both Houses of Parliament. The sidewalls are adorned by two large paintings by the Scottish artist Daniel Maclise, one representing the meeting of Wellington and Blucher after the Battle of Waterloo, the other, the death of Nelson at Trafalgar. It seems totally appropriate that in past years Presidents Giscard D'Estang and Mitterand of France were entertained in the room displaying so graphically two of their greatest defeats!

I still sit in wonderment in the Lords' Chamber itself, with the ornate gold throne and the red leather benches. In this place of course is enacted the most splendid of all State Ceremonies – the Opening of Parliament, when, wearing the Imperial Crown, the sovereign reads the speech from the throne to the assembled Lords and Commons.

Composition of the Lords

The following are members of the House of Lords (at the time of writing), provided they are not under the age of twenty-one:

- Lords Spiritual:
  - the Archbishops of Canterbury and York
  - the Bishops of London Durham and Winchester
  - twenty-one other diocesan bishops of the Church of England according to seniority of appointment
- Lords Temporal
  - Lords created for life under the Appellate Jurisdiction Act 1876 (as amended) to serve as Lords of Appeal in Ordinary (the Law Lords)
  - Life Peers created under the Life Peerages Act 1958
  - 90 Hereditary Peers elected pursuant to the House of Lords Act 1999
  - The Earl Marshall
  - The Great Lord Chamberlain.

Disqualification for Membership

The following are disqualified for membership:

- Those under twenty-one

- Aliens
- Those convicted of treason are disqualified for sitting and voting *until they have suffered their term of imprisonment or received a pardon* (my italics).
- Bankrupts are disqualified for sitting and voting. The court notifies the Lord Chancellor and it is recorded in the Journals of the House.

With regards to the italics, it seems remarkable to me that bankrupts are treated far more harshly than criminals, so that convicted perjurer Jeffrey Archer can sit, whilst a Peer made bankrupt, perhaps through no fault of his own, is disqualified. It says a lot about priorities when these rules were promulgated.

Legislative sittings of the House of Lords are presided over by the Lord Chancellor, although at the time of writing the Prime Minister has announced a separation of powers, with the creation of a new Department of Constitutional Affairs. The first Secretary of State of this department is Lord Falconer of Thoreton, the new Lord Chancellor. Once the details are worked out, it is understood he will no longer be the 'speaker' in the Lords and has already ceased to sit as a judge.

My time in the Lords has also seen Lord Irvine of Lairg sitting as Lord Chancellor on the Woolsack with the Mace behind him. The Bishops sit immediately on his right, in front of and to the left of the government peers. Peers of the opposition parties sit on his left, with non-party peers (including Law Lords) sitting on the cross benches facing him.

The House of Lords is also the final judicial court of appeal for Great Britain and Northern Ireland and sits in the morning for the hearing of appeals. In recent years the judges, sitting without wigs, sat in a committee room upstairs with only opinions and judgments being delivered to the House itself.

At either side of the chamber are the voting lobbies with the 'not content' lobby being to the left of the Lord Chancellor and the 'content' lobby being to his right. When a division is called Peers have to vote physically by walking through either lobby from the chamber. Eight minutes is allowed for Peers outside the chamber to get back to vote, which can be quite demanding for elderly peers who are outside the Palace when a division is called.

Leaving the Lords chamber from the opposite end to the throne leads into the Peers' Lobby and into the Peers' Corridor, where, there hangs a painting by Charles West Cope, of the last Sovereign to set foot in the House of Commons. This was Charles I in 1642 when he attempted to arrest five Members of the Commons. He went there with soldiers, stormed in and said, 'I am sorry on this occasion to have come unto you.' He then asked for the whereabouts of the five members, Pym, Hampden, Hazelrigg, Hollis and

Strode. The Speaker, a man called Lenthall is shown kneeling before the King and saying, at great risk to himself it has to be said, 'Sire, I have neither eyes to see nor tongue to speak except as this House doth command me, whose servant I am.'

The King said, 'I see the birds have flown,' and left the chamber. As he did so the assembled members shouted 'Privilege, privilege, privilege!' Since then no reigning Sovereign has been allowed to enter the House of Commons. That is where the Black Rod ceremony springs from when, as the Monarch's representative, he has the House of Commons' door slammed in his face and the Sergeant at Arms looks through the grill in the door, to check that there are no soldiers present, before letting Black Rod in to summons members to the Lords Chamber, to hear the Queen's speech. Charles I paid with his life of course, when he was arrested by Oliver Cromwell for High Treason, tried in Westminster Hall and beheaded in Whitehall on 30 January 1649.

The Central Lobby stands between the Lords and the Commons and is where visitors and constituents, having entered through the main St Stephen's Entrance, wait for Members of Parliament. The mosaics above the four great arches in the Lobby represent St George (England), St Andrew (Scotland), St David (Wales) and St Patrick (Ireland).

CHAPTER 15

A Growing Compensation Culture

O NE OF MY deep concerns whilst heading the Superintendents' Association had been the growing tendency for people to sue for compensation at the drop of a hat. This was assisted by the introduction of 'no win – no fee', legal representation which increased litigation and of course, was costing the public in two ways. Courts and their staff are funded from the public purse and, when the organizations being sued are in the public sector, any damages awarded, again, come out of the pocket of the public.

Having gone into the House of Lords I was able to continue expressing my concerns about these issues. There was, I recall, a particularly annoying tendency for some chief constables when they were sued for damages following alleged malpractice by police officers, to settle out of court on the basis of legal advice which put simply, was, that it was the cheapest option! This took no account the message it sent to the public, who clearly thought that the accusations were substantiated even though the settlements were 'without admission of liability'. Even worse in my judgment, was the effect all this had on police morale! If officers knew, for example, that the allegation was false, they wanted their day in court and the support of their chief officer. To see the matter 'settled' was a slur on their integrity. So I continue to speak on such matters both in the press and in parliament, if the opportunity arises.

Then there was evidence that police officers were increasingly suing their employers over matters which clearly were part of their job. I know that I ruffled a few feathers in the Police Federation, some officials of which saw it as a betrayal of the their members. It was no such thing of course, as I had been saying the same things throughout my presidency of the Association.

I believed the police service was being damaged by an over-emphasis on 'stress' and the provision of 'counselling'. There were cases reported of officers suing their respective forces for a variety of bizarre reasons, which I thought were unreasonable, such as:

- an officer transferred back to frontline duties claiming £100,000 for psychological damage
- an officer whilst having a shower at work, slipped and hurt his back and was given £100,000 in an out of court settlement
- two police marksmen who saw a burglar shot dead by one of their colleagues claimed compensation for 'psychiatric injury'.

Police *magazine cartoon.*

I said in an article in the *Sunday Times* in October 1998 and I quote, 'There is a growing compensation culture and it is enfeebling the force. I am particularly concerned at officers seeking compensation for stress caused by incidents, which they knew they would have to deal with.'

The whole question of the ridiculous position we have got into was illustrated recently by a case, which would have been funny if it was not so serious. It was demeaning and outrageous to see the Metropolitan Police Commissioner Sir John Stevens and his predecessor, Lord Condon, paraded at the Old Bailey to stand trial on criminal charges brought by the Health and Safety Executive following the tragic death of an officer who fell through a roof whilst bravely doing his duty. Did those who brought the case really think through the consequences of a finding of guilt in such circumstances? Thankfully they were rightly acquitted but it has come to a pretty pass when such a prosecution is launched!

As for stress counselling, I get most concerned when I read or see on television details of tragic accidents which people have witnessed, or in which a child or children are killed in tragic circumstances, and where whole communities or schools are offered counselling. Again I believe that this disables people from using their natural immune system to deal with the aftermath of trauma. It is similar to the over use of antibiotics which disables the body's immune system over time.

It was put well by an expert in the field, Angela Patmore, who explains that the body produces adrenalin at times of stress in preparation for 'fight' or 'flight'. Counselling was the equivalent of switching off a burglar alarm during a burglary and simply reduces the body's natural mechanisms for dealing with matters, which are perfectly natural emotional challenges. There is a growing body of medical opinion in this field that argues that requiring people to 'talk through' stressful events soon after they have happened, is at least unhelpful and at most, is counter productive. A whole 'stress' industry has grown up around disaster management and produced an army of 'counsellors', who in my view do not add a great deal of value, other than to increase the 'blame' culture which now pervades society.

In any event, legal claims are costing the government and the public a great deal of money, and Jack Straw the then Home Secretary went public and supported my concerns regarding the growing compensation culture and certain sections of the legal profession hitching a ride on growing a gravy train.

Hillsborough

The issue was brought to a head in the courts in the Hillsborough case during December of 1998. No one can deny the trauma felt by all those who witnessed the terrible events at the stadium in Sheffield nearly ten years earlier, when a crush at the Leppings Lane end of the stadium killed 96 fans and injured hundreds more.

The House of Lords sitting judicially had to consider an appeal from the chief constable of South Yorkshire against a lower court finding that he was to blame for psychiatric injuries caused to police officers present witnessing events, as the disaster unfolded. By a majority of three to two, the Law Lords ruled that the officers were not entitled to compensation. I wrote an article in the Express newspaper on December 5, stating that

> I believe that in its landmark judgment, the Lords has thrown the police service a lifeline. One only has to think of air and rail crashes over the years – Lockerbie, Piper Alpha, Clapham and Kings Cross as well as Aberfan a generation earlier. It is the ability to deal with such incidents without hesitation that makes the police, ambulance and fire services special.

The then chief constable of South Yorkshire Police, Richard Wells put it succinctly when he said, 'When members of the public take the oath of allegiance for the office of constable they are to expect hardship, danger, death and to some extent, disaster.' How right he was and, hopefully the judgment will stem some of the more outrageous claims.

Press Interest

The press both locally and nationally were taking an interest in the newly appointed Peers and soon picked up on the fact that Brian Mackenzie and his old school pal, Tom Sawyer, from the terraced streets of Darlington, had arrived at the Palace of Westminster together. The *Northern Echo* in Darlington ran a feature on 4 December, headed 'The raggy-arsed lads who ended up Lords,' with a picture of Tom and me in the Library Corridor of the Lords.

The *Independent* did better and identified the fact that both Tom and I had attended Dodmire School in Darlington, where we had spent our infancy being educated in a 'temporary' tin hut, next to the main building which, as I mentioned earlier had been there since 1920. The local education authority had decided to demolish the 'temporary' hut after 79 years and thought it would be nice if the two 'old boys' now in the Lords, attended and presided over the occasion. So we were invited back in the summer of 1999 to make speeches and say cheerio to our old, early seat of learning.

The press were still taking an interest in Superintendent Ray Mallon who was still suspended by Cleveland Police. The then chairman of the Police Complaints Authority, which was overseeing the inquiry, blamed the length of time the inquiry was taking, on the officers being investigated, who were 'dragging their feet'. I was astonished at the suggestion, bearing in mind that our Association had suggested ways of speeding up the complaints process, which advice had been ignored. I published a press statement saying,

> Any probationer police officer knows that it is for the prosecuting authorities to prove criminal allegations and not for the suspect to assist in that process. Is Mr Moorhouse suggesting that there should be different rules for police officers being investigated? To blame the officers who are being investigated for any delay therefore is utter nonsense. Any inquiry should be focussed and properly resourced to enable it to be completed within a reasonable time.

Even Jack Straw started to comment on the cost of the inquiry and demanded to know how the money was being used. My main complaint was also the lack of accountability as to how the soaring bill for the inquiry was being spent. So I was out of favour with the Police Complaints Authority too, although I have to say that when I came into contact with the then, deputy chairwoman of the authority, Molly Meacher, some time later when she took over the chair of the newly formed Security Industry Authority, I got on extremely well with her and her chief executive, John Saunders as they set about regulating Britain's burgeoning security industry – another issue which I have campaigned about since Adam was a boy!

My contributions to the media were not all serious! In April of 1999, I was invited to answer questions in an end piece column of the *Police Review*, which is the national magazine of the police service. It is entitled 'verbals' and is a question and answer session. It was an enjoyable piece and I set out to entertain as well as inform. I repeat it so that the reader can judge whether I succeeded on either count.

Is there truth in the rumour that you've dropped your trousers in front of home secretary Jack Straw?
Yes. When Jack Straw was in opposition, I did a photo opportunity with him, which entailed me getting changed into uniform in his office. He has never let me forget it and even mentioned it during a speech. I got my own back the other week when chairing a conference at which the Home Secretary was speaking, by inventing the following conversation. 'Where should I put my clothes Jack?' 'On the floor next to mine!'

What has been the worst car journey of your life?
Undoubtedly, during the summer of 1995. I attended the Police VJ Service at Coventry Cathedral with the then home secretary Michael Howard, ACPO and colleagues when I took ill. I drove home to Durham, counting every milestone, hunched over the wheel. I was having a heart attack and when I got home I was admitted straight into intensive care. I can only explain my irresponsibility in driving by saying that when you are as ill as that, you get a tremendous homing instinct. I am thankfully, absolutely fine now.

Have you ever considered a life of crime?
If I ever did, I rejected it almost immediately. I don't know any really successful

criminals – and in any case I have always had a passionate belief in justice. Thinking about it now, if I had turned to crime I think I might have made quite a good con man. How else could the son of a council worker from the northeast end up in the House of Lords?

What's the funniest thing that has happened to you so far in your career?

Leading a serial of officers to a pub disturbance on a Friday night, we had to squeeze past customers in a corridor. A young woman, slightly worse for drink, looked at my superintendent's cap, smiled and unbelievably squeezed me in an unmentionable place. I looked straight into her eyes and, hardly moving my lips said, 'If you don't let go, your feet won't touch the ground.' It is the one and only time I have been indecently assaulted on duty!

What is you favourite Monica Lewinsky joke?

I frequently get into trouble for being politically incorrect. I think therefore that it might be better to do what Monica should have done and keep my mouth shut!

Do northerners have more fun?

Newcastle is the 'fun' city of Europe and it has a tremendous buzz. I think northerners do have a natural friendliness and are used to working hard and playing hard. My mother told me years ago that crime was so rare you could leave your doors wide open and she would describe how her family huddled round the open fire to keep warm in winter. Why they didn't just close the doors I'll never know!

What was your proudest moment as a police officer?

As a lad I did not do particularly well at school (I failed the 11 plus), passing my sergeant's exam for the first time and coming top in the force. Then passing the same exam the following year to qualify for the 'Special Course' interviews and coming top in the force again! (Incidentally, I failed the interviews on both occasions).

How would you like to be remembered?

I would like to be remembered for helping to make the Superintendents' Association a valued and effective influence on government policy (of both parties) and also for translating the vision of a paedophile register (against the counsel of some colleagues who did not think it achievable) into a successful conference debate and pursued to success in the Sex Offenders Act 1997.

[*Police Review*: 2 April 1999]

I was now getting into the routine of commuting each week between Durham and London. I mixed and matched between flying from Teesside and Heathrow and using GNER trains. I have to say there is not a lot between them from door to door in terms of time, but the train is far more amenable to doing some work. I always consider that travelling time is wasted time and therefore plan essential reading for any journey I have to make. The problem with flying is that the journey is in short segments and you never get settled. I had to drive to Teesside, go through check-in, fly for 45 minutes, and then commute from Heathrow to central London. As I have said earlier, you get a good 3-hour spell on the train to do as you wish. I still carry my small radio headset so that I can catch my beloved Radio 4.

Hot Desking

I mentioned that newly appointed Peers were given a peg and a locker on arrival at the Lords. We could also apply for a computer and a printer. I had used a hand held and a desk computer at home for writing speeches and surfing the Internet for a few years and found it invaluable for researching a whole range of topics. I was also getting into the use of electronic mail although I was just a novice in the mid nineties. I duly got my allocated laptop computer and printer and was shown how to get onto the parliamentary website to access *Hansard*, the library and, a whole range of other sources of information, including the World Wide Web itself.

I was also given software which would enable my computer at home in Durham to access the parliamentary system, which was a real boon because I could continue working at weekends without carrying bundles of paper with me. I did not intend to carry the laptop around with me and therefore needed a base. I discovered a delightful room in the Lords' committee corridor called the Peers' Writing Room. It was a wonderful room with leather chairs and tables to write at, with tea making facilities and newspapers delivered there daily. A veritable oasis!

I selected a desk near the window where I could use the large sill to place papers and books. I connected my computer and printer and decided that this was my home for the foreseeable future. I knew that it was against all the rules to use the same desk on a permanent basis, but there was no way I was going to disconnect my computer every evening and become an itinerant Peer. I heard on the grapevine that there were mutterings from some of the old guard, but I stuck to my guns and was never officially asked to move. The downside of the Peers' Writing Room is that some of the elderly, usually, I have to say, hereditary Lords, used it as a smoke room and the place was occasionally enveloped in plumes of cigar, pipe and cigarette smoke. Even worse, they would nod off after lunch and snore for England! These were the trials and tribulations of ennoblement in the late nineties.

They were however, lovely people. Mostly very elderly and somewhat infirm but with minds as sharp as razors. I was seen as the new whiz kid on the block I believe, particularly sitting as I did, using the computer on the desk each day. Len Murray, the former general secretary of the TUC was a regular, as was the delightful Jack Ashley, a consummate parliamentarian who was always helpful and friendly. I got particularly friendly with the late

Baroness (Beatrice) Serotta, a former Health Minister, who looked on me as her computer adviser. I was always happy to help of course and it never ceased to amaze me how these elderly people, who were in their seventies and eighties, took to computers with gusto. There was always a will to embrace new ideas and technology.

It was not just an office. On one memorable occasion the House sat right through the night, I forget what the Bill was, and rather than attempt to get home, I slept on a settee in the Peers' Writing Room. A cleaning lady, bringing me a cup of tea around 6:30 a.m., woke me. That was a memorable night for another reason. We were hanging around waiting for votes in the Bishops' Bar, which is situated just off the Prince's Chamber.

It would be about 2:00 am when Cecil Parkinson walked in. I remember he was wearing a black tie and dinner suit and we struck up a conversation. 'Hello, you won't know me, I'm Brian Mackenzie,' I said. 'Of course I know you, I listen to you on the *Today* programme,' he said with a smile. He then told me how he still retained an interest in politics and always awoke to the *Today* programme on Radio 4. I remember after about ten minutes conversation he stopped me and said, 'For God's sake Brian, will you stop calling me Michael!' I was very embarrassed at getting my Parkinsons mixed up!

That old warhorse, Norman Tebbit, then joined us. After about thirty minutes, Norman left, and Cecil and I resumed our conversation. By now we had both had a few drinks during a very long evening. 'I suppose you think Norman and I are good friends, do you?' I told him that that would be a reasonable conclusion.

'Well let me tell you a story,' he said. 'Can you remember the spot of trouble I had with Sarah Keyes a few years ago?'

'Of course.' I said inquisitively.

'Well,' continued Cecil, 'when it all broke, I had to get it off my chest and tell someone about it so I took Norman, a fellow member of the cabinet, to one side. I told him the story and how it would be all over the papers the next day, and do you know what he said in reply?'

'I have not got the foggiest idea!' I said through the smoke and alcoholic haze.

'Well what do you think of this?' Cecil said, 'He said to me, 'well there were three contenders, now there are only two'. He was talking about the next potential leaders of the party, Myself, Michael Heseltine and Norman. He had written me out of the script. How's that for a shoulder to cry on?'

I couldn't believe my ears and thought about what I'd heard as I nodded off to sleep on my settee in the Peers' Writing Room when I eventually retired for the night.

Another amusing aside in relation to the Peers' Reading Room was the retirement of Betty Boothroyd, the formidable and well-respected former Speaker of the House of Commons. She came into the Lords about the same time as I was allocated an office in 2001. I bumped into her in the corridor of the Palace one day and, we were chatting when she said, 'You must be the policeman.' I told her that she was quite correct and that I was a former police officer, but why did she ask? 'Well, I was not allocated an office to my satisfaction when I first came into the Lords, so I used to sit near the window in the Peers' Writing Room. Somebody came up to me one day and said, "You can't sit there Betty, you'll get into trouble. That desk belongs to the policeman!"' I have to say what a delightful lady Betty Boothroyd is – known throughout the world, the salt of the earth and a joy to be with. The House is all the stronger with people of that stature.

I was showing more and more visitors around the Palace and my knowledge of the history, procedures and traditions of the place was building up. It was about this time that Colin Appleby, a former superintendent from Durham rang me and asked if he could bring a Polish visitor to tour the Lords. She was called Teresa Stochel, a pleasant, attractive, athletic looking English teacher from Krakow who took a great deal of interest in our parliamentary traditions of Westminster. I readily agreed and we had a splendid day culminating with a glass of wine on the terrace. I have found that foreign visitors, unlike some of us, do not take our democracy for granted, particularly if at some stage in their history they have, for whatever reason, been denied their freedom.

CHAPTER 16

Confrontation in the Chamber

M Y FIRST set piece debate after my maiden speech in October was during the debate on the Queen's Speech, which was held on 2 December 1998. After the State Opening of Parliament has taken place, which is usually in November following the spill-over period, when there is a rush to try and complete outstanding business, there is a debate for about a week on the general provisions outlined in Her Majesty's Gracious Speech, as it is referred to.

I remember sitting in the study at home pouring over what to say when Jean popped her head into the room. For all her many skills and talent, what Jean is not, is a political animal. She said, 'What are you doing?' 'The Queen's speech', I said without further explanation. 'Really', she said seriously, 'Is that the one she gives on Christmas Day?' Only Jean could have said that, and we roared with laughter.

When I gave the speech, I was on home ground talking on a subject with which I had spent all of my adult life dealing – crime. I quoted Sir Kenneth Oxford the distinguished former Chief Constable of Merseyside, who knew a bit about fighting crime, as saying in 1978, 'If we cannot prevent the dreadful increase in crime, or at least contain it, the freedom and way of life we have been accustomed to enjoy for so long will vanish!' [*Hansard* 2 Dec 1998: Column 528]

I then further stated that we have a duty on behalf of all our people, together with the defence of the realm, to fight crime on every front. In continuing my speech I went on to say something, which I cannot explain, don't know why I said it and, cannot remember where the information came from, but I must have said it because it is recorded in *Hansard*. I will explain the significance of all this in a moment. I said, (and I quote) 'The consequences of not doing so (fighting crime) are graphically illustrated by the tragic events in the emerging democracy of Russia over recent months. They culminated in the contract killing of Galina Starovoitova, a distinguished democratic spokeswoman.' [*Hansard* 2 December 1998: Column 528]

Now the spooky thing about naming the St Petersburg murder victim, which I did not recall doing, until researching this book, was that I was to meet the victim's ex-husband in 2001, some three years later. He was the distinguished Professor, Michael Borschevsky, who is now a British citizen, who told me about the killing. Yet when I listened spellbound to his story three years later, I still did not recall that I had named his former wife, Galina in my speech in the Lords in 1998. I still see Michael and count him as an extremely good friend. Again, it was a strange act of fate, which threw us together after naming her in the Lords.

In that speech, I spoke about the scourge of juvenile crime, particularly from a northeastern perspective, where we spawned 'blip' boy, 'balaclava' boy and 'rat' boy: juvenile offenders who single-handedly caused a 'blip' in the crime figures through continuous re-offending, were interviewed on television wearing a balaclava to hide their identity, or lived like rats, hiding from the police. We had coined the phrase 'revolving door justice', which referred to the phenomenon of arrest, charge, court, bail, arrest, charge, court, and bail; like a revolving door. I was in my element, debating on the side of the victim, and speaking from the heart on issues I really felt I knew something about. I soon found out however that whereas in the real world, as people get older they seem to move to the right politically, in the House of Lords (I can't speak for the Commons), people seem to move to the liberal left!

Even former Tory home office ministers seem to forget about the innocent victims and talk continuously about terrible prison conditions and how community punishment, without any evidence of reduced recidivism, is a better option than custody. They seem to forget that bad behaviour should have unpleasant consequences and talk about 'having a debate around what causes this behaviour, such as burglary, which in any event is not violent.' You tell that to the pensioners who are frightened to leave their own homes or the victims of burglary who see their life's possessions trashed!

As I have stated earlier, I often point out in speeches, both inside and outside the House, that the victim of crime is the only participant in the criminal justice process who is not a volunteer. We must never forget that fact! So in the address on the Queen's speech I talked about victims, juveniles, witness intimidation, sexual offences (in the context of women being forced to parade their sexual history in court when it bears no relevance to the case being heard) and finally, the unaccountability of the Police Complaints Authority. I am pleased to say that all of these matters have been addressed by the New Labour Government against strenuous opposition, quite often from lawyers, in the House of Lords.

I finished once again, on a humorous note, and I quote:

> In conclusion, I remember sitting through a civil case in the United States following a road accident, where a man had been knocked from his motor cycle by a horse which had reared up and trampled a dog which had run on the road. The plaintiff was suing for traumatic shock and stress injury caused by the accident.

Cross examined by the defence attorney, the plaintiff was asked if he told a policeman at the scene that he had never felt better in his life. 'Yes', said the plaintiff. The defence naturally rested their case.

The plaintiff's attorney then re-examined his client and asked him to elaborate. 'Well', said the plaintiff, 'I was lying dazed on the ground when a police officer arrived at the scene, he went over to the injured dog, put his revolver to its head and shot it. He then went over to the lame horse, put his gun to its head and shot it. He then came over to me and asked me how I felt. I told him that I had never felt better in my life!' [*Hansard* 2 Dec 1998: Column 531]

I then told their Lordships that they could determine from that, that the answers to questions always need to be seen in the context of the circumstances in which they are asked!

Drugs

Another campaigning topic of mine over the years, which cropped up fairly early on in my parliamentary career, was drugs. I saw that there was to be a debate on 3 December 1998, on a report by a Lords' Select Committee dealing with scientific and medical evidence on the use of cannabis and recommended relaxing the law. As I listened to the debate develop, I realized that everyone, apart from me, who was speaking in it, had been a member of the committee. It became clear to me that it was an exercise in self-congratulation. I was having none of it and said so. 'I suspect that had I been a member of the committee,' I said, 'there might have been one dissenting participant.' [*Hansard* 3 Dec 1998: Column 685]

Although the committee accepted the dangers of cannabis and were against legalization for recreational use, they were recommending that doctors should be able to prescribe and, pharmacists supply, the drug for medical purposes. As I said in the debate, 'There is a contradiction. Throughout the report, it is stated that the most common method of taking cannabis is to smoke it.' I went on, 'Professor Heather Ashton of the University of Newcastle is reported as saying that smoking cannabis leads to three time greater tar inhalation than tobacco. Chronic use increases the risk of cardiovascular disease, bronchitis, emphysema and lung cancer.' [*Hansard* 3 Dec 1998: Column 686]

My objection has never been to the use of the properties of cannabis in medicine, providing it is in the form of a pill, but why a responsible body such as this committee, should be recommending the use of a disease-causing and life-threatening method of treatment in order to alleviate pain and suffering is beyond me! In any event the government has ordered medical trials and I am delighted that they ignored the recommendation of this learned committee on this occasion. I have seen the misery that drug misuse has brought to families and communities and will continue to fight against its legalization, with all the misery and social problems that would go with such a decision.

In my early months in the Lords I was continuing to better understand the protocol and procedures. My history studies had gone well and I was showing more and more visitors round the Palace as well as hosting lunches and receptions in the various function rooms. The summer of 1999 was pleasant on the Lords' Terrace on the bank of the River Thames and I thought how lucky I was to part of it all.

I was still enjoying each weekend at home and it was usual on a Saturday for Jean and me to dine locally with friends. As I was still the Billet Master, I would occasionally don my superintendents' uniform and lead the Mayoral Bodyguard at the various parades and processions when required.

Back in the Lords a throwaway remark in a question caught the media's attention. I suppose it was because it was almost 'silly' season. During questions to the government in July 1999, I had light-heartedly suggested that unlike begging, busking was not illegal, as the busker was providing a service in return for payment. I then went on to point out that on a tube train, the audience were like 'prisoners' and some of the singing was dreadful. I suggested, tongue in cheek, that in such cases perhaps action should be taken under the 1968 Trades Descriptions Act.

Well I did not bargain with the media frenzy, which followed. I was called by reporters, broadcasters and a London television station even asked me to do a piece on film in a tube station, talking to a busker, who in fact turned out to be a professional musician. Ken Bruce on Radio 2 the next morning even had a phone-in session on the subject. One thing about public life is that you tend to forget that people are hanging on your every word and we all know, particularly the jeweller Gerald Ratner, how that can get you into trouble occasionally!

It was on 19 July 1999 that Tom Sawyer and I went back to Dodmire School in Darlington to a nostalgic re-union in the tin-hut classroom of the infants' school before it was demolished. Tom and I were last there as 5-year olds in 1948 and here we were half a century later returning to the scene of the crime. It was a tremendous day. Tom and I gave speeches to all the children dressed in 1920s attire with their parents and staff. The press and television were there in abundance of course and it was a great occasion, which certainly brought back memories. As I said earlier, even the national media took an interest.

Stephen Lawrence
I was still writing articles in the newspapers from time to time and, one topic which exercised my mind in that summer of 1999 was the report into the tragic murder of the black teenager, Stephen Lawrence many years earlier.

Demolition of the tin hut.

This had been published on 15 February 1999. The report had found the Metropolitan Police to be 'institutionally racist' and the Commissioner Sir Paul Condon accepted that fact. This admission brought an outcry from officers on the ground and from the London Federation. I was worried that such a finding would reinforce negative stereotypes about all police officers, particularly those in ethnic communities.

Particularly worrying was the fact that officers were reluctant to use stop and search powers, which was causing an increase in street crime. It had gone up 35 per cent in the three months since the report was published. I knew that it was the commonest ploy in the book for anyone arrested to shout 'police harassment' or 'racism', but in the climate prevailing, the last thing an officer wanted was to be labelled a racist. I therefore went public in supporting the police in their pilot schemes of 'targeted' stops and search, which were having some success with arrests jumping from 11 per cent to 18 per cent. Since then Sir John Stevens has done a tremendous job in tackling street crime and at the same time making it clear that racial attitudes within the police service will simply not be tolerated.

An Englishman's Home

I was finding, as we rolled into 1999, that in a sense my life had not changed a great deal since stepping down from the Superintendents' Association. I was still commuting south, still doing media work on important issues of crime, sentencing and criminal justice reform and I was still attending Jack Straw's weekly ministerial meetings and keeping my finger on the pulse of the government's reforming agenda. One topic that had been recurring throughout my period in the Association had been the question of victims, in defence of themselves or their property, inflicting injuries on criminals. There had been one or two high profile cases of members of the public tackling offenders in the act of stealing cars or burgling houses and finding themselves being arrested and taken to the police station and in some cases, being charged with assault.

I have dealt with allegations of assault made against schoolteachers by pupils, or more accurately by their parents, and I never found the need to arrest the teacher in order to interview him. Again I went public and spoke on the *Today* programme and elsewhere. Michael Howard had agreed with me in 1996 that it was not a satisfactory state of affairs and, asked the Director of Public Prosecutions to provide clearer guidance to the police. For the life of me I could not understand why the police had to formally arrest people simply to inquire into the circumstances of an altercation between a burglar and a householder, just because the burglar came off worse! After all, the innocent householder was not going to run away so there wasn't much of a risk.

New guidance came out, but it did not seem to make much difference to the police and it all added to the public's perception of a criminal justice system protecting the villain rather than the victim. I suppose the police were looking over their shoulders and wanted to be seen to be fair, but I simply couldn't understand why they had to be so heavy handed. On the odd occasion that prosecutions were brought, juries were very reluctant to convict.

The law is straightforward; a person can use as much force as is reasonable in the circumstances in the prevention of crime. The difficulty is determining what is reasonable. The test which I always used as a police officer was that you could use fist against fist; club against club, knife against knife or, firearm against firearm. The latter justifies the police shooting armed assailants. I also insisted that there was a discount for the victim, if they were elderly or infirm, or if the incident happened in your own home with a trespasser, particularly at night.

At the end of the day, it was a matter for the police to make a judgment early on, and if they did not pass the matter on to the Crown Prosecution Service then the matter stopped there and then and, in most cases so it should! I cannot think of any circumstances of someone being injured when in the act of burglary, unless fatal, which would justify the householder being hauled off to the police station to be interrogated. They could be interviewed at home or, at the most, invited to attend the police station for interview later. It is often thought that the police have to be neutral in these matters. I disagree – if prima facie, the injured party was the author of his own misfortune by trespassing in a dwelling, the police should take account of that in deciding how to proceed.

Tony Martin

The whole matter was brought into sharp focus in 1999 by the case of Tony Martin. He was the Norfolk farmer who shot two burglars who were burgling his home, 'Bleak House', during the night in August 1999, killing a teenager and injuring his older companion. Martin was arrested, charged, tried and convicted of murder, which was later reduced to manslaughter and was sentenced to five years. I did not hear the evidence and therefore cannot judge whether that was a just sentence. I am however convinced that in a case where a householder, in defending himself or his property, injures a burglar, the burglar forfeits the normal application of the criminal law. I am not saying that the use of excessive force should be encouraged and, it may well be that a specific offence of 'Excessive Force' should be created, but it would be far less severe that the present arrangement.

By a remarkable co-incidence, at the time of writing this chapter of the book, Tony Martin has just been released on 19 July 2003, having served two-thirds of his five-year sentence, and a debate is raging on whether he should have been imprisoned. Most opinion polls are on the side of Martin not being sent to prison!

I wrote a newspaper article pointing out that the offence might not have been committed had the rural community been better policed and, the judiciary had used their powers more effectively. I quote,

> For example, Darren Bark, involved in the attack on Tony Martin's farm, had 52 convictions, ranging from assault, theft criminal damage, affray and burglary. So the police had clearly got his number. They regularly arrested his colleague in crime, Brendan Fearon, who had 33 convictions to his credit... As for Barras – when he was shot dead at the age of 16 years – he already had a record of 29 offences and had been in court on five occasions, had spent time in a young offenders' institution and was on bail for theft.
>
> Had those men been behind bars, the fateful raid on Bleak House would not have taken place and Fred Barras would be alive and Tony Martin a free man. [*Daily Mail* 24 April 2000].

Since that time I have been speaking out in favour of a re-balancing of the criminal justice system and whilst this finds favour with Tony Blair and David Blunkett, it is an uphill battle in the House of Lords, and on these issues at any rate, their Lordships' appear to be out of step with the majority of people in the country.

I raise these matters time after time in the Lords but still invariably find myself a lone voice in the wilderness in a House full of lawyers. In November 1999 I again went on the offensive in the Queen's Speech debate and, I quote:

> When I saw the reaction of the various vested interests to the proposals in the Queen's Speech, it took me back to the days when I was a police officer and so saddened by the claptrap I used to hear then. I passionately believed in liberty and freedom: the liberty to walk the street without being attacked; the freedom to enjoy the comfort of your own home without being burgled; and the joy of bringing up a family without worrying about the threat of pornographers or paedophiles.

I then continued in lighter vain,

> We all suffer crime, even police officers. A colleague said to me last week that his wife had her credit card stolen. He told me that he had not reported it to the police because the thief was spending less than she was! [*Hansard* 24 Nov 1999: Column 511]

Incidentally, the following day a lady stopped beside me in a corridor whilst I was making a telephone call. When I had finished she said, 'Lord Mackenzie, you don't know me but I work in the *Hansard* Office. I just want you to know you had the whole office falling about with your comments about the credit card.' It reinforces the point that you never know who is listening!

Indeed in the same debate I again railed in favour of the government's proposals in the Crime and Public Protection Bill, to prevent people with a history of sex offending working with children. Similarly an extension of mandatory drug testing was also welcomed by me, as were many of the provisions in this and other Home Office Bills.

An example of the uphill task I had arose the following month when during a debate on the Mode of Trial Bill, there was a reference to my earlier comments in the Queen's Speech debate, by Lord Thomas of Gresford. I stood to intervene, 'My Lords, I thank the noble Lord for giving way. During the debate on the Queen's Speech I said that these points were being made by vested interests, and being a former president of the Police Super-intendents' Association, I can recognize a vested interest when I see one.'

That comment really ruffled the feathers of the noble Lord, who launched a vitriolic attack on the police. 'My Lords, I am not going to be lectured by representatives of police organizations when some of the problems that have occurred in the criminal justice system in this country over the past 10 or 15 years have been caused by failures and negligence of the investigators and not by the lawyers the courts or the juries.' [*Hansard* 2 Dec 1999: Column 931]

I was still attending FBI re-training sessions in Europe and the Americans were extremely pleased to have had one of their graduates elevated to the Lords, although I am not sure they understood much about it. Through the good offices of former graduates, David O'Dowd and Keith Povey, both of whom have held the post of Chief HMI, I was asked to attend a photo opportunity with Luis Freah, Bill Clinton's FBI Director, which I was more than happy to do.

Back Home
Meanwhile my social life at home was lively with Friday night usually taken up with a visit to the pub, or the Dunelm Club in Durham City, to catch up on the week's events in the north. The word 'Dunelm' is apparently Viking for 'Durham'. Saturday evening was usually an evening out for a meal with Jean and friends. The house which we lived in at Etherley Close had been extended and we had three mature trees in the garden. It had three lawns front and back, which although not enormous, took time to keep trimmed. The leaves in the autumn were a greater burden and my weekend would be eaten away by working outside if the weather allowed, or working on speeches or business matters, if it was wet or cold. Having set up my limited company, Framwellgate Resources, any monies from speeches and freelance journalism were channelled through that. I found it demanding but interesting and even offered Jean a job as my secretary!

One very lucrative speech I was invited to give was in December 1999 by the Social Market Foundation, which was a think-tank based in Westminster. Two leading lights in the organization at that time were Katharine Raymond, a bright young lady from Liverpool, whom I had met at the Labour Party Conference when I was the President of the Superintendents' Association. She is now an advisor to David Blunkett. The other was Helen Brown, a diminutive lady with short, dark hair, who later became a leader-writer on the Times and is now happily married and self-employed.

In any event, I was asked to speak on the 'Black Economy' and the venue was Rome! That sounded very attractive until I found that it clashed with a long arranged visit to Parliament by my son Brian, his girlfriend Lisa and Lisa's parents, Tim and Janice Whitehead. There was no way I could cancel that, so I declined the speaking engagement sorrowfully. However, Helen rang me and told me that she had mixed the dates up. They would fly me out the night before for an early speech and I could be back to the Lords by lunchtime next day to meet my guests. I did just that, flew to Rome the night before, spoke before 9 a.m. and hosted a very agreeable lunch in the House with my guests.

I occasionally met sociably in Durham with a local building developer, Mike Williams, who I had come across years earlier when he bought a car from me. He was now in partnership with Trevor Graham, a former banker. I was invited by Mike to join the board of their company, Kingslodge, based at Meadowfield, just outside Durham City, which I did, together with another acquaintance Sam Stoker, a character if ever there was one. Sam had been a lecturer at Durham University for many years and had just retired from being Principal of St Cuthbert's Society, one of the colleges there. He was a keen sports fan and after dinner speaker and we got on famously.

One of the first public engagements I had done following my appointment to the Lords was to open the 'Busy Bees' nursery in August 1998, at Framwellgate Moor. Kingslodge Developments owned it and, it was a pleasure to perform the ceremony and make a brief speech.

Christmas of 1999 went well and I was looking forward to my life in the Lords into the new Millennium year of 2000. We returned to Westminster after the Christmas break and got into the swing of things again. The Westminster Village, as it's called, is a wonderful community and I was settling in well to my new life. In the evenings if it was quiet, I would have a drink in one of the various 'watering' holes in the Lords, or even go down to the Strangers' bar in the Commons, where MPs, journalists and researchers would mix.

I had been approached to chair the Lords' Home Affairs Committee and was quite happy to take it on, arranging for outside speakers to come and address interested peers. Sir John Stevens was one of the early guests who came and generated a great deal of interest. The problem with Westminster is the vast number of competing interests, with meetings, receptions, launches and the like. I found it very difficult to estimate how many colleagues would turn up at meetings and sometime it was quite embarrassing to find that a high-powered guest was addressing only a handful of Peers, but I think most people understood the difficulty.

It was in April of 2000 that I found myself listening to Questions at the usual afternoon slot, on Thursday 13th. Larry Whitty was the minister in the firing line and was answering a bizarre question about the lack of police action in ensuring Peers' constitutional right to get clear access to parliament. The problem it appears was that the utility companies were digging holes in the roads, which meant that Peers' cars were diverted, causing delays. The minister was asked why there was not a requirement to notify the Commissioner of the Metropolitan Police each time there was to be a hole dug, so that proper traffic diversions could be arranged?

The debate was in full flow and all manner of issues were discussed and I found it quite amusing. Lord Whitty was doing his best to placate their Lordships.

'My Lords, although the general impression is that those disruptions are present for a long time, in fact most are there for an extremely short time. Therefore quite often, very temporary measures are needed. Indeed, although, as the noble Baroness says, the portable traffic signals are vehicle-activated, there are situations where, for a short period, the traffic may be judged better by human involvement rather than by automated traffic signals.'

I could not stand any more of this! I rose to speak, 'My Lords,' I bellowed, 'I am not sure the police would welcome being notified every time that a hole is dug in the road. Certainly, when I was a divisional commander and somebody complained about a hole appearing in the road, my stock response was that the police would be looking into it!' [*Hansard* 13 April 2000: Column 285]

That is the one and only time I have seen Margaret Thatcher, all in blue on the front bench opposite, roaring with laughter. What an achievement!

I was also chairing conferences for a company called 'Infolog' whose managing Director is a delightful dapper Chilean former immigrant called Luis Macchiavello, who had come to Britain with his family to escape persecution. The company was expanding and ran mainly public sector conferences, which I would often chair, and I would also invite chief constables and ministers to address them. It was a useful opportunity to meet serving chief constables such as Richard Childs from Lincolnshire, Sir David Phillips from Kent, Maria Wallis, the new chief constable of Devon and Cornwall and the genial Irish chief constable of Surrey, Denis O'Connor, who I knew when he was an assistant commissioner in the Metropolitan Police. A delightful and very professional officer, he subsequently invited me to speak at the Surrey officers' mess dinner, which I did.

CHAPTER 17

Election 2001

EARLY IN 2000 I bumped into a former Superintendents' Association pal of mine, Dai Davies, who had been in charge of the Royalty Protection Squad at Scotland Yard and, you will recall, played a very prominent part in our firearms debate following the Dunblane tragedy, just before we both retired. He was now working with a former CID officer from London called David Ledward and they had formed a company called The Agency. I was invited to join them in a venture, which looked extremely interesting.

They were to make a fact-finding trip to Russia in May 2000, through the auspices of Prince Michael of Kent, who has a great interest in Russia, not least because of his family connections with the former Russian Romanov royal dynasty. A lunch was organized in London hosted by Prince Michael and a businessman with a great interest in security matters, James Brown from Kent, the Managing Director of a successful export company called Selectamark. I got on very well with Jim, who was a small, dapper man in his seventies, with the enthusiasm of a twenty-year old, and I later had the privilege of showing his family round the Lords.

I had also attended a lunch at Lumley Castle in Durham some time before, when Prince Michael launched a project for the Durham Agency Against Crime, again supported enthusiastically again, by James Brown. Prince Michael, or 'Mick' as Dai would call him, not least to disguise to whom he was referring, was a splendid host, and regaled us with the customs and practice in the former Soviet Union. I have to say I liked the idea of standing in for Prince Michael of Kent and readily agreed to lead the delegation. However, I had to clear it with Jean and found that there was a problem. We were to go on a family holiday in Tenerife with Max and Marion Currah, the dates clashed and the arrangements for the holiday had all been made. Max of course was my former detective colleague from Peterlee, now long retired.

I was going to decline the invitation to visit Russia and discussed it one Friday evening with Arthur Walsh, the licensee of the Rose Tree in Shincliffe Village. 'Brian', he said, 'You've got to go, you can go to Tenerife anytime, this is the chance of a lifetime!' The more I thought about it, the more I knew he was right. In the end I made a good old British compromise. Jean, with Max and Marion Currah, would fly to Tenerife and I would join them from Russia about three days into the holiday. Try as I could, I could not get a flight direct from Moscow to Tenerife, so arrangements were made for me to fly back to Heathrow and then pick up a flight from Gatwick to Tenerife. But more of that journey later.

We were travelling to Moscow first class by Aeroflot and I set off for Heathrow Airport on Monday 22 May 2000. There were five of us going on the trip. All were former police officers, except Nicholas Kullman, an academic with a Russian background and an excellent knowledge of Russian culture. The others were Dai Davies, David Ledward, Alan Hedley, another former detective and myself. The arrangements were superb. It was the first time I have flown anywhere where I did not see my luggage from start to finish. It was all arranged for us. The flight to Moscow was excellent and we were picked up at Moscow Airport in a limousine with a police escort. Throughout the trip I had a close protection security guard, whom I dubbed 'Ivan the Terrible'. He never left my side, even when I went to the gents! He was a mountain of a man and I was pleased he was on our side!

As we drove from the airport to the hotel in the centre of Moscow I noticed a row of young women standing side by side on the edge of the dual carriageway. I asked what they were doing and we were told that they were prostitutes on display. Cars would draw up and the driver would select the girl he wanted and she would go with him in the car. I asked if it was legal and our escort said, 'No it's illegal, and they keep getting arrested from time to time!'

We got to the hotel and checked in, still closely guarded by our escorts, and had dinner in the hotel. On Tuesday we had lunch in a Ukrainian restaurant, again travelling with a full police escort – virtually knocking other motorists off the road to allow us to travel freely. I soon learned that the Russian police were all powerful. Another custom I soon got into was the practice of toasting with vodka everybody and everyone. The Queen, Tony Blair, the Russian President so it went on, and each time you emptied your glass, it was refilled.

That afternoon we met the deputy minister of the interior Col-Gen Igor N Zubov and his colleague Eugene Ruzalev and had interesting talks on Terrorism, including Chechnya. This was followed by talks with the Russian Head of the International Cooperation Department, Alexander N Malinovsky and colleagues, again discussing aspects of terrorism. I recall that he issued a specific invitation to Jack Straw to visit Russia. We had an evening of culture at the Moscow Opera House where we saw a performance of *La Bohème*. There were nine curtain calls, which I thought were never going to end.

Wednesday involved a fascinating meeting with Deputy Minister of Justice Yuri Kalinin and head of the prison service. Prison conditions were discussed and I was surprised at his liberal values and condemnation of prison conditions in Russia, where tuberculosis was rife. This was followed by a demonstration by the OMON anti-terrorist police. They gave a unique insight into the use of protective shields and the mock storming, by abseiling, of a house holding kidnap victims. Travelling back for lunch I was struck by the sight of plasterers in overalls, standing on scaffolding on the gable end of a building – they were all women!

A fairly uneventful meeting with the head of the Russian section of Interpol followed and that evening we had dinner in a Moscow beer restaurant.

The following day we met Colonel Nickolay Pankratov, who was the head of the Department of Permissions and Licensing in the Ministry of the Interior. What really interested me here was that the private security industry in Russia was fully regulated and those authorized could also get permission to carry and use firearms! We had been advocating regulation of the security industry in the UK for many years.

The old KGB Headquarters, now known as the Federal Security Service (FSS), was next on our itinerary, and it was an impressive old building, which I am sure, had many a story to tell! The head of the anti terrorist unit Lieutenant General Ivan Mironov greeted us and, we discussed respective methods of dealing with kidnap and extortion. He described how in Chechnya houses were constructed with cellars to hold kidnap victims. Crime was endemic with certain families in Groznyy where as standard, they had rings cemented to walls where victims of extortion would be held, sometimes for up to 12 months, in shocking conditions. It was apparent that the Russians were paranoid about western criticism of their conduct of the war in Chechnya.

At lunchtime we were met by Alexander Gurov, the Chairman of the Security Committee of the State Duma (Lower House of Parliament) of the Russian Federation. Mr Gurov gave us an analysis of his party called UNITY, which has become an effective force in the centre of the Russian political spectrum. It was a very interesting and fascinating meeting. Being the only parliamentarian in our delegation, I led all the meetings and I was extremely pleased that over the years I had taken an interest in international affairs and could at least hold my own in the many conversations that we had. As all the meetings were through an interpreter, it at least gave me a little thinking time!

Siberia
At 6.30 p.m. we flew to Irkutsk in Siberia which took about five hours, arriving in the early hours of Friday morning. The head of security at the hotel, Vladimir Litvin who was a locally born former secret policeman, met us and I learned that prisoners still worked in gangs in the area, reflecting the

tradition of the Siberian Gulag. We were also warned that there were brown bears in the area, which could be dangerous. At 11:00 a.m. we met the Head of the Interior Department of the Irkutsk Region, Major General Alexander Rossov, who commanded a vast area in Siberia, with a population of only 2.8 million. A very violent area we were told, with a murder rate last year of 1,700. This compares with Britain's murder rate of 750 for a population of 56 million!

We then visited an oil complex and met Fyodor Serdyuk, the General Director, who gave us a brief presentation. Throughout the visit we were plied with brandy and vodka. A lavish lunch followed with more toasts in a local restaurant and then to Irkutsk itself for a cultural visit to churches and a Gulag prison where men and women had toiled. We finished that evening with a delightful tour of the 'December' Museum where I signed the visitors book on behalf of the delegation. I noticed that Vladimir Putin the Russian President had signed it only a short while earlier!

Saturday was a leisure day and we visited the open air Wooden Museum near to Baikal Lake where we were sung and danced to and, had a walk through Siberian history. The weather was absolutely glorious and surprisingly hot – not at all what I expected of Siberia.

Going back to the hotel for dinner, a superb trio of mother, father and son, entertained us with fine singing. I retired to bed before midnight as I was rising early to catch my flight to Heathrow. I duly rose and my police escort and minders drove me to the airport where I was presented with a large presentation case about 3 feet long as a parting gift. I opened it and when I saw the gift I knew it was a nightmare! It was a set of very fancy duelling pistols with what appeared to be ball bearing missiles. I knew that I was in trouble, smiled nonetheless, and expressed my thanks. I then went to the VIP lounge.

When I declared my 'gift' the captain of the aircraft flying back to Moscow, quite rightly, insisted on the 'weapons' travelling with him on the flight deck. When we got to Moscow I managed to transfer all right to my connecting flight to Heathrow. That is where the trouble started! I landed at Heathrow and was directed to the Customs and Excise Office where I had to explain my possession of 'guns'. Having been on the move for 17 hours I was in no mood for protracted discussions and in any event had to catch my connecting flight at Gatwick to join Jean and the others in Tenerife. I told the customs officer that I was quite happy for the guns to be seized but he would have none of it and said that I would have to stay with them until we determined whether they were real. I was getting annoyed now and he could see that. Eventually he said, 'Ok, I'll give you the benefit of the doubt, off you go, but don't take them out of the box!'

It was the decision I had been dreading. I had decided that there was no

Fact finding in Siberia, May 2000.

way I was going to take the guns to Tenerife from Gatwick only to bring them back again. Walking through Heathrow with my suitcase and this large presentation case some 17 hours after setting off from Siberia, I had a brainwave! I went across to a uniformed policeman and told him my identity. 'I'm a personal friend of Sir John Stevens,' I said. 'The police in Russia gave me this present for the Commissioner.' I lied. The constable then started to examine the firearms and asked me if they were real and I told him I did not know. He then called his sergeant on the radio and I thought the saga was never going to end. By now I was totally exhausted and his sergeant arrived and agreed to take the firearms from me. Success!

I got my flight to Tenerife, enjoyed the break in the sun and thought nothing more of the deadly present. It was some two months later when I got a call at the House of Lords from Sir John Stevens' staff officer. He told me that they had had the 'present' examined at the laboratory and they were indeed Section 1 firearms, requiring a licence! I told him to find a nice display room in Scotland Yard and to keep them for posterity. All in all a remarkable visit which will live with me for the rest of my life. I have dined out on the stories many times since.

The Agency team have now unfortunately broken up, but I recall having lunch with some other Russians discussing business proposals around that time, when in the middle of lunch, the Russian Interpreter said that he wanted to speak privately to me. We left the table, as though to visit the the gents. In the corridor he said, 'Where are you tomorrow?'

'In the Lords', I said, 'Why?'

'Well Mr X (I'll not identify him) wants me to bring you a present.'

'What kind of present?' I asked curiously.

'5000 dollars', he replied.

I was incredulous and said I couldn't possibly accept any money under those circumstances and that any financial dealings would have to be discussed in the open meeting with my colleagues present. He looked disappointed and said, 'Mr X will not be pleased!' Whereupon I gave him a short lecture on the way that the John Major government had fallen through bribery and sleaze and, brown paper envelopes. I believe he got the message, but it illustrated to me the culture of Russian business and it put me on my guard.

The Julie Hogg Murder

When I first entered the Lords, David Hines who lived on Tyneside and whose daughter had been killed, had invited me to become a Patron of the North of England Victim's Association (NEVA). I was more than happy to oblige, as the plight of victims had been an issue for me throughout my police service, particularly in my later years as an officer of the

Superintendents' Association. David works at a Magistrates' Court Office on Tyneside and NEVA was his big passion. He worked tirelessly to improve the lot of victims.

I was invited to address a NEVA conference on Saturday 23 September 2000, where I met Ann Ming, the mother of Julie Hogg, a pizza delivery girl who had gone missing. Despite a search of her home, the police found nothing. Three months later, Ann Ming found Julie's body behind the bath of the house. A local man, Billy Dunlop was arrested and charged with Julie's murder but the jury failed to convict him.

He later confessed to the killing but could not be prosecuted again as he had been acquitted, so he was prosecuted for perjury whilst giving evidence during his murder trial. He was convicted and received six years. This was the issue, you will recall, double jeopardy, which I had raised at my final superintendents' conference in 1997 with the new Home Secretary, Jack Straw. I therefore spoke out strongly again at the NEVA conference in favour of abolishing the ancient rule, so that justice could be done for Ann Ming and her husband Charlie.

Since that conference, Mrs Ming has continued to campaign tirelessly for justice to be done and I have supported her in every way possible, including raising the case on the floor of the House of Lords. It is extremely satisfying therefore to have attended a meeting in July 2003, in parliament, with Ann and her husband, chaired by the Attorney General Lord Peter Goldsmith, where a commitment was given to abolish the double jeopardy rule in the Criminal Justice Bill then before parliament.

Since going to the Lords, I have made a point of attending the meetings of the Northern Group of MPs, the chairmanship of which rotates annually. It is a useful source of party activity in the northeast and over the years has been attended by Peter Mandelson, Stephen Byers, Alan Milburn, Doug Henderson and other northeast ministers who had generally become known as the 'North East Mafia'.

My connection with Durham City council was cemented by my role as Billet Master, referred to earlier and I also regularly attend liaison meetings with the Durham County Council arranged by the very able chief executive, Kingsley Smith who I knew from my policing days in Durham. He would make regular forays south with his leader of the council, Ken Manton, who recently replaced the old warhorse Don Robson, one of the stalwarts responsible for Durham's excellent Test Cricket ground at Chester-le-Street. It is a very useful lobbying meeting and the elected members would bring the county officers for Education, Finance and the like. The indomitable Lord (Jack) Dormand, the former MP of Easington, attended these meetings and brought tremendous experience to the table. I always knew he was around when I heard those familiar words of his 'Now bonny lad'.

Election Year

It was felt that the year 2001 might be a significant one for the government as it was believed that Tony Blair would call a general election. It was and he did!

It was significant also, because in the still running Operation Lancet inquiry by Cleveland Police into the conduct of Ray Mallon, the long suffering detective who had been suspended since 1997, he was informed in February that he would face no criminal charges. At an estimated cost of £7m, the whole basis of the suspension, 'for matters which could be construed as criminal' had been destroyed, following the decision, which, was announced by the Crown Prosecution Service. I again raised the question of the methods employed by the Police Complaint Authority in such cases and called for a public inquiry. There were calls for the chief constable Barry Shaw to resign and local MPs were divided on where the blame lay.

The newspapers sensed that an election was imminent and early in 2001 the *Daily Telegraph* ran a story by Rachael Sylvester entitled, 'Labour launches new charm offensive to woo the boys in blue'. The article started,

> Fifty years ago two small boys used to play football together in the playground at a Darlington primary school. Their names were Tom Sawyer and Brian Mackenzie.
>
> One went into politics and became the general secretary of the Labour Party; the other joined the police and ended up as the president of the Police Superintendents' Association.
>
> Now both are Labour Peers and their long-standing friendship has been a key factor in improving relations between the party and the police.
>
> In the past, Labour MPs believed the Tories had a virtual monopoly over the boys in blue. One chairman of the Police Federation abandoned all pretence of neutrality, declaring in 1994 that Michael Howard was 'the best Home secretary in 30 years'. [*Daily Telegraph* 18 January 2001]

I wrote an article in the *Express* entitled 'Have Labour finally won our trust on crime?' and I quote

> The Tories always claimed to be the party of law and order but when Tony Blair became shadow home secretary in the early nineties, he set about changing that perception with his slogan 'Tough on crime and tough on the causes of crime'. Now Labour, which yesterday unveiled its 10-year crime plan, boasts that it is the first government for 50 years to have less crime at the end of its term in office than when it came in.
>
> I can recall when I was the president of the Police Superintendents' Association in 1995, complaining to the last government about the organization of the Crown Prosecution Service and its poor relationship with the police; about criminals owning and working in security firms; about paedophiles;

about a growing yobbishness on the street. With the exception of paedophiles the last government took no action, but all these issues have been tackled by Jack Straw, who has also built on Michael Howard's anti-paedophile measures.

It concluded

Labour's reputation for being soft on criminals cost it votes in previous elections. Since Tony Blair gave the party a policy makeover it has become increasingly hard to distinguish between Labour and the Tories in their rhetoric about the issue. With the election looming, the government will be hoping that it has done enough to convince voters that it really is prepared to get tough.

So on Tuesday 8 May 2001, the Prime Minister Tony Blair announced that the general election would take place on Thursday 7 June, and the battle commenced to see if he could be the first Labour Prime Minister to win two consecutive election victories.

Victory!

In the event, it was no contest. William Hague, the young Tory hopeful, who had fared very well in the setting of the Common's debating chamber, was well and truly trounced. Whilst he had performed well in parliament, he had a negative image in the country and the general consensus was that the government needed a second term to deliver the results promised, particularly with regard to the public services. Labour won another massive majority of 166 on a turnout of 59.4%, the lowest since 1918.

I had joined a reforming parliament in 1997 with major constitutional changes under its belt, such as the creation of the Scottish Parliament, the Welsh, Northern Irish and London Assemblies being set up, as well as reform of the House of Lords. Over 700 hereditary peers had gone, out of control legal aid expenditure was tackled and an attempt was made to reduce the number of cases eligible for jury trial. It was a fascinating time to be in the Lords. Indeed at the time of writing, Tony Blair has broken Attlee's record as the longest continuously serving Labour prime minister.

When the new parliament was opened in June 2001, I once again put my name down to speak in the debate on the provisions in the Queen's Speech. Lord (Jeff) Rooker had been elevated from the Commons and joined the government front bench with a Home Office brief. When my turn to speak came round I congratulated Lord Rooker on his appointment and then again used humour to soften up the audience.

My Lords... I read a survey recently which stated that people's biggest fear is the fear of dying! People's second biggest fear is the fear of speaking in public! I am told that there is a third fear; that is the fear of dying whilst speaking in public! I know that your Lordships will not allow that to happen to me this evening! [*Hansard* 27 June 2001 Column 413]

I welcomed the contents of the Queen's speech, particularly with regard to the proposed Criminal Justice Bill, which concentrated on putting victims first, and declared my interest as a patron of the North of England Victims' Association. I then got on my hobbyhorse. This, remember, was the suggestion dismissed by all when I first raised it at my final Superintendents' Conference in September 1997. I quote:

> I start with the proposal to abolish the double jeopardy rule. In 1997, as president of the Superintendents' Association, I addressed the national conference, which was to welcome for the first time the new Home Secretary, the Right Honourable Jack Straw. In my speech in 1997, I called for the abolition of the archaic double jeopardy rule. We had been through a period in which a number of wrongful convictions had been identified for various reasons. Those miscarriages, quite rightly had been corrected.
>
> I recalled many years previously, long before I was a police officer, the case of a man called Stanley Setty who had been murdered. His dismembered body parts had been thrown from an aircraft into the North Sea. I recall graphically the trial of one Donald Hume for that grotesque murder. He was eventually acquitted.
>
> As a young student of the criminal law at the time, I remember my horror at reading for the first time the gruesome details of the murder by none other than the self-confessed murderer himself, Donald Hume. He wrote his story in a Sunday tabloid – I think it was the *Sunday Pictorial* and that shows how long ago it was – detailing the murder, how he chopped up the body and distributed the body parts from a light aircraft. I have little doubt that he earned quite a fat fee for his memoirs.
>
> I was even more disturbed when I realized that for all his admissions, he could not be prosecuted because of that ancient common-law doctrine of autrefois acquit, which in essence, meant that an accused could not be put in jeopardy twice for the same offence. It was a rule that was introduced in ancient times, when the odds were stacked against the criminal. For example in those days the accused could not give evidence in his own defence. It seemed to my simple mind at that time, that the interests of justice would be served by accepting the principle that a wrongful acquittal was just as much a miscarriage as a wrongful conviction. Times change, and it appeared to me that with modern forensic evidence and other legal safeguards, the time had come for a change. Justice should reflect the public interest.
>
> There have been more recent cases in the northeast, for example a man was charged with the murder of his girlfriend, whose body was suddenly found by her mother hidden behind the bath. The man was acquitted and following an indiscreet admission of guilt when in prison, he was subsequently charged with giving false evidence at his own trial. He was sentenced to six years in prison for perjury. Understandably, the victim's mother, as an innocent victim of the murder, has ceaselessly fought for justice. [*Hansard* 27 Jun 2001: Column 414]

I also took the opportunity to talk about proposed police reforms with particular reference to the Ray Mallon case and the need to improve the police complaints system. I concluded on an issue that has been brought home to me even more graphically since commuting to London – rough sleeping. I quote:

> The public are entitled to a reasonable quality of life. Only today in an underground station at Hyde Park Corner I had difficulty walking past two settees, which were clearly the beds of two poor individuals who presumably slept there at night. In 2001 that is simply unacceptable. That is a social problem that needs dealing with. I despair. In this new century I believe that the police and social services should take action to deal with such difficulties. There must be better ways of dealing with people than allowing them to sleep in such places. Tourists were falling over them. It was quite disgraceful. [*Hansard* 27 Jun 2001: Column 416]

An Office at Last

I was now a full member of the 'Westminster Village', getting on very well with all the staff, above and below stairs, and at last I was allocated an office! An ex-church commissioners' building in Millbank, just opposite the Lords' Victoria Tower, had been renovated and, I put my name down for a room. I have to say that it exceeded all my expectations. It is large and spacious; we have an armchair and a settee, as well as a modern computer desk. I even had wall-shelves fitted next to my desk and the building has a nice canteen as well as printing, copying and fax facilities. My normal routine is to walk from my flat to the office, a journey of about fifteen minutes, for about 9:30 a.m. I then deal with my e-mails and the considerable bundle of mail that we all receive. A lot of it is general lobbying literature, but many people write to me with a whole range of problems and I deal with it as an MP would. I write to the minister concerned and forward the reply to the 'constituent'. What with meetings and phone calls, it seems no time at all before the House sits at 2:30 p.m.

I had a verbal complaint from Richard Hopps, a local farmer at Shincliffe. He rightfully complained of the growing volume of fly tipping that was taking place on his land. I researched the matter and found that it had been discussed in debates in the Lords and was being dealt with in proposed future legislation. I wrote several times to Richard, supplying him with information which I had gleaned. I also discussed it with him in the pub and I remember him saying, 'Why don't you stand as MP?' I took that as a compliment!

It was in May of 2001 that I was invited to speak to the Law Society Annual Dinner at the Café Royal in London. There were about 500 people there and as well as a minister from the Lord Chancellor's Department. I found that speaking before me was the distinguished former chairman of the

Criminal Bar Association, Anthony Scrivener QC. I was a little concerned at having to follow such a proficient orator, but I need not have worried. He ruined the opportunity by reading from a prepared brief, making very political points and attacking the government's policies. He even attacked the House of Lords, knowing I assume, that I was to follow him to the rostrum.

When I got to the rostrum, I could not miss the opportunity to get back at him. Totally ad-libbing I said, 'Ladies and Gentlemen, I am delighted to speak to this annual dinner for the very first time. It is particularly gratifying to follow such a distinguished speaker as Anthony Scrivener QC, probably one of the finest speakers of the day.' And then the punch line, 'It's a pity something seems to happen to him at night!'

It brought the house down and I had them eating out of my hand after that. Indeed I got a lot of offers for future speeches from that one night at the Café Royal. As an end piece, the icing on the cake was a couple of days later when I was walking into the Lords' Old Palace Yard; a large car which was leaving stopped beside me. The window wound down and I saw that it was Lord Goldsmith, the Attorney General. 'Brian, I just wanted to tell you that I thought it was brilliant the way you put down Anthony Scrivener at the dinner the other night.' 'Thank you, Peter', I said, 'Who told you about it?' The Attorney smiled and said, 'I was in the audience.' Which brought home to me yet again, that you never know who is listening when you speak in public!

People in the Lords are continually moving on and I have got used to parliament going into recess, in the full knowledge that some of the elderly peers would not be coming back. I had seen it with Lord Montague, Baroness Barbara Castle, Lord Longford and Beatrice Serotta. The Gentleman Usher of the Black Rod, Sir Edward Jones, retired and was replaced by the diminutive, but extremely smart and effective, Lt Gen Sir Michael Wilcocks.

My old pal Mick Skelton, the principal doorkeeper, was due to retire towards the end of 2001, and I was quite sad at the prospect of losing such a good friend and adviser in the Lords. A couple of months before he was due to retire, Mick developed what appeared to be a sore throat and he lost his voice. I became very concerned when it did not improve after a couple of weeks, as I remembered my problems years earlier. So I strongly advised Mick to seek medical advice, which he did.

He was eventually referred to a specialist and an operation was found to be necessary. I am delighted that the operation was successful and Mick eventually recovered his voice. I went off to the Christmas recess with a sad heart knowing that I would not see him in uniform with his beaming, florid features, or hear him shout in the Peers Lobby, 'Please be upstanding for the Lord Chancellor.' But I needn't have worried, he still comes back to the

Lords and usually gives me a ring, so that when possible, we meet up and have a drink.

I was delighted with Mick's replacement as Principal Doorkeeper. John 'Geordie' Kirtley is a no-nonsense former warrant officer in the Royal Marines, who as his nickname implies, come from Newcastle upon Tyne. John has a great sense of humour and so we get on extremely well also, often sharing jokes and a chat when the opportunity arises. Another lovely character on the staff is Keith Phipps, a senior doorkeeper who served formerly as a warrant officer in the Coldstream Guards. All wonderful people, who I suppose I hit it off with because of my disciplined background.

Another new acquaintance I made was a genial Northern Irishman called George Fleck who works in the commons as a messenger. George had formerly been a builder and lives in Pinner with his delightful wife, Veronica. I found him extremely good company and we often have a drink together after work in the Sports & Social Club. Keith Best occasionally comes down to London, particularly if the HOP Club is staging a Karaoke night. We had attended a couple of times and thoroughly enjoyed the evenings. I am not sure whether I am the first Peer to sing karaoke in the Palace of Westminster. If I'm not, there can't have been many others. George came to a Karaoke night with us and he even invited Keith and me to stay with him and Veronica in Pinner one Saturday evening. We had a hilarious evening in the local pub with our hosts and their friend Gordon, who is in insurance, and their other friends Jim and Annette.

Indeed I have since returned the hospitality by inviting George and Veronica to stay with us at the cottage in Shincliffe Village, when they visited Durham in August 2003.

Barcelona

Early in 2002, Jean and I decided to have a holiday in Barcelona, and stayed in a nice hotel near The Ramblas. We went to see the magnificent architecture of Gaudi and I recall on our last evening, Jean fancied an Indian meal. We asked the friendly waiter in the Meridion Hotel, where we were staying, where the nearest Indian Restaurant was and he gave us directions. We walked and walked and walked. In the end we took a taxi, named the restaurant and the driver took us right back to where we had started! It was about 50 yards away from the hotel. Then, when we got there, we found it did not open until 8:00 p.m., so we went for a drink and went back after eight.

Looking forward to our Indian meal we scoured the menu and although regular dishes were there, it did not indicate whether it was beef, chicken or pork. When I queried this, the waiter told us it was a vegetarian restaurant! Not to be deterred, I told Jean that vegetarian food is often just as good with spices and told her we could enjoy a nice bottle of wine. I called the waiter again and yes, you've guessed, it was a teetotal restaurant as well! Jean nearly murdered me.

Whilst on the subject of food, I had noticed that I was starting to get heavier and that my waistline was expanding. It is so easy in the Lords to attend lunches, dinners and the multitude of receptions in between and nibble away all day. I knew I would have to tackle the problem head on.

I had been to a dinner with Stan Henry and his lovely wife, Avril, who is extremely slim, had told me that her secret was that she did not eat bread. Whilst I did not eat butter, I loved bread with soup and had toast with my kippers on the train, so I decided to give it a try and cut out bread. I suppose it is a form of the controversial Dr Atkins diet. In any event, the weight just dropped off me! I lost two inches off my waistline and a stone in weight in about 2 months. I have stayed off bread since then, still eating potatoes and pasta, and I still like a pint or two. I weigh in at 12 stones 8 pounds, which is not bad for a man who stands 6 feet 2 inches tall.

CHAPTER 18

Campaigning to the End

IT WILL NOT HAVE GONE unnoticed that many of my friends over the years were licensees and that my wife and I regularly frequent the Rose Tree and the Seven Stars in the delightful village of Shincliffe, just 2 miles south of Durham City. It was our ambition to move to a house, which was bright and sunny, but without the responsibility and work of maintaining a large garden. I therefore tasked Jean with looking in the property advertisements for an appropriate place, which suited us both. It seemed logical therefore to consider Shincliffe Village as a venue and we actually looked at one or houses there, but saw nothing which we both liked.

I had also decided to buy a new car and had set my heart on a BMW convertible, although it was hardly justified in terms of the car journeys I made. Nevertheless I decided to treat myself and specified the full works to BMW with a satellite GPS navigator, dashboard television, and a steering wheel cruise button, together with automatic gears, none of which I had ever had in my life. In late May of 2002 I took delivery of the car at Park Lane in London and therefore had to drive it home. It should be remembered that I rarely drive to London, always flying or travelling by train, but this was a necessity.

I do not normally believe in fate, but on this occasion travelling north, I left the A1 motorway at the Bowburn turn-off in Durham, to drive along the A177 towards the city. Why I did this I do not know, as I would normally go to the next junction to join the A690 which takes you into the city further north, which was where we lived at Framwellgate. As I drove towards Shincliffe Village I saw that the cream cottage, about 100 yards south of the Seven Stars Inn, had a 'For Sale' sign up. When I got home I asked Jean why she had not mentioned the cottage and she said she had not seen it advertised. I thought it was worth a look at so we went back and took the telephone number of the estate agent and arranged a viewing.

It was just what we were looking for. Built into the hillside, the living quarters are upstairs with the bedrooms below. It was completely modern inside with a hardwood conservatory built upstairs at the back and facing south. The top of the garage had been made into a sun deck, with a rockery garden, requiring little maintenance, sloping up to the fields above. Needless to say, we made an offer, which was accepted, and we moved into our new house on 29 July 2002. I often ponder 'what if' I had not picked the car up that day, 'what if' I had gone home by my normal route? But then you can apply these thoughts to every event in your life! I even purchased a surprise present for Jean, which was an aerial photograph of the cottage with a suitable caption commemorating the house-move. We have great neighbours across the road, with Irene and Jim Milburn and Tommy and Julie Shepherd, with whom we often socialize at the nearby Seven Stars. We also meet other locals such as the local farmer Richard Hopps and his wife Susan, Ron Stark and Anne, David and Lorraine Boyd, Dr John Harrison as well as many others. It is everything we could have wished for!

Our sons now were settled down. Brian, the eldest, a computer consultant, lives with his girlfriend Lisa in Bury, Greater Manchester in a nice detached house. Andrew lives a little nearer us in Newcastle with his girlfriend Tina, and they have just recently moved into a larger house with a large south-facing back garden. Jean and I encouraged them to buy rather than rent, having ourselves discovered the difficulty of getting into the house market rather late, due to living in police provided accommodation for many years. It is often said that you can choose your friends but you cannot choose your family – well all I can say that whoever chose my family did me a great service!

It was about this time that I was stopped in the Lords by Lord Stanley Clinton-Davis, a solicitor and former aviation minister. He told me that he was the president of the British Airline Pilots' Association (BALPA) and asked if I was interested in becoming vice-president. I was honoured to be asked, let him have a brief biography of myself, and following lunch with the general secretary, Jim McAuslan and chairman, Mervyn Granshaw, took up the post in early 2003, having declared the interest with the House of Lords Registrar. The interest in selecting me, for this position, was clearly security related following the terrible events of September 11 2001.

Anti-social Behaviour

There was still great public concern about the levels of yobbery and anti-social behaviour on the streets. Indeed, the prime minister was reported as suggesting that such behaviour should attract a fixed penalty ticket rather like speeding, and there was talk of youths being marched to cash-point machines by the police. This caused derision in the media, so I went public and stated my long-held view that there was merit in any system which prevented an officer being detained in a police station for hours preparing court papers. I don't know where the silly cash-point suggestion came from, but the fixed penalty option at the police station was a good one, and I said so. In the event it became a provision in the Queen's Speech in November 2002 and a number of pilot schemes have been highly successful.

Street crime had rocketed, mainly because of the theft of mobile phones, to such a degree that the prime minister himself called a high profile meeting in Downing Street and the 'Street Crime Initiative' was set up. Again there was opposition derision when Tony Blair announced that the problem would be under control by September. A review by Sir Keith Povey, Her Majesty's Chief Inspector of Constabulary, who reported in July 2003, showed that the initiative was highly successful in reducing street crime by 17,000. That amounts to 17,000 less victims!

The thrust of the Home Office agenda for the forthcoming year was a rebalancing of the criminal justice system, with another attempt to reduce trial by jury in complicated fraud cases and where juries had been tampered with. Again there was widespread opposition in the Lords. In the Queen's Speech debate I quoted a top police officer and said:

Perhaps I can quote a Commissioner of the Metropolitan Police:

'What we know about trials in higher courts doesn't justify any complacency. Indeed, there is one fact I can mention which should be enough in itself to justify some kind of enquiry. This is the rate of acquittal... The English criminal trial never decides whether the accused is innocent. The only question is whether according to the rules of evidence, the prosecution has proved that he is guilty – and this is not at all the same thing.

'There must be a failure rate – we can't always expect to convict the guilty or never to prosecute the innocent. But in my opinion a failure rate of one in two is far too high.'

He then went on to talk of some defence advocates. I quote:

'We see the same lawyers producing, off the peg, the same kind of defence for different clients... witnesses suddenly and inexplicably change their minds. Defences are concocted far beyond the intellectual capacity of the accused. False alibis are put forward. Extraneous issues damaging to police credibility are introduced. All these are part of the stock in trade of a small number of criminal lawyers. The truth is that some trials of deliberate crimes for profit – robbery, burglary and so on – involve a bitter struggle of wits and tactics between the detective and the lawyer'.

Sir John Stevens? The noble Lord, Lord Condon? The noble Lord, Lord Imbert? No. Those are the words of Sir Robert Mark, who was commissioner in the 1970s, in his Dimbleby Lecture over 30 years ago!

I make no apology for quoting his words. They illustrate that there has been, certainly during my many years of police service, an ongoing debate – quite rightly – on the efficacy of the criminal justice system in its efforts to protect our most vulnerable citizens from violence. I, for one, welcome the provisions in the Gracious Speech dealing with double jeopardy and court procedures; indeed re-balancing the justice system itself. I believe that they go some way towards giving more support to the victims in society and I welcome them unreservedly [*Hansard* 21 Nov 2002: Column 484]

I was delighted to receive a personal letter from the Home Secretary, David Blunkett, on 29 November, which was short and to the point:

Dear Brian,

I just wanted to say how grateful I was for the support you gave the Criminal Justice Bill during the Debate on the Address on 21 November. We need more people like you in the Lords!

I enjoyed meeting you last week at the Police Review Awards. We must try to have a cup of tea together at some point.

Best wishes.

David Blunkett

A little encouragement works wonders, and he kept his promise.

It was in December 2002 that Jean and I attended a reception and dinner at Durham County Hall, the host being the chairman of the Durham County Council. We all dutifully attended and had a drink with the new chief constable of Durham, Paul Garvin and his wife. There was a rumour that there was a surprise guest arriving and it did not take long to establish that it was the Prime Minister Tony Blair, who was to address the dinner.

I recall that the night was quite foggy and as we trooped through to the dining room, it was clear that something was wrong. People were scurrying about and Kingsley Smith, the chief executive, stood up and apologized to the expectant guests. Mr Blair had an important meeting with the Irish Prime Minister, Bertie Ahearn, and because of the fog, Prime Minister Blair's flight had been diverted back to London.

Everybody was clearly disappointed at the principal guest not appearing, including the crew and master of the Durham's adopted warship, who were present at the dinner. Kingsley Smith came over to the table where I was sitting with other guests, which included one of the Banks brothers and his wife, whose opencast mine I had defended all those years ago during the coal dispute. Kingsley whispered to me 'Brian, Will you stand in for the Prime Minister and say a few words after the dinner.' 'Of course,' I said, 'Give me a couple of minutes to think.' I jotted down a few thoughts, asked Kingsley to let me know the name of the naval captain and prepared myself to speak.

After a very agreeable dinner, I was called upon to say a few words. I went to the lectern in the corner and started with a regular opener about an early speaking engagement as a detective inspector on the drug squad, at Winterton Psychiatric Hospital in Sedgefield, which is Tony Blair's constituency. I quote, 'Throughout the early part of my speech at the hospital, a man at the front kept shouting "Rubbish! Rubbish!" I put up with this for so long and then I turned to the doctor next to me and said, "Do you want me to continue?" "Of course you should continue", he said, "it's the first sensible thing he has said since he came in here!"'

I then took a risk by picking on one of the guests from the Royal Navy warship, the captain, who I will call Captain Kelly. 'I am delighted to see our guests from the Royal Navy at the dinner this evening. I can let you all into a secret, including his colleagues who are with him. Captain Kelly is no shrinking violet. In fact I can disclose on good authority, that he joined the navy so the world could see him!'

It went down extremely well, particularly with the other members of the crew with him at the dinner. It was a great night and Chief Constable Paul Garvin asked me if I would speak at a future Durham Constabulary Officers' Mess Dinner, which I was more than happy to agree to.

Suffer Little Children

Rebecca Sawyer's is a tragic case, which occurred on New Year's Eve 2002 in Ashington, Northumberland. Ian Carr drove a stolen car and crashed it into the saloon car of the Sawyer family, killing little Rebecca aged 6 years and seriously injuring her baby sister. Ian Carr fled the scene. He was found to have 89 previous convictions, one of which was for causing death by dangerous driving, on which occasion he had again fled the scene, leaving his friend to die. I argued strenuously that the law needed beefing up with a higher maximum sentence. At the time of writing it carries ten years. I also argued for an indeterminate sentence for repeat offenders such as Carr.

I was invited by officials to attend the Home Secretary's office for tea on 11 February 2003, at 5:15 p.m. and took advantage of the visit to raise the question of the importance of the double jeopardy changes being retrospective and also the case of little Rebecca Sawyer, whose parents had written to me.

When I saw David Blunkett, he listened intently. He had his new guide dog Sadie at his feet and I recall that as we talked over tea and biscuits, Sadie playfully rolled onto her back and in doing so, kicked the table, spilling the tea. I remember thinking, 'I hope David doesn't think that was me!' David Blunkett agreed with me that changes were needed and that they would be in the Criminal Justice Bill. I followed up with television and newspaper interviews and raised it on the floor of the House of Lords in March, asking Her Majesty's Government:

'Whether they have any plans to change sentencing provisions for causing death by dangerous driving?'

I was very pleased by the reply of the then Home Office Minister, Lord Falconer of Thoreton, who said:

'My Lords, we intend to increase the maximum penalty for the offence of causing death by dangerous driving from 10 years' imprisonment to 14 years' imprisonment. That follows our report on the review of road traffic penalties published in July of last year. We intend to legislate as soon as parliamentary time allows.

The Criminal Justice Bill contains provisions that will empower the courts to impose indeterminate sentences on dangerous drivers causing death who are assessed as presenting a significant risk of significant harm to the public.' [*Hansard* 12 March 2003: Column 1309]

I was absolutely delighted that the efforts of myself and the family's local MP Denis Murphy had paid dividends, and I was particularly pleased for Mr and Mrs Sawyer who had suffered such a tragic loss that fateful night.

I was in a celebratory mood that day and being naturally gregarious, I went to the HOP Inn, where I saw that the French lady, who was in her mid thirties, was sitting by herself at one of the tables. People tell me that my police background leads me to continually ask questions when meeting people, and I soon established that she was an interpreter, spoke five languages and that her name was Salima Kabache, but the rest, as they say, is history...

Index